WJEC/Eduqas

Religious Studies
for A Level Year 1 & AS

Judaism

Helen Gwynne-Kinsey

Edited by Richard Gray

Illuminate Publishing

Published in 2016 by Illuminate Publishing Ltd, P.O Box 1160, Cheltenham, Gloucestershire GL50 9RW

Orders: Please visit www.illuminatepublishing.com
or email sales@illuminatepublishing.com

British Library Cataloguing-in-Publication Data

A catalogue record for this book is available from the British Library

ISBN 978-1-911208-01-3

Printed by Ashford Colour Press

10.16

The publisher's policy is to use papers that are natural, renewable and recyclable products made from wood grown in sustainable forests. The logging and manufacturing processes are expected to conform to the environmental regulations of the country of origin.

Every effort has been made to contact copyright holders of material reproduced in this book. If notified, the publishers will be pleased to rectify any errors or omissions at the earliest opportunity.

This material has been endorsed by WJEC/Eduqas and offers high quality support for the delivery of WJEC/Eduqas qualifications. While this material has been through a WJEC/Eduqas quality assurance process, all responsibility for the content remains with the publisher.

WJEC/Eduqas examination questions are reproduced by permission from WJEC/Eduqas

Series editor: Richard Gray
Editor: Geoff Tuttle
Design and Layout: EMC Design Ltd, Bedford

Acknowledgements

Cover Image: © Eddie Gerald / Alamy

Image credits:

p. 1 Eddie Gerald / Alamy; **p. 11** mountainpix; **p. 20** jorisvo; **p. 30** Stavchansky Yakov; **p. 31** aastock; **p. 33** Sean Pavone; **p. 39** robert_s; **p. 41** Tania Karant; **p. 42** Phonlamai Photo; **p. 43** (left) Public domain; (right) Moody Publishers / FreeBibleimages.org; **p. 44** Fulcanelli; **p. 53** (top) Robert Hoetink; (bottom) Renato Seiji Kawasaki; **p. 54** (top) Blambi at English Wikipedia, Creative Commons Attribution-Share Alike 3.0 Unported; (bottom) Howard Sandler; **p. 55** Howard Sandler; **p. 57** david156; **p. 72** Noam Armonn; **p. 73** Original uploader and author was Yukeldukel at en.wikipedia [Public domain], via Wikimedia Commons; **p. 79** Howard Grill; **p. 82** Arkady Mazor; **p. 84** CE Photography; **p. 89** James Steidl: **p. 93** blueeyes; **p. 98** Tupungato; **p. 99** Berthold Werner, Public domain; **p. 100** George Dukinas; **p. 101** Ferenc Somorjai [CC BY-SA 3.0 (http://creativecommons.org/licenses/by-sa/3.0), GFDL (http://www.gnu.org/copyleft/fdl.html) or CC-BY-SA-3.0 (http://creativecommons.org/licenses/by-sa/3.0/)], via Wikimedia Commons; **p. 103** www.BibleLandPictures.com / Alamy Stock Photo; **p. 104** יורד הירא, ARIE DARZI (http://yavan.org.il/pws/gallery!826) [CC BY-SA 3.0 (http://creativecommons.org/licenses/by-sa/3.0)], via Wikimedia Commons; **p. 111** Irmhild B; **p. 112** Noam Armonn; **p. 113** (left) Creative commons; (right) ASAP / Alamy Stock Photo; **p. 120** (top) vita pakhai; (bottom left) Sergei25; (bottom right) rmnoa357; **p. 121** tomertu; **p. 122** Hanan Isachar / Alamy Stock Photo; **p. 123** Shuki (Own work) [CC BY-SA 2.5 (http://creativecommons.org/licenses/by-sa/2.5)], via Wikimedia Commons

Ilustration by: Daniel Sanchez Limon/Beehive Illustration: **p. 6**.

Contents

About this book

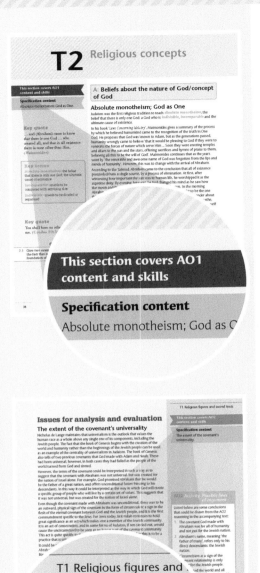

With the new A Level in Religious Studies, there is a lot to cover and a lot to do in preparation for the examinations at the end of AS or the full A Level. The aim of these books is to provide enough support for you to achieve success at AS and A Level, whether as a teacher or a learner.

This series of books is skills-based in its approach to learning, which means it aims to combine covering the content of the Specification with examination preparation from the start. In other words, it aims to help you get through the course whilst at the same time developing some important skills needed for the examinations.

To help you study, there are clearly defined sections for each of the AO1 and AO2 areas of the Specification. These are arranged according to the Specification Themes and use, as far as is possible, Specification headings to help you see that the content has been covered, for both AS and A Level.

The AO1 content is detailed, but precise, with the benefit of providing you with references to both religious/philosophical works and to the views of scholars. The AO2 responds to the issues raised in the Specification and provides you with ideas for further debate, to help you develop your own evaluation skills.

Ways to use this book

In considering the different ways in which you may teach or learn, it was decided that the books needed to have an inbuilt flexibility to adapt. As a result, they can be used for classroom learning, for independent work by individuals, as homework, and, they are even suitable for the purposes of 'flip learning' if your school or college does this.

You may be well aware that learning time is so valuable at A Level and so we have also taken this into consideration by creating flexible features and activities, again to save you the time of painstaking research and preparation, either as teacher or learner.

Features of the books

The books all contain the following features that appear in the margins, or are highlighted in the main body of the text, in order to support teaching and learning.

Key terms of technical, religious and philosophical words or phrases

> **Key terms**
>
> Patriarch: the term given to denote the male head of a family or tribe

Quickfire questions simple, straightforward questions to help consolidate key facts about what is being digested in reading through the information

> **quickfire**
>
> 1.1 What is the meaning of the name 'Abraham'?

Key quotes either from religious and philosophical works and/or the works of scholars

> **Key quote**
>
> The life of a community is conceived of and described in vividly individual terms; and … a representative individual can embody the life of the community in what he is, does, and experiences. (G.W. Anderson)

Study tips advice on how to study, prepare for the examination and answer questions

Study tip

There are many symbolic elements within the story of the Abrahamic Covenant, and it is important that you are able to discuss the deeper meaning behind each one rather than just telling the story in an examination answer. This shows that you understand and can interpret the text. Your ability to do this would distinguish a high level answer from an answer that is simply vague or general.

AO1 Activities that serve the purpose of focusing on identification, presentation and explanation, and developing the skills of knowledge and understanding required for the examination.

AO1 Activity

After reading the section on 'Abraham's belief in One God as creator of Heaven and earth' write a Twitter entry of no more than 140 characters which explains why Abraham's view about God was revolutionary at that time.

AO2 Activities that serve the purpose of focusing on conclusions, as a basis for thinking about the issues, developing critical analysis and the evaluation skills required for the examination

AO2 Activity *Possible lines of argument*

Listed below are some conclusions that could be drawn from the AO2 reasoning in the accompanying text:

Glossary of all the key terms for quick reference.

Specific feature: Developing skills

This section is very much a focus on 'what to do' with the content and the issues that are raised. They occur at the end of each section, giving 12 AO1 examples and 12 AO2 examination-focused activities.

The Developing skills are arranged progressively, so as to provide initial support for you at first, and then gradually encourage you to have more independence.

AO1 and AO2 answers and commentaries

The final section has a selection of answers and commentaries as a framework for judging what an effective and ineffective response may be. The comments highlight some common mistakes and also examples of good practice so that all involved in teaching and learning can reflect upon how to approach examination answers.

Richard Gray
Series Editor
2016

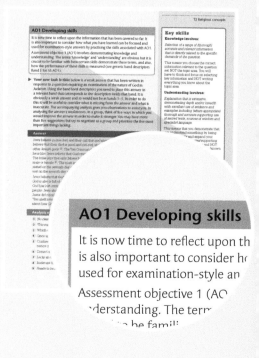

T1 Religious figures and sacred texts

A: Abraham and the establishment of the covenant of circumcision

Specification content

Abraham as Father of the Jewish people (Genesis 12:1–3); Abraham's belief in One God as creator of Heaven and Earth.

Abraham as Father of the Jewish people (Genesis 12:1–3)

According to Jewish tradition, the history of the Jewish people begins with a man named Abraham who was born circa 1800 BCE in the city of Ur in Mesopotamia: an area that we call Iraq today. Jews regard Abraham as the first Patriarch of the Jewish people. A Patriarch is the term given to denote the male head of a family or tribe; and Abraham is therefore known as the Father of the Jewish people, and as such, has been held in high esteem throughout the history of the Jewish people and up to the present day.

Key quote

Texts from widely separated periods and from different parts of the Near East show that in such communities it was common for the cult to be traced back to a special relationship between the deity and the clan chief or cult founder. (G.W. Anderson)

Key quote

The life of a community is conceived of and described in vividly individual terms; and … a representative individual can embody the life of the community in what he is, does, and experiences. (G.W. Anderson)

Key terms

BCE: Before the Common Era

Patriarch: the term given to denote the male head of a family or tribe

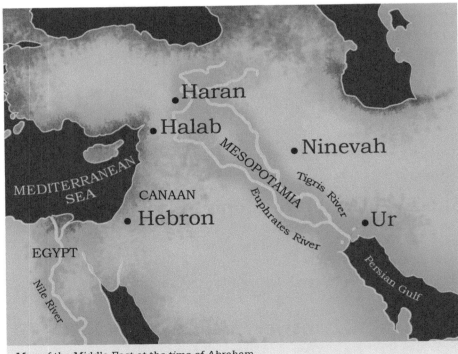

Map of the Middle East at the time of Abraham

quickfire

1.1 What is the meaning of the name 'Abraham'?

B.W. Anderson notes that '… the religion of Israel's ancestors was characterised by a strong clan or family solidarity. Even the names borne by individuals suggest the close personal relationship between the clan and the deity who was regarded as "father, " … for instance, the name Abram, which contains the element "father" means "The (Divine) father is exalted".' The Hebrew Scriptures tell us that God changed Abram's name to Abraham, which means 'the father of many', and in order to find out the background to this title we need to look at the relationship between God and Abraham.

Abraham's belief in One God as creator of Heaven and Earth

There is very little biographical information about Abraham, and he is first mentioned in Genesis chapter 11, where he is known as Abram. His family initially led a nomadic lifestyle as shepherds, but they eventually settled in Haran. As far as religion was concerned, Abram lived in a polytheistic age where people believed in, and worshipped, many gods. We find reference to this in Joshua24:2: 'Joshua said to all the people, 'This is what the LORD, the God of Israel, says: "Long ago your ancestors, including Terah the father of Abraham and Nahor, lived beyond the Euphrates River and worshipped other gods."' Indeed, Abram's father, Terah, was a merchant who sold idols for worship.

However, tradition tells us that Abram had already begun to question the accepted view about there being many gods. Abram's response to God was revolutionary as he was the first to teach that there was One God, creator of Heaven and earth. In Genesis 14:22 Abram states: 'With raised hand I have sworn an oath to the LORD, God Most High, Creator of Heaven and earth.' Monotheism had been born as a result of Abram accepting and realising that there is only one true God.

However, the concept of monotheism is not without its problems, as a number of Old Testament scholars have pointed out that we are using an anachronistic understanding of the term in relation to the events at the time of Abram. Abram may not have been a monotheist in the current sense of the concept, but that is not to say that he doesn't exemplify the beginnings of practical monotheism: '... that although there is at this stage no explicit denial of the existence of other gods, the germ of monotheism is already present'. (G.W. Anderson)

Key quote

It is sometimes thought that monotheism is at its heart a modern philosophical construct, one that should not be retrojected to the biblical context. (Mark S. Smith)

> ## Key terms
>
> **Anachronistic:** to attribute something to a historical period in which it did not exist
>
> **Monotheism:** belief that there is only one God
>
> **Nomadic:** not living a settled life in one place
>
> **Polytheism:** belief in more than one god
>
> **Retroject:** to project into the past

Key quote

Although a case may be made for an original monotheism in early Israelite history, it is far more likely that monotheism was a relatively late theological development of Israelite religion, perhaps in the sixth century BCE. (Walls)

AO1 Activity

After reading the section on 'Abraham's belief in One God as creator of Heaven and Earth' write a Twitter entry of no more than 140 characters which explains why Abraham's view about God was revolutionary at that time.

Specification content

The nature of the covenant between
God and Abraham – the promise of
land and offspring (Genesis 12:7;
13:14–17).

Key quote

Noah had no faults and was the only
good man of his time. He lived in
fellowship with God . . . I am now
making my covenant with you and
your descendants … I promise that
never again will all living beings be
destroyed by a flood.
(Genesis 6–9)

Key quote

Then the LORD appeared
to Abram, and said, 'To your
descendants I will give this land.'
(Genesis 12:7)

quickfire

1.2   Why, according to Genesis, was
       Abram singled out by God?

Key terms

Covenant: an agreement or contract

Idolatrous: worship of idols

The nature of the covenant between God and Abraham – the promise of land and offspring

At the beginning of Genesis chapter 12, we read that God called to Abram and
made a covenant with him: a covenant is an agreement or contract. This is known
as the Abrahamic covenant:

> The LORD had said to Abram, 'Go from your country, your people and your
> father's household to the land I will show you.
>
> I will make you into a great nation,
> and I will bless you;
> I will make your name great,
> and you will be a blessing.
> I will bless those who bless you,
> and whoever curses you I will curse;
> and all peoples on earth
> will be blessed through you.'
>
> (Genesis 12:1–3)

However, the idea of a covenant relationship in itself was not something new at the
time of Abram. The making of covenants between individuals was commonplace
in the ancient world, as were covenants made between kings and their conquered
subjects. The covenant structure at the time had a set format, usually in a number
of parts, which included the following elements: identifying the two parties who
were making the agreement; information concerning the background to the
covenant; the terms of the covenant; and sanctions which would come into force
if the terms of the covenant were broken. They were made for a variety of reasons,
including for strength, protection or to keep a people in submission. At the time of
Abram, animal sacrifices were also an integral part of the covenant ceremony.

The Torah recounts two earlier covenants that God had made prior to Abram: one
was with Adam, and the other with Noah, and both had been universal covenants
with humankind rather than just the Jewish people. God made an agreement with
Noah that the world would never be destroyed by water again, and the rainbow
was a sign of this particular covenant.

The Abrahamic covenant was initiated by the word of God: it was authoritative and
full of promise and would establish the Abrahamic community within the protection
of God. The terms of the covenant were set out as follows: if he would leave his home
and family, then God would make three promises: Abram would be the father of a
great nation; would have numerous descendants, and would be given a land to live
in. Why was Abram singled out by God? According to Genesis 17:1, it was because he
was considered to be 'blameless' amongst those in his generation.

The requirement for Abram to leave his homeland was a symbol of him moving
away from the idolatrous practices of his family. It also showed that God had chosen
Abram to be a spiritual as well as a physical leader. Abram and his descendants would
establish a nation which would be an example to the world that God was the one and
only all-powerful God, whom people should follow and worship.

AO1 Activity

Focus on selecting relevant information in order to show knowledge.

After reading the section on 'The nature of the covenant between God and
Abraham', close the book and write down the three terms of the covenant
which God made with Abram.

Abram was concerned, however, as both he and his wife, Sarah, were old and did not have any children. As well as leaving their homeland, it seemed to be an impossible set of promises for God to keep. Nevertheless, Abram did what he was asked and placed his trust in this nameless God.

By accepting the terms of the covenant, the relationship between the Jewish people and God was established. As a result of his faith, God changed Abram's name to Abraham, meaning 'the father of many':

'No longer will you be called Abram; your name will be Abraham, for I have made you a father of many nations.' (Genesis 17:5)

The Abrahamic covenant is what is known as an unconditional covenant, which is an agreement between two parties, but when only *one* of the parties is required to do something. It was also an everlasting covenant. The covenant ceremony is recorded in Genesis chapter 15, and depicts a ritual, which was customary at the time when making treaties. We have evidence of just such a ceremony in the texts of the Mari people of Mesopotamia, which mention the sealing of covenants by killing an ass. After being slain, the animal would be cut in half and the two participants of the covenant agreement would pass between the two parts. The slaying and cutting in two of the animal was a symbol of what would happen to anyone who broke the terms of the covenant. However, it is significant that in the ritual with Abram, God alone moved between the halves of the animals represented by a smoking furnace and a flaming torch. Such an act should be shared by both parties, but God caused sleep to come upon Abram so that he would not be able to pass through. This act highlights the unconditional nature of the covenant. The covenant is eternal and it is God, not Abraham, who binds to the covenant; it is a promise made by God alone and is symbolised by God's flaming torch moving between two halves of an animal's carcass. Its sign is circumcision.

AO1 Activity

Read 'The nature of the covenant between God and Abraham', and then answer the following question: What evidence do we have that points to the fact that the covenant between God and Abraham was an unconditional covenant?

This practises the AO1 skill of being able to use relevant evidence in order to give depth to your answer.

Brit milah (circumcision) as a sign of the covenant (Genesis 17)

According to the Torah, Abraham was commanded by God to circumcise himself, all the male members of his household, as well as all of his descendants. This, according to the book of Genesis, was to be a sign of the covenant relationship between God and the 'chosen people':

'Then God said to Abraham, "As for you, you must keep my covenant, you and your descendants after you for the generations to come. This is my covenant with you and your descendants after you, the covenant you are to keep: Every male among you shall be circumcised. You are to undergo circumcision, and it will be the sign of the covenant between me and you."' (Genesis 17:9–11)

The ritual of circumcision would have been a procedure which was already known to Abraham, as it was widely practised in the ancient Near East. However Abraham was given a specific reason for carrying it out: circumcision was to be an outward, physical sign in the flesh of the eternal covenant between God and the Jewish people, and was the first commandment specific to the Jews. The Torah also says

Key quote
They venture forth in faith, trusting that their family life is in the hand of their mobile God, who leads them into the future, towards the realisation of the divine promises. (B.W. Anderson)

quickfire
1.3 What is an unconditional covenant?

Key quote
The account, though overlaid with later theological interpretation, preserves a very ancient ritual of covenant-making in which the deity makes a binding commitment, sealed by the power of a curse, to fulfil a promise. (B. W. Anderson)

Key terms
Abraham: meaning 'the father of many'

Unconditional covenant: an agreement between two parties, but when only *one* of the parties is required to do something

Specification content
Brit milah (circumcision) as the sign of the covenant (Genesis 17).

quickfire
1.4 What specific reason was Abraham given for carrying out circumcision?

Key quote
Just as he has entered into the covenant, so may he enter into Torah, marriage and good deeds. (Translation of words spoken at the brit milah ceremony)

that: 'Any uncircumcised male, who has not been circumcised in the flesh, will be cut off from his people; he has broken my covenant.' (Genesis 17:14)

Abraham did as required, and he himself was circumcised at the age of ninety-nine years (Genesis 17:24).

The ceremony of **brit milah** is still practised amongst Jews today, and is an important event for the family of a Jewish son as it gives them the feeling of being linked in a long chain reaching all the way back to Abraham. The ceremony is usually carried out by a qualified **mohel**, usually on the eighth day after birth.

However, brit milah has greater significance for Jews than just being merely a physical operation. For many Jews it is seen as the act which makes one a member of the Jewish community. On a spiritual level, it is an act of **consecration** which signifies that the individual is under divine authority, and, as such, is subject to God's commandments. It is restricted to males, as in Jewish tradition it is the male Jew who is obliged to remember and transmit the faith to his descendants. He is therefore ever to be reminded, by the sign on his body, of his duties to God. Indeed, such is its importance that not carrying out this particular term of the covenant would signify in some forms of Judaism that the un-circumcised would no longer be considered to be part of the covenant community.

Key terms

Brit milah: circumcision

Consecration: the act of dedicating to God's service

Mohel: a qualified person who carries out the rite of circumcision

---

AO1 Activity

After reading the section on 'Brit milah (circumcision) as a sign of the covenant', explain the significance of circumcision as part of the covenant relationship.

This practises the AO1 skill of being able to show an accurate understanding of religion and belief.

The significance of Abraham's faith and test of obedience

Key quote

With ten tests our father Abraham was tested and he withstood them all in order to make known how great our father Abraham's love [for God] was. **(Ethics of the Fathers)**

One of the promises of the covenant was that Abraham would be the father of a great people, and when he was 100 years old, and Sarah, his wife was 90, God promised them a son. Sarah conceived and gave birth to a baby boy whom they named Isaac, which means 'laughter', and which is an expression of joy at having a son at such old age. By doing this, God showed control of the world and that in order to keep the promise to Abraham was prepared to intervene in the natural processes of nature.

The ultimate test of Abraham's faith and obedience to God, however, comes in Genesis 22 when he is asked to sacrifice Isaac: 'Sometime later God tested Abraham. He said to him, "Abraham!" "Here I am," he replied. Then God said, "Take your son, your only son, Isaac, whom you love and go to the region of Moriah. Sacrifice him there as a burnt offering on a mountain I will show you."' (Genesis 22:1–2)

Specification content

The significance of Abraham's faith and test of obedience (Genesis 22).

quickfire

1.5　How was Abraham shown that God was in control of the world?

God had promised that Abraham's descendants would come through Isaac, and yet now God was telling Abraham to kill his only son. Abraham's willingness to perform the task shows the exceptional level of faith which he displayed in God. He therefore took Isaac, as directed, up the mountain and prepared to slay him. At the very last minute, God intervened and spared Isaac's life by providing another animal, a ram, for sacrifice. The test is complete and God once more reiterates the promises to Abraham of land, descendants and a personal relationship.

Rabbinic tradition relates that God tested Abraham ten times; however the Mishnah does not tell us what those tests were. Nevertheless, the Akedah, (referring to 'binding' of Isaac), is considered to be the final one. This passage has caused much debate amongst rabbis as to the meaning behind the incident. Rabbi Joseph Leiner suggests that the story allows us to gain an appreciation of God's rules of moral conduct, and that Abraham achieved this when he came to the realisation that killing was wrong. For Maimonides, people and God are on opposite sides of a divide which can never be bridged, therefore he claims that when Abraham 'heard' the voice of God, he had, in reality become attuned to the will of God and was able to interpret it. The event has also been seen as the culmination of a period in Abraham's life when he had been struggling to understand what God wanted from him.

AO1 Activity

After reading the section on 'The significance of Abraham's faith', prepare a 30-second response from Abraham in answer to the question 'How strong is your faith in God?'

The covenant relationship between God and Abraham is unique. For the first time, there is a two-way relationship between God and man with God doing something for Abraham, and yet Abraham is not being required to do anything specific in return for God: '... the covenant was based upon the deity's oath, not upon human performance'. B.W. Anderson.

Abraham's faith is significant as, through him, God established a special covenant relationship. This new relationship offered unconditional future blessings to the descendants of Abraham, and thus Abraham becomes the way in which God will create a people who will live by a certain set of values.

Abraham's test of obedience

quickfire

1.6 What was the ultimate test of Abraham's faith?

Key terms

Akedah: referring to 'binding' of Isaac

Mishnah: meaning 'a teaching that is repeated'; a collection of oral laws

Rabbinic tradition: teachings which come from the rabbis

Study tip

There are many symbolic elements within the story of the Abrahamic covenant, and it is important that you are able to discuss the deeper meaning behind each one rather than just telling the story in an examination answer. This shows that you understand and can interpret the text. Your ability to do this would distinguish a high level answer from an answer that is simply vague or general.

Key skills

Knowledge involves:

Selection of a range of (thorough) accurate and relevant information that is directly related to the specific demands of the question.

This means you choose the correct information relevant to the question set NOT the topic area. You will have to think and focus on selecting key information and NOT writing everything you know about the topic area.

Understanding involves:

Explanation that is extensive, demonstrating depth and/or breadth with excellent use of evidence and examples including (where appropriate) thorough and accurate supporting use of sacred texts, sources of wisdom and specialist language.

This means that you demonstrate that you understand something by being able to illustrate and expand your points through examples/supporting evidence in a personal way and NOT repeat chunks from a textbook (known as rote learning).

Further application of skills:

Go through the topic areas in this section and create some bullet lists of key points from key areas. For each one, provide further elaboration and explanation through the use of evidence and examples.

AO1 Developing skills

It is now time to reflect upon the information that has been covered so far. It is also important to consider how what you have learned can be focused and used for examination-style answers by practising the skills associated with AO1.

Assessment objective 1 (AO1) involves demonstrating knowledge and understanding. The terms 'knowledge' and 'understanding' are obvious but it is crucial to be familiar with how certain skills demonstrate these terms, and also, how the performance of these skills is measured (see generic band descriptors Band 5 for AS AO1).

Obviously, an answer is placed within an appropriate band descriptor depending upon how well the answer performs, ranging from excellent, good, satisfactory, basic/limited to very limited.

For starters, try using the framework / writing frame provided to help you in practising these skills to answer the question below.

As the units in each section of the book develop, the amount of support will be reduced gradually in order to encourage your independence and the perfecting of your AO1 skills.

EXAM PRACTICE: A WRITING FRAME

A focus on examining the role of Abraham in Judaism

According to tradition, the Jewish religion began with a man called Abraham …

Jews regard Abraham as the first Patriarch of the Jewish people. A Patriarch is …

Monotheism was born as a result of …

Genesis chapter 12 tells us that …

The terms of the covenant were as follows …

The Abrahamic covenant was known as an unconditional covenant, which means …

The outward, physical sign of the covenant was …

Abraham's total faith in God can be seen in Genesis 22 when …

In conclusion …

Issues for analysis and evaluation

The extent of the covenant's universality

Nicholas de Lange maintains that universalism is the outlook that values the human race as a whole above any single one of its components, including the Jewish people. The fact that the book of Genesis begins with the creation of the world and humanity rather than the beginnings of the Jewish people can be used as an example of the centrality of universalism in Judaism. The book of Genesis also tells of two previous covenants that God made with Adam and Noah. These had been universal; however, in both cases they had failed as the people of the world turned from God and sinned.

However, the terms of the covenant could be interpreted in such a way as to suggest that the covenant with Abraham was not universal, but was created for the nation of Israel alone. For example, God promised Abraham that he would be the father of a great nation, and offers unconditional future blessing to his descendants. In this way it could be interpreted as the way in which God will create a specific group of people who will live by a certain set of values. This suggests that it was not universal, but was created for the nation of Israel alone.

Even though the covenant made with Abraham was unconditional, there was to be an outward, physical sign of the covenant in the form of circumcision: a sign in the flesh of the eternal covenant between God and the Jewish people, and it is the first commandment specific to the Jews. For Jews today, brit milah continues to hold great significance as an act which makes one a member of the Jewish community. It is an act of consecration, and in some forms of Judaism, if not carried out, would cause the uncircumcised to be seen as no longer part of the covenant community. This act is quite specific to the Jewish people, and doesn't imply that this is to be a practice that is universal.

It could be argued that the covenant is universal in its outlook, with God's role for Abraham as being the one who would lead his descendants both spiritually and literally to the establishment of a nation. This would be done in such a way as to show the world that God was the one and only all-powerful God, whom people should follow and worship.

Many scholars agree that the call of Abraham undoubtedly introduces a new phase in God's story of redemption. When Abraham is promised by God that '... all peoples on earth will be blessed through you', we could interpret the reference to 'all peoples on earth' as applying to humankind in general rather than solely to the Jewish community. In this way, God's promises to Abraham, promises sealed by God's covenant with him, become the foundation for Israel's mission to the world. As a result of his faith, God changed Abram's name to Abraham, meaning 'the father of many'. This is another indication that the covenant was universal.

In conclusion, there are two distinctive lines of argument in relation to the universality of the covenant in Judaism and the process of reasoning for each argument depends upon how the covenants in Judaism are interpreted. On the one hand, clearly the 'universal' covenants with Adam and Noah were seen to be failures by some within Judaism and that the covenants between Abraham and Moses are exclusive to the Israelites and their descendants which is consequently exclusive to Judaism. On the other hand, despite the exclusive nature of the covenants between Abraham and Moses, some argue that the covenant still remains open to all today. The debate continues amongst those who study Judaism today.

This section covers AO2 content and skills

Specification content

The extent of the covenant's universality.

AO2 Activity *Possible lines of argument*

Listed below are some conclusions that could be drawn from the AO2 reasoning in the accompanying text:

1. The covenant God made with Abraham was for all of humanity and not just for the Jewish nation.

2. Abraham's name, meaning 'the father of many', refers only to his direct descendants: the Jewish nation.

3. Circumcision as a sign of the covenant relationship is only meant for the Jewish people.

4. God created the world and all that is in it, therefore God would not restrict the promises made in the covenant to just one group of people.

5. Even if the covenant was made for the Jewish people originally, this does not mean that it cannot extend to all people today.

Consider each of the conclusions drawn above and collect evidence and examples to support each argument from the AO1 and AO2 material studied in this section. Select one conclusion that you think is most convincing and explain why it is so. Now contrast this with the weakest conclusion in the list, justifying your argument with clear reasoning and evidence.

Specification content
Covenant as a privilege or
a responsibility.

AO2 Activity *Possible lines of argument*

Listed below are some conclusions that could be drawn from the AO2 reasoning in the accompanying text:

1. God has promised to protect the Jewish people, therefore they have a responsibility to keep their side of the covenant.

2. Jews have been chosen by God to be an example to the nations: it is a privilege to have been chosen.

3. It can be a great burden trying to maintain a Jewish lifestyle in a secular society.

4. The requirements of the 613 commandments given by God were meant to help the Jews to establish themselves as a nation during their time in the wilderness and are no longer relevant in the 21st century.

5. Circumcision is outdated for some Jews and so the idea of both privilege and responsibility are not as important.

Consider each of the conclusions drawn above and collect evidence and examples to support each argument from the AO1 and AO2 material studied in this section. Select one conclusion that you think is most convincing and explain why it is so. Now contrast this with the weakest conclusion in the list, justifying your argument with clear reasoning and evidence.

Covenant as a privilege or a responsibility

The strength of the covenant relationship between God and the Jewish people remains. Jews have the privilege of being able to look back at times when the strength of God has helped them in times of trouble, and this, in turn, helps them to continue to move forward with purpose and faith.

There is also the privilege of knowing that God has promised to stay with them, and will never abandon them because they are the chosen people; therefore, the strength of the covenant relationship between God and the Jewish people endures.

Jews can also look forward to the future fulfilment of the covenant with the coming of the Messiah. The Messiah will bring peace to the world; Jerusalem will be rebuilt, and the Jews will have their freedom as well as their Promised Land.

The fact that Jews understand their relationship with God in terms of a covenant in which God has promised to make them a great nation suggests a responsibility to live in obedience to God. Jews believe that they are God's chosen people: chosen in the sense that they are to be examples to the world of the way in which God wants people to live.

Maintaining a life of obedience to God through religious living brings with it great responsibilities when living in a secular society which does not cater specifically for a Jewish way of life. Nevertheless, Jews accept their responsibility to set a good example by ensuring that their lifestyles are in accordance with the mitzvot which God has set out for them to follow. The 613 mitzvot (commandments) cover all aspects of a Jewish person's life. They incorporate ways in which to worship God, how and when to pray, festivals and rites of passage as well as practical rules for living, including food laws (kosher). Life lived under such restrictions may well be seen as a burden, especially when life in the 21st century is so very different from the early years of the Jewish nation when they were wandering in the desert and required such rules for their survival. It can be especially difficult to keep these rules when living as a Jew in a society such as Britain which does not cater for such a lifestyle. For example, it can be burden upon a young Jewish person who attends a non-Jewish school, and who is unable to buy food from the canteen, or go out for a meal with friends because of the requirement to keep the kosher food laws. Neither are they able to go out with non-Jewish friends during the Sabbath.

The Abrahamic covenant established the covenant of faith between God and the Jewish people. Yet even though it was an unconditional covenant, its sign was to be that of an outward, physical act: that of circumcision. For Jews today, the continuation of this ritual highlights their responsibility to act upon God's requirements.

One possible conclusion could be that to ask whether it is one or the other – privilege or responsibility – is really a misconception of covenant as it is clearly both as evidenced from the discussion above. However, this conclusion does not address the issues of whether or not there is equal emphasis on both for Jews today and throughout their history. Clearly, the debate about the application of the religious laws within Judaism between Reform and Orthodox Jews indicates that this is not, and possibly will never be, solved to everyone's satisfaction. The answer to any question about 'privilege or responsibility' will therefore be dependent upon how one interprets the religious rules within Judaism.

AO2 Developing skills

It is now time to reflect upon the information that has been covered so far. It is also important to consider how what you have learned can be focused and used for examination-style answers by practising the skills associated with AO2.

Assessment objective 2 (AO2) involves 'analysis' and 'evaluation'. The terms may be obvious but it is crucial to be familiar with how certain skills demonstrate these terms, and also, how the performance of these skills is measured (see generic band descriptors Band 5 for AS AO2).

Obviously, an answer is placed within an appropriate band descriptor depending upon how well the answer performs, ranging from excellent, good, satisfactory, basic/limited to very limited.

For starters, try using the framework / writing frame provided to help you in practising these skills to answer the question below.

As the units in each section of the book develop, the amount of support will be reduced gradually in order to encourage your independence and the perfecting of your AO2 skills.

Have a go at answering this question by using the writing frame below.

EXAM PRACTICE: A WRITING FRAME

A focus on assessing whether the covenant God made with Abraham was ultimately a covenant for all nations of the world and not just for the Jewish people

The issue for debate here is ...

There are different ways of looking at this and many key questions to ask such as ...

The covenant God made with Abraham was the third covenant, which is recorded in the book of Genesis. The first two, which had been made with Adam and Noah, had both been universal, but both had failed as the people of the world had turned from God and sinned. It could be argued that as a result of this, God had given up on humanity and ...

It could be argued that the covenant with Abraham is unique because ...

However, there could be another way of interpreting the covenant relationship such as ...

In light of all this, it could be argued that ...

Nevertheless, it is my view that ...

and I base this argument on the following reasons ...

Key skills

Analysis involves identifying issues raised by the materials in the AO1, together with those identified in the AO2 section, and presents sustained and clear views, either of scholars or from a personal perspective ready for evaluation.

This means that it picks out key things to debate and the lines of argument presented by others or a personal point of view.

Evaluation involves considering the various implications of the issues raised based upon the evidence gleaned from analysis and provides an extensive detailed argument with a clear conclusion.

This means that the answer weighs up the various and different lines of argument analysed through individual commentary and response and arrives at a conclusion through a clear process of reasoning.

Study tip

Where analysis and evaluation are concerned, it is important that you have a clear understanding of the issue raised by the question set. You will not be able to produce a high level answer if you have misunderstood the question.

Specification content
The nature and significance of the Mosaic covenant both at the time of Moses and today (Exodus 19–20).

quickfire

1.7 Who is known as the Law-giver within Judaism?

quickfire

1.8 How did the Pharaoh attempt to weaken the Hebrew nation?

Key terms

CE: referring to the Common Era; the period beginning with the traditional birth year of Jesus

Divine: belonging to; relating to; or coming from God

Moses: which means 'to draw out' or to 'extract'

Pharaoh: the title of the kings of ancient Egypt

Promised Land: the land of Canaan which had been promised by God to Abraham and his descendants

Prophet: a person chosen to express the will of God

Prophetic: having the characteristics of a prophet

Theophany: the manifestation of God to humans

quickfire

1.9 What was the nature of the theophany that Moses experienced?

B: Moses and the establishment of the covenant of law

Background information

Moses is considered, after Abraham, to be the second most important leader of the Jews. If Abraham was the Father of the Jews, then Moses was the Law-giver, the one who gave the Jewish faith a foundation as the chosen people of God. In c. 1160, Maimonides (1135–1204 CE), a prominent rabbi and Jewish philosopher, composed 'The Thirteen Principles of Faith' which, in his view, contained the essential tenets of the Jewish religion. Such is Moses' importance within the Jewish faith that number 7 of the thirteen principles states that he is the highest in rank of all of the prophets.

The Bible tells us that the descendants of Jacob lived in Egypt for 450 years and during this time grew into a nation called Israel. However, it also reflects a political situation in which the Israelites became enslaved. It is difficult to pinpoint a definite date, but historians and scholars believe that the enslavement occurred when the Pharaoh Rameses II came to the throne in around 1290 BCE. The Pharaoh enslaved many groups of people in Egypt in order to use them to carry out work on a series of massive building projects. This matches a Biblical description, which says that the Children of Israel, or Hebrews as they are also known, were put to work in this way: 'So they put slave masters over them to oppress them with forced labour, and they built Pithom and Rameses as store cities for Pharaoh.' (Exodus 1:11)

In an attempt to weaken the Hebrews further, the Pharaoh ruled that all male newborn Israelite babies should be killed. It is at this point in the narrative that Moses is introduced. The tradition of Exodus chapter 2 relates the miraculous account of Moses' escape from death. He was born to a Hebrew mother who, in order to save him from being killed, placed him in a basket on the River Nile leaving his fate up to God's will. He was subsequently found and rescued by the Pharaoh's daughter, and brought up in the palace as a royal prince. He was named 'Moses', which means 'to draw out,' to or to 'extract': an indication that he would be the one who 'extracted' or took the Israelites out of slavery in Egypt.

Other aspects of his life were also to have great significance in relation to the escape from Egypt. His upbringing in the Egyptian court gave him valuable knowledge that he would use to great advantage in later life when dealing with the Pharaoh. Also, despite his nurture in Pharaoh's court, he continued to have a strong feeling of identification with his own Hebrew people. As an adult he killed an Egyptian who was beating a Hebrew slave, and it was as a result of this that he was forced to flee. He was driven into exile to the land of Midian where he married the daughter of a priest named Jethro. He spent forty years as a shepherd, living in the desert, a period in his life which would equip him with the survival skills required during the time of wandering in the wilderness after the escape from Egypt.

It was while tending the flocks in the wilderness that Moses heard the voice of God speaking to him through a bush, which flamed but did not burn: God called to him from within the bush: '"Moses! Moses!" And Moses said, "Here I am"' (Exodus 3:4). God asked Moses to lead the Israelites out of slavery in Egypt and deliver them to the Promised Land. Such an event is known as a theophany, which refers to the manifestation of God to humans, and Bernhard W. Anderson says that this account 'portrays the divine calling and commission of a prophetic figure. ... Moses was given a task and was summoned to take part with God in the historical drama.' Moses was uneasy about the call but finally returned to Egypt and demanded freedom for his people.

After a number of confrontations with the Pharaoh, followed by a series of ten plagues upon Egypt, which culminated in the death of the first-born sons in every Egyptian household, Pharaoh was finally persuaded by Moses to release the Israelites. Yet, as they fled, he changed his mind and set out to bring them back.

The Hebrew scriptures give a clear picture of their route of escape, and tell of them approaching a body of water called 'Yam Suf', the 'Sea of Reeds' which is usually translated as the 'Red Sea'. The narrative expresses the conviction that God was guiding them as the waters parted, the Israelites walked through, then the waters returned and destroyed the Pharaoh's army.

The deliverance of the people of Israel from slavery is known as the **Exodus** from Egypt. Exodus means a departure, a going out, usually of a large group of people.

Key quote

While we have no extra-biblical record of the ten plagues or of a mass escape of slaves from Egypt, natural disasters did take place periodically, and mass escapes of slaves are known from elsewhere in the ancient world … Moreover, if the Israelites had invented their history, it seems more likely that they would have portrayed themselves as the original inhabitants of their land rather than interlopers with a humiliating background as slaves. (Tigay)

> ### AO1 Activity
>
> After reading the information in the 'Introduction', note down examples of evidence that could be used to show that Moses was destined to play a significant part in the history of the Israelite nation.
>
> This will help you to select key, relevant information for an answer to a question about the role of Moses and the establishment of covenant law.

The nature and significance of the Mosaic covenant at the time of Moses (Exodus 19–20)

After leaving the land of Egypt the Israelites set out for the Wilderness of Sinai, the place to which Moses had been directed by God: '… when you have brought the people out of Egypt, you will worship God on this mountain' (Exodus 3:12). The journey itself was challenging: the **wilderness** environment was hostile, with little food or water. It was also a time when the people were discontented and voiced their complaints about God: 'Is the LORD among us or not?' (Exodus 17:7). It has been interpreted as a period in which the people were 'tested' to see if they could live in complete and daily dependence upon God providing **mercy**.

Key terms

Exodus: a departure, a going out, usually of a large group of people

Mercy: the characteristic of God to be forgiving

Wilderness: a wild and uncultivated region: in this case, a desert

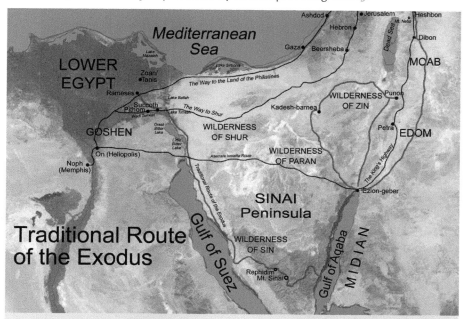

Map of the route of the Exodus journey

quicKfire

1.10 What is a 'conditional covenant'?

quicKfire

1.11 What made the Mosaic covenant different from the one made with Abraham?

Key terms

Benevolence: act of kindness or generosity

Conditional covenant: a covenant in which two or more parties agree to look after each other's interests so that they will all benefit

Hittite: the name given to a nation of people from Asia Minor

Mosaic: relating to Moses

Parity: the condition of being equal

Subordinate: lower in importance or rank

Suzerain: a ruler that exercises control over another state, whilst allowing it to retain some autonomy

Key quote

To make a covenant in no way infringes upon the sovereignty of the great king. And yet the covenant is not just an assertion of power over an inferior, as though the vassal were forced into obedience. The most striking aspect of the suzerainty covenant is the great attention given to the king's deed of benevolence on behalf of the vassal, deeds which evoke a response of grateful obedience.
(B. W. Anderson)

It was at Mount Sinai that the second covenant between God and the Israelites was established. The Mosiac covenant, as it is known, is a conditional covenant. A conditional covenant is one in which two or more parties agree to look after each other's interests so that they will all benefit. In the covenant made with Moses, God promised to be God of the Israelites only if they obey a set of divine laws. It was a covenant that reinforced the covenant that God had given to Abraham; however, the Jews were now told what they were required to do as their side of the agreement.

However, we need to look in more detail at the particular form of the Mosaic covenant. Bernhard W. Anderson draws attention to a study of international treaties of the late second millennium BCE, which have been found chiefly in Hittite archives. He claims that an analysis of the form and content of these treaties reveals that there two distinct types of conditional covenant: parity and suzerainty.

A parity covenant is one in which both parties, being equal in rank, bind themselves to each other by reciprocal obligations. The suzerainty covenant, however, is more unilateral, for it is made between a suzerain, a great king, and his subordinate. In this particular relationship, it is the suzerain who 'gives' the covenant, and within its terms, the subordinate party receives his protection. However, the subordinate is under an obligation to obey the commands issued by the suzerain.

Scholars have identified six characteristics of a suzerain treaty:

1. Preamble – states the name of the sovereign.

2. Historical prologue – the suzerain makes reference to previous deeds of benevolence performed on behalf of the subordinate.

3. Conditions imposed upon the subordinate – the most important requirement is that an oath of loyalty must be made by the subordinate, and in doing so, must pledge not to recognise the sovereignty of any other powers.

4. Attention to the treaty document – this requires that copies of the treaty be preserved in the temples of both countries, and that it is to be read publicly in the subordinate state once a year.

5. Witnesses to the treaty – although the gods of both countries are invoked as witnesses, precedence is given to the Hittite gods. Moreover, included among the witnesses are natural powers such as Heaven and earth, winds and clouds, mountains and rivers.

6. Penalties – blessings in the form of protection will result from obedience to the treaty, but curses will fall upon the subordinate if unfaithful.

There are so many similarities between this form of treaty and the Mosaic covenant in Exodus 19–24, that some scholars have concluded that it must have provided the model in terms of which Israel portrayed the relationship which Yahweh had initiated with the people.

For example, the preamble seems to be present in God's self-identification: 'I am Yahweh, your God.' (Exodus 20:1). The historical prologue may be found in the affirmation that Yahweh delivered the people from slavery in Egypt (Exodus 20:2 cf. 19:4). Furthermore, the Decalogue of Exodus 20 provided the stipulations, which Moses wrote in a document called the 'book of the covenant' and read in the hearing of the people (Exodus 24:4a, 7).

Notwithstanding, other elements are *not* present, but, as Anderson points out, we should not expect the witness clause, at least in the same form, because Yahweh does not recognise other 'gods'.

It has therefore been proposed that Moses became acquainted with this form of treaty in Egypt, which had a long history of dealing with the Hittites, and that he used it to interpret the meaning of Yahweh's initiative in freeing the people. The

Mosaic covenant was in no sense a parity contract in which both parties were equal and mutually dependent. It was not a relationship between equals. 'The covenant was *given* by God; the relationship was conferred upon the people by their Sovereign … Yahweh initiated the relationship and, …Yahweh was free to terminate it, with the result that Israel would no longer be the "people of God."' (B.W. Anderson)

Moses ascended the mountain and God called to him stating the promise to stay with the Jews and never to abandon them because they were now a divinely chosen people: 'Now if you obey me fully and keep my covenant, then out of all nations you will be my treasured possession' (Exodus 19:5).

God is telling the people that they have a responsibility too: they must dedicate themselves to serving the Lord forever, and to make the world a better and holier place by obeying God's laws. In return for this, God will never abandon them.

The nature and significance of the Mosaic covenant for Jews today

One of the most significant things about the Mosaic covenant is that it was made with the whole nation rather than with an individual, as in the case of Abraham. Furthermore, it is a covenant which still provides the basis for the Jewish faith today.

Under the Mosaic covenant, the Law was given to the Jewish people and such is its significance, that the practices of Jews today can be seen as a development of those laws into a distinct lifestyle. The five books of Moses contain 613 mitzvot (commandments) which set out the ethical ideals of the Jewish people, set within an account of their historical background. By living according to the mitzvot, Jews can maintain their relationship with God, thus cultivating a lifestyle which reflects the holy nature of the covenant relationship. It is also the means by which the Jewish people can witness to other nations: 'Be holy because I, the Lord your God, am holy.' (Leviticus 19:2)

E.W. Heaton identifies the four distinctive features of the faith, which grew up as a result of the Mosaic covenant:

1. It was a faith which originated in response to God's self-disclosure to Moses and the conviction that it was God who had delivered the Israelites from their bondage in Egypt.

2. It was a faith which discerned the grace of Yahweh in the creation of Israel as a covenant people and in his guidance and protection through all the vicissitudes of its history.

3. It was a faith which demanded total trust in God's purpose and power.

4. It was a faith which demanded absolute moral obedience.

AO1 Activity

Write down five statements which illustrate the significance of the Mosaic covenant for Jews today.

This practises the AO1 skill of selecting the key relevant information.

AO1 Activity

After reading the section on 'The nature and significance of the Mosaic covenant at the time of Moses', create a mind map that includes:

(a) a simple explanation of the term 'conditional covenant',

(b) the terms of the Mosaic covenant and

(c) the evidence which scholars have suggested shows that the Mosaic covenant may have been based upon a suzerainty covenant.

This will help you to gain a detailed knowledge and understanding of the nature of the Mosaic covenant.

quickfire

1.12 How can Jews today maintain their relationship with God?

Key quote

By its very nature…. (it was) a tradition which was didactic rather than cultic … a moral faith … (E.W. Heaton)

Key terms

Didactic: intended to teach or instruct

Ethical: to live according to a set of moral principles

Mitzvot: commandments (plural)

Vicissitudes: unpredictable changes of circumstance

Specification content

The recording of the covenant by
Moses (Exodus 24:4, Exodus 34:1–2,
27–28); the importance of God's
protection for obedience
(Exodus 34:10–11).

The recording of the covenant by Moses (Exodus 24:4, Exodus 34:1–2, 27–28); the importance of God's protection for obedience (Exodus 34:10–11)

After receiving all the laws and recounting them to the people, the narrative tells us that Moses returned to Sinai, at God's request, accompanied by two sons of Aaron (brother of Moses), and seventy elders who acted as witnesses for the people. The elders remained at the foot of Sinai, and the sons of Aaron ascended part of the way. However, it was Moses alone who went up to the summit where he recounts and records the laws of God: 'Moses then wrote down everything the LORD had said.' (Exodus 24:4)

Although tradition has it that the laws of God were originally written upon tablets of stone, the written text, believed by many Jews to contain the actual words of God to Moses, exists today in the form of the **Torah**: the name given to the Five Books

Moses with the two tablets of stone

of Moses. In giving the Law to the people, Moses taught the Israelites what God expected of them, and by keeping these rules they would become God's servants, helping to fulfil the divine plan.

It is at this point that the covenant is sealed, formally and legally, by means of a sacrificial ceremony: 'He got up early the next morning and built an altar at the foot of the mountain and set up twelve stone pillars representing the twelve tribes of Israel.' (Exodus 24:4)

It was common practice for covenants in the ancient world to be **ratified** by a special ceremony, and these took a variety of forms. For example, by eating salt together (Numbers 18:19); by partaking of a sacrificial meal (Genesis 31:54); by passing between the divided pieces of slaughtered sacrifice (Genesis 15:10), but especially by the use of blood. In this particular instance, an altar was built surrounded by twelve pillars symbolising the twelve tribes, and the covenant was ratified by a blood sacrifice.

Key quote

Moses received the Torah from Sinai, he gave it to Joshua, Joshua gave it to the Elders, the Elders to the Prophets, and the Prophets to the men of the Great Assembly. **(Ethics of the Fathers)**

Key terms

Ratify: to give formal consent to a treaty or agreement

Torah: means 'instruction' or 'teaching' and refers to the first five books of the Jewish scriptures; it can also refer to the whole of Jewish teaching

It was not long, however, before the people strayed from their promises to God. They became discontented that Moses had gone back up the mountain but had failed to reappear, and their discontent was shown in the creation of an **idol**, a calf, made of gold that they worshipped in pagan ways. When Moses appeared and saw their **debauched** behaviour, he was angry and smashed the tablets upon which the Ten Commandments were written, thereby demonstrating that the people had broken their part of the covenant.

Nevertheless, the importance of Moses' role as leader and **mediator** cannot be under-estimated and Exodus 34 tells us that he ultimately **interceded** for the people and received assurance that God's love included the capacity to forgive.

The covenant was renewed through a new declaration of the law of the covenant, again given by God, but Moses was to prepare the tablets on this occasion: 'The Lord said to Moses, "Chisel out two stones like the first ones, and I will write on them the words that were on the first tablets, which you broke. Be ready in the morning, and then come up on Mount Sinai. Present yourself to me there on top of the mountain."' (Exodus 34:1–2)

The destruction of the first stone tablets on which the Ten Commandments were recorded provided for a new edition as a symbol of the renewal of the covenant:

'And he said, "Behold, I make a covenant. Before all your people I will do marvels, such as have not been wrought in all the earth or in any nation; and all the people among whom you are shall see the work of the Lord; for it is a terrible thing that I will do with you. Observe what I command you this day. Behold, I will drive out before you the Amorites, the Canaanites, the Hittites, the Perizzites, the Hivites, and the Jebusites."' (Exodus 34:10–11)

This passage states that God will re-establish the covenant, and will lead Israel to the Promised Land with unprecedented miracles. In return, the people are to obey the terms as set down by God. 'Then the Lord said to Moses, "Write down these words, for in accordance with these words I have made a covenant with you and with Israel" … and he (Moses) wrote on the tablets the words of the covenant – the Ten Commandments.' (Exodus 34: 27–28)

Scholars have noted that the second set of tablets, although meant to be a copy of the first, differs in a number of areas. J.H. Tigay, for instance, notes that in view of the people's recent religious sin, they are in some ways stricter than the first edition, with the laws against idolatry appearing first and in greater detail. The second set of laws is also sometimes referred to as the 'ritual **decalogue**', owing to their concentration on **cultic** matters such as the seasonal festivals or the prohibition against the Canaanite practice of boiling a young goat in its mother's milk: 'Perhaps they presuppose the later situation of Israel's settlement in Canaan, when agricultural festivals were adopted and some Canaanite practices repudiated.' (B.W. Anderson)

AO1 Activity

After reading this section on the covenant, close the book and, making use of the following words: mediator; idol; intercede; covenant (which you can use in any order); note down Moses' role in the renewal of the covenant.

This will help you to practise using specialist language and vocabulary in context.

Key terms

Cultic: a system of religious beliefs

Debauched: immoral, corrupt behaviour

Decalogue: the Ten Commandments

Idol: an image or symbol, especially of a god, which is used as an object of worship

Intercede: to make an appeal on someone's behalf

Mediator: someone who acts between two parties in order to bring about an end to a disagreement

Key quote

These narratives in Exodus … show that Israel could not claim to be better than other nations, either morally or religiously, for the people displayed the same weaknesses and strength that are found in the life of any people. If there was any difference, it lay in the extraordinary experience that had formed them into a community, and the destiny to which they were called in the service of God. (B.W. Anderson)

Study tip

There is a variety of terms used to describe the Jewish people: Children of Israel; Israelites; Hebrews. Your ability to use these terms accurately would distinguish a high level answer from one which has limited depth of understanding.

Key skills

Knowledge involves:

Selection of a range of (thorough) accurate and relevant information that is directly related to the specific demands of the question.

This means you choose the correct information relevant to the question set NOT the topic area. You will have to think and focus on selecting key information and NOT writing everything you know about the topic area.

Understanding involves:

Explanation that is extensive, demonstrating depth and/or breadth with excellent use of evidence and examples including (where appropriate) thorough and accurate supporting use of sacred texts, sources of wisdom and specialist language.

This means that you demonstrate that you understand something by being able to illustrate and expand your points through examples/supporting evidence in a personal way and NOT repeat chunks from a textbook (known as rote learning).

Further application of skills:

Once you have made your choices and selected your information, compare them with another student. See if together you can decide on six and their correct order, this time, in sequence for answering a question.

AO1 Developing skills

It is now time to reflect upon the information that has been covered so far. It is also important to consider how what you have learned can be focused and used for examination-style answers by practising the skills associated with AO1.

Assessment objective 1 (AO1) involves demonstrating knowledge and understanding. The terms 'knowledge' and 'understanding' are obvious but it is crucial to be familiar with how certain skills demonstrate these terms, and also, how the performance of these skills is measured (see generic band descriptors Band 5 for AS AO1).

▶ **Your new task is this:** from the list of ten key points below, choose six that you feel are the most important in answering the question above the list. Put your points in order of priority, explaining why they are the six most important aspects to mention from that topic. This skill of prioritising and selecting appropriate material will help you in answering examination questions for AO1.

A focus on outlining the nature and significance of the Mosaic covenant at the time of Moses.

1. In the covenant made with Moses, God promised to be God of the Israelites only if they obey a set of divine laws.

2. The terms of the covenant set out what God expected of the Israelites, and by keeping these rules, they would become God's servants, helping to fulfil the divine plan.

3. Events from his early life indicate that Moses was destined to play a significant part in the history of the Israelite nation.

4. According to Jewish tradition, the history of the Jewish people begins with the covenant that God made with Abraham. Abraham was the first Patriarch of the Jewish people.

5. The Mosaic covenant is a conditional covenant.

6. Under the Mosaic covenant the Law was given to the Jewish people and such is its significance, that the practices of Jews today can be seen as a development of those laws into a distinct lifestyle.

7. Scholars have suggested that the Mosaic covenant is a form of suzerainty covenant. In this particular relationship, it is the suzerain who 'gives' the covenant, and within its terms, the subordinate party receives his protection.

8. It was a covenant that reinforced the covenant that God had given to Abraham; however, the Jews were now told what they were required to do as their side of the agreement.

9. God is telling the people that they have a responsibility too: they must dedicate themselves to serving the Lord forever, and to make the world a better and holier place by obeying God's laws. In return for this, God will never abandon them.

10. Moses was the Law-giver, the one who gave the Jewish faith a foundation as the chosen people of God.

Issues for analysis and evaluation

Whether covenant is a method of religious control

When the covenant was first established, it could be perceived to have been a form of religious control. The Israelites had been taken from Egypt, a place where they had been immersed in Egyptian culture, and they were not prepared for the religious and cultural changes that were taking place. It was therefore imperative that they remained faithful solely to the God of Abraham, living as they did in a region that was resolutely polytheistic. Religious control in this context could therefore be seen in a positive light, by providing a framework in order that they would not be tempted by the religion of the Canaanites, which they would encounter once they had settled in the Promised Land.

It was important that the people had a structure upon which to establish the covenant community, and this structure encompassed more than just things which we would recognise as belonging to religious practice. Thus the 613 mitzvot covered all aspects of daily life, both practical as well as religious, and gave the Jews their special identity as the chosen people of God. Adherence to the mitzvot continues today, with Jewish communities abiding by God's laws as a means by which they continue to show their loyalty within the covenant relationship.

The conditional nature of the Mosaic covenant, however, means that it is not one that is built upon an equal partnership between God and human beings. The power and holiness of God is emphasised and, in accepting the terms of the covenant, the Israelites were beholden to keep the requirements of the commandments. In the covenant made with Moses, God promised to be God of the Israelites only if they obey a set of divine laws. We are therefore able to identify a controlling element within the relationship; in that it is incumbent upon the Jews to live according to God's laws in order to preserve God's promise of protection. God is the suzerain, and the Jews the subordinate.

By agreeing to enter into the covenant with God, they were acknowledging their gratitude, and showed their obligation by promising to keep the commandments. In this context it *is* about religious control, because such are the terms of the covenant, that if the Jews disobey God then they will lose God's protection.

Nowadays, keeping the mitzvot is seen as a discipline rather than a control mechanism as they bring discipline to every aspect of Jewish life. For example, keeping the kosher food laws can be seen as a test of faith rather than a means of control as no specific reason is allocated to them.

Some would claim that it is also possible to live a Jewish life without keeping all of the mitzvot, and such is the case within Reform Judaism. Therefore, in these circumstances, the covenant is not considered to be a method of religious control.

Ultimately, it could be said that keeping the requirements of the covenant can be seen as a means of communicating with God, and underlines the fact that the Jews continue to acknowledge the responsibility they have as partners in the covenant which God made with them through Moses at Mount Sinai: its aim being to bring the world, through Judaism, to ethical monotheism.

This section covers AO2 content and skills

Specification content

Whether covenant is a method of religious control.

AO2 Activity *Possible lines of argument*

Listed below are some conclusions that could be drawn from the AO2 reasoning in the accompanying text:

1. In its historical context, the covenant was established as a form of religious control.

2. A person can't be Jewish unless they want to be controlled by God.

3. The emphasis has changed nowadays, and keeping the terms of the covenant is seen as a religious discipline.

4. It is possible to retain Jewish identity without following all of the requirements of the covenant.

5. Living according to the terms of the covenant is one of the ways in which a Jew communicates with God.

Consider each of the conclusions drawn above and collect evidence and examples to support each argument from the AO1 and AO2 material studied in this section. Select one conclusion that you think is most convincing and explain why it is so. Now contrast this with the weakest conclusion in the list, justifying your argument with clear reasoning and evidence.

How far covenant is of legal value

The word 'covenant' is a legal term which refers to a binding contract or agreement. It therefore follows that the Mosaic covenant is a legal contract, in which two parties have responsibilities towards each other. As a result of this, the Torah has been described as the 'eternal law', and it is possible to obtain guidance from it in modern-day society. The mitzvot contained within it offer guidance, yet they require further explanation, and it is the halakhah which explains how the commandments are to be kept; thus the divine law continues to be universally applicable in every age and at every time.

When properly and devoutly observed, the mitzvot can enhance the spiritual element of a person's life by turning the everyday things of their daily routine into acts that have religious significance. Jews believe that when they keep God's laws, they bring holiness into the world and prepare it for the time when all human beings will know God. This is especially evident within the Hasidic branch of Judaism where the concept of devekut (clinging to God) is of utmost importance. God must be kept constantly in the mind, and every thought and action is considered to be a holy act that brings the individual closer to God.

However, we need to take account of the fact that times have changed since the establishment of the Mosaic covenant. It could be argued that it was only of legal value in ancient times when the covenant between God and the Israelites was first established. It was important at that time that the people had a structure upon which to build their community as the chosen people of God. This required laws which would cover all aspects of their lives.

It has been suggested that the covenant no longer has 'legal' value as the focus on the keeping of the mitzvot reduces the religion to a set of rules, thus suppressing spirituality. It also marks out the Jewish lifestyle as being different, and this could be a problem when living in a society where they are in the minority, leading ultimately to discrimination.

Many of the laws are out-dated, and are no longer representative of the majority of issues that are faced in modern-day life. Medical issues such as fertility treatment and organ transplantation, for example, were not evident at the time of the making of the original covenant.

Reform Jews do not follow the mitzvot in their entirety or original form, and are not afraid to discard aspects of the law which they believe have no relevance for them in modern society. Nevertheless, they continue to live a Jewish lifestyle which is relevant within society.

Perhaps it is more appropriate to view the Torah as more than just a legal 'rule' book, and accept it in a much wider sense as a guide for the establishment of a moral and ethical code of conduct.

AO2 Activity *Possible lines of argument*

Listed below are some conclusions that could be drawn from the AO2 reasoning in the accompanying text:

1. The laws contained within the covenant were initially important when the Israelites were establishing themselves as a new nation.

2. The laws bring holiness into the world and set the Jews apart as examples of the way in which God wants people to live.

3. Spirituality is in danger of being suppressed if Judaism becomes just a set of rules.

4. The Torah is more of a moral and ethical guide rather than merely a legal rulebook.

5. The laws are out-dated and are not representative of the majority of issues faced in modern-day life.

Consider each of the conclusions drawn above and collect evidence and examples to support each argument from the AO1 and AO2 material studied in this section. Select one conclusion that you think is most convincing and explain why it is so. Now contrast this with the weakest conclusion in the list, justifying your argument with clear reasoning and evidence.

Study tip

Remember that AO2 assessment objectives are testing your ability to analyse and evaluate a particular issue. Therefore you don't need to include detailed explanations of terms such as 'covenant', for example, or biographical facts about Moses.

Developing skills for AO2

It is now time to reflect upon the information that has been covered so far. It is also important to consider how what you have learned can be focused and used for examination-style answers by practising the skills associated with AO2.

Assessment objective 2 (AO2) involves 'analysis' and 'evaluation'. The terms may be obvious but it is crucial to be familiar with how certain skills demonstrate these terms, and also, how the performance of these skills is measured (see generic band descriptors Band 5 for AS AO2).

Obviously an answer is placed within an appropriate band descriptor depending upon how well the answer performs, ranging from excellent, good, satisfactory, basic/limited to very limited.

▶ **Your task is this:** from the list of the ten key points below, select six that are relevant to the evaluation task below. Put your selection into an order that you would use to address the task set. In explaining why you have chosen these six to answer the task you will find that you are developing a process of reasoning. This will help you to develop an argument to decide how much legal value the covenant with Moses has within Judaism.

'A focus on evaluating whether the covenant made with Moses is any longer of legal value.'

1. It is possible to retain a Jewish identity without living according to the mitzvot. Reform Jews do not consider that they are breaking any laws when they decide not to follow all of the mitzvot.

2. Even though the covenant was established in ancient times, the laws are still relevant and are constantly being discussed and re-interpreted to ensure their relevance for modern-day living.

3. Religious laws are of no value in societies ruled by secular laws which are set by a government.

4. The covenant only really had legal value when the nation of Israel was being established in the wilderness. It was important at that time that there was a firm moral and ethical structure within which the new community could be established.

5. They don't have any legal value for me at all because I am not a religious person, and I think that it is ridiculous to have to follow rules such as what you can or cannot eat.

6. There is a danger that focusing on following the rules can mean a loss of opportunities for spiritual development.

7. Keeping the rules shows discipline and turns everyday acts of daily life into opportunities for worshipping God.

8. I say 'live and let live'. If Jews want to carry on following these laws than that's their business.

9. Many of the laws are out-dated, as there are many issues in modern-day society, such as advances in medicine, which are not covered by the original covenant.

10. The covenant made with Moses is an eternal covenant, and therefore still has legal value as both parties have a responsibility to keep the terms of the agreement.

Key skills

Analysis involves identifying issues raised by the materials in the AO1, together with those identified in the AO2 section, and presents sustained and clear views, either of scholars or from a personal perspective ready for evaluation.

This means that it picks out key things to debate and the lines of argument presented by others or a personal point of view.

Evaluation involves considering the various implications of the issues raised based upon the evidence gleaned from analysis and provides an extensive detailed argument with a clear conclusion.

This means that the answer weighs up the various and different lines of argument analysed through individual commentary and response and arrives at a conclusion through a clear process of reasoning.

Specification content

The receiving of the Torah at Sinai
and the significance of the written
law (Exodus 19–20).

quickpire

1.13 What is the literal meaning of the
word 'Torah'?

quickpire

1.14 Name the first five books of the
Hebrew Scriptures.

Key term

Yahweh: a form of the Hebrew name
for God

Key quote

Israel is called to be a 'holy nation'.
This means that Israel belongs
to Yahweh … this relationship
was expressed in a covenant
… as represented by the Ten
Commandments. (G.W. Anderson)

C: The Torah as a source of wisdom and authority – its use and treatment in worship and daily life

The receiving of the Torah at Sinai and the significance of the written law (Exodus 19–20)

The word Torah literally means 'instruction' or 'teaching' and refers to the first
five books of the Hebrew Scriptures: Genesis, Exodus, Leviticus, Numbers, and
Deuteronomy. However, it can also mean the whole of Jewish teaching. It is the
central and most important document of the Jewish religion and has been used as
the basis of the Jewish faith throughout its history.

The story related in Exodus chapters 19–20 deals with God's revelation at Sinai, the
giving of the Law, and the making of the covenant.

According to Exodus 19:3–6, God had brought the people to Mount Sinai for a
particular purpose: 'You yourselves have seen what I did to Egypt, and how I carried
you on eagles' wings and brought you to myself. Now if you obey me fully and
keep my covenant, then out of all the nations you will be my treasured possession.
Although the whole earth is mine, you will be for me a kingdom of priests and a
holy nation.'

Bernhard W. Anderson says 'Whether in fact these people would be the people of
Yahweh depended upon a condition: "… if you will obey my voice and keep my
covenant." Then they would be Yahweh's personal possession, the community that
belongs to Yahweh in a special sense and whose vocation is to order its entire life
according to Yahweh's sovereign demands.'

The narrative of Exodus 19–20 describes the divine appearance on Sinai, and the
giving of the laws to Moses.

Most Jews believe that God dictated the Torah to Moses during the forty days he
spent on Mount Sinai. When he descended from the mountain and returned to
the people, he was carrying two blocks of stone with writing cut into them. These
tablets of stone contained the Ten Commandments; a set of principles which set
out the general limitations which are defined by the covenant relationship. During
his time on the mountain, Moses was also learning all the other commandments
that God wanted him to teach to the people. These were to become known as the
Law, and in giving the Law to the people, the Jews were now fully aware of what
they were required to do in order to fulfil their side of the covenant agreement.

The five books of Moses are therefore of the greatest importance to Jews as they
contain the mitzvot (commandments) by which they are to live as people chosen
by God. The five books of Moses contain 613 commandments in all, which show
how God wants Jews to live. They also set out the ethical ideals of the Jewish
people, set within an account of their historical background:

- Genesis deals with the creation of the world; the patriarchs; and concludes with
  the settlement of the Hebrew people in Egypt.
- Exodus tells of Moses leading the Israelites to freedom; the revelation of the
  Torah on Mount Sinai, and the beginning of the journey in the wilderness.
- Leviticus contains instructions about ritual as well as legal and moral practices,
  and its emphasis is upon the rules that would enable people to attain the state of
  holiness that is required by God.
- Numbers demonstrates the importance of holiness, faithfulness and trust as the
  people make their journey to the land that God promised their fathers.

- Deuteronomy takes the form of speeches made by Moses, which were made on the borders of the Promised Land. It also contains laws, ethical teachings, and ends with the death of Moses.

Therefore, Jews believe that the Torah shows them how God wants them to live in order that they might uphold their commitment to the covenant relationship. Furthermore, the significance of the written Law, contained within the five books of Moses, is such that the practices of Jews today can be seen as a development of these laws into a distinct lifestyle.

AO1 Activity

After reading the section 'The receiving of the Torah at Sinai and the significance of the written law', close the book and finish off the following sentences:

a. The word 'Torah' means …

b. The Torah refers to …

c. The Torah is the basis of …

d. Most Jews believe that God …

e. Jews believe that the Torah shows them …

Compare and discuss your sentences with someone else who has also completed the task.

This will help to gain a summary of the relevant facts about the Torah.

The nature and purpose of Torah in Orthodox and Reform Judaism

The Jewish faith is centred upon the Torah, which acts as the primary means by which God communicates with human beings. The Torah contains all of the mitzvot required in order to practise the religion; and acts as the means by which Jews can maintain their part of the covenant relationship that was made with God at Sinai.

However, the term 'Torah' can mean different things. Apart from referring to the first five books of the Hebrew Scriptures, the word 'Torah' can also be used to mean the whole of the Jewish Bible. The Jewish Bible is known as the **Tanakh** or written Torah. The written Torah is divided into three sections:

- Torah – the Five Books of Moses
- Nevi'im – the books of the Prophets
- Ketuvim – holy writings.

The name 'Tanakh' comes from an **acronym** of the three subsections of the written Torah: T, N, K.

However, when considering the Torah, in the sense of the Five Books of Moses, we need to be aware that different groups within Judaism interpret its nature and purpose in different ways.

The Jewish religion is made up of many different branches, and the term 'Orthodox' can be used to refer to Jews who uphold the chain of tradition, which goes all the way back to the founding of their religion. Orthodox Jews accept, without doubt, that the Torah really is the word of God, which was revealed to Moses on Mount Sinai. As a result of this, they accept its authority without question as the direct **revelation** of Divine Law. In studying the Torah, an Orthodox Jew believes that they are in contact with the will and the mind of God, and as such, are carrying out one of the highest forms of religious activity. They see the purpose of the Torah as setting out clearly what God requires of them in life.

Key quote

The momentous encounter with God at Sinai is, for Judaism, the defining moment in Jewish history, the moment when God came down on earth and spoke to all Jews, present and future, giving them His rules for life, which they accepted enthusiastically. These laws … became the basis of all Judaism. (Tigay)

Specification content

The nature and purpose of Torah in Orthodox/Reform Judaism.

quickfire

1.15 What is the Tanakh?

Key terms

Acronym: a word made from the first letters of other words

Revelation: the act of revealing a divine truth

Tanakh: Hebrew name for the Bible

Key terms

Cohen: a man descended from the old priestly families of ancient Israel

Halakhah: literal meaning: 'the path that one walks'; Jewish law

Progressive Revelation: the concept that old laws of the Bible are no longer applicable in modern society in which new ethical, moral and spiritual values have been 'revealed'

As a result of this, they continue to live according to the 613 mitzvot, as their sole guide for everyday life and behaviour, as far as is practicable.

Orthodox Jews believe that they will be judged eventually on the way in which they have, or have not, kept the covenant commandments. Indeed, they believe that everything that is done by a Jew; from preparing and eating food to their business practices with others, should reflect the commandments given by God. Being true to the Torah also links them to the past with the Patriarchs such as Abraham.

The significance of the Torah is evident in the care that is taken when copying the Five Books of Moses onto new scrolls; making sure that there are no mistakes that could change the word of God. Maimonides states in his 'Thirteen Principles of Faith' that: 'The work of Moses is true work (number 7); The Law now is the same as when it was first given (number 8); The Law is going to be the same for ever (number 9).' This is the traditional Orthodox opinion.

Reform Jews follow a more liberal, modern form of Judaism. They believe in God's revelation and that the Torah contains many divine truths, but they attribute the authorship of the Torah to divinely inspired humans. Brian Close says: 'The Biblical writers were men inspired by God, but they were not superhuman and there can be no guarantee that they were equally inspired in everything they wrote'.

Nevertheless, the Torah is still instructional and inspiring, and a necessary resource. Reform Jews argue that Judaism is not something static, but a religion that is developing and changing all the time. As a consequence of this, it is possible to re-interpret the mitzvot according to the current needs or situation of the individual. As a result of this, they do not feel the need to adhere to all of the original 613 commandments.

In order to keep Judaism ever relevant, practices which no longer serve any helpful purpose may be rejected. This is known as the concept of **Progressive Revelation.** This concept proposes that the old laws of the Bible, which were relevant at one time, are no longer applicable in modern society in which new ethical, moral and spiritual values have been 'revealed'. Here is an example: According to the **halakhah** (Jewish law), a **Cohen** (a man descended from the old priestly families of ancient Israel) may not marry a divorced woman. The Reform view on this is that the Cohens in modern life no longer carry out priestly functions and so should not be required to be different from other Jewish men when it comes to whom they may or may not marry.

The Reform movement became a strong force in America in the second half of the nineteenth century, and in 1885, its views were expressed at a meeting of Reform rabbis in Pittsburgh. In a statement produced there, known as the Pittsburgh Platform, they set forth the Reform view on the nature of the Torah:

'We recognise in the Mosaic legislation a system of training the Jewish people for its mission during its national life in Palestine, and today we accept as binding only the moral laws, and maintain only such ceremonies as elevate and sanctify our lives ... We hold that all such Mosaic and rabbinical laws as regulate diet, priestly purity, and dress originated in ages and under the influence of ideas altogether foreign to our present mental and spiritual state ... Their observance in our days is apt rather to obstruct than to further modern spiritual elevation ... We consider ourselves no longer a nation, but a religious community, and therefore expect neither a return to Palestine, nor a sacrificial worship under the sons of Aaron, nor the restoration of any of the laws concerning the Jewish state.'

The Pittsburgh Platform statement called for the following things: A rejection of laws that have a ritual rather than a moral basis, such as rejection of the Jewish dietary laws, for example. Nevertheless, this does not mean that Reform Jews are not concerned about the halakhah at all: they continue to regard the Torah as being instructional and of great value.

quickfire

1.16 What do Reform Jews reject as a result of the Pittsburgh Platform?

> ## AO1 Activity
>
> Work with a partner: one of you is to take on the role of an Orthodox Jew, and the other a Reform Jew. Give a verbal explanation to each other of your particular Jewish points of view towards the nature and purpose of the Torah. Find a new partner, and swap roles so that you have considered both points of view.
>
> This task will help you to develop a deeper understanding of the diversity that can be found within the Jewish religion. It will help you to demonstrate depth and breadth in an examination answer about the nature and purpose of the Torah.

The pre-existent and eternal relevance of Torah

Specification content

The pre-existent and eternal relevance of Torah.

The notion of the pre-existence of the Torah has been a basis for philosophical rabbinic debate throughout the centuries. Jewish tradition tells us Moses received the Torah from God at Mount Sinai. However, according to rabbinic tradition, the Torah is one of seven things which were created before the world existed, and that it was present in Heaven before God revealed it to Moses. This suggests that the Torah was pre-existent and represented the plan which God had established before the world even began.

quickfire

1.17 Name two rabbis who argued for the pre-existence of the Torah.

Rabbi Eliezer ben Yose claimed that the Torah existed for 974 generations before the creation of the world. Rabbi Shimon ben Lakish taught that the Torah was 2,000 years older than the world, and was originally written in black fire upon white fire. Rabbi Akiva called the Torah 'the precious instrument by which the world was created'. Indeed, Jewish mysticism presents the Torah as an architectural blueprint for the creation of the world; according to Midrash Konen (2:24), God drew three drops of water and three drops of fire from the **celestial** Torah, and from them made the world.

However, the concept of pre-existence has also been rejected. For example, it was rejected by Rabbi Saadia Gaon, a prominent Jewish philosopher, on the grounds that it contradicted the principle that the world was created '**ex nihilo**'; whilst Judah ben Barzillai contended that the Torah pre-existed only as a thought in the mind of God. Rabbi Yehuda Halevi spoke of the Torah as preceding the world by design, arguing that because God had the Torah in mind when creating the world, and 'the first thought is the end of the work', the Torah can be said to have existed before the world.

Jews also believe that the Torah received at Sinai is eternal, and this concept is found repeatedly in the Torah: '… for the generations to come … (it is) a lasting ordinance'. (Exodus 12:14) In other words, the Torah is an eternal law which will continue to exist and to be relevant for all future generations.

> **Key terms**
>
> Celestial: relating to heaven
>
> Ex nihilo: a Latin phrase meaning 'out of nothing'

Specification content

Use and treatment of the Torah: Sefer Torah; Torah reading (in the synagogue and home), Torah study at a yeshiva (institute for Tanakh and Talmudic studies) and the role of the oral Torah.

Key quote

One should not live in a town that has no sofer. (The Talmud)

Key terms

Aron Kodesh: the 'Holy Ark' or cabinet in which are kept the Sefer Torah scrolls at the synagogue

Etz chaim: meaning 'tree of life'; the name given to the wooden pole on a Sefer torah scroll

Kosher: means 'fit' or 'proper'

Parshiot: sections of the Torah read in the synagogue

Sefer Torah: 'Scroll of the Torah'

Shabbat: the seventh day of the week; the day of rest according to the Ten Commandments

Sofer: Scribe

Sefer Torah

The Sefer Torah is a parchment scroll upon which the Five Books of Moses are written, and it is the holiest item in a synagogue. The 613th mitzvah sets out the obligation for every Jew to write a Torah scroll: 'Now therefore write this song, and teach it to the people of Israel; put it in their mouths that this song may be a witness for me against the people of Israel.' (Deuteronomy 31:19)

According to Orthodox Jewish tradition, the first Sefer Torah was dictated by God, and written by Moses. Identical copies have been made ever since throughout the generations, and because of the great care that has been taken in their writing, there has been little room for error or change over the years.

A sofer (scribe) writing part of a Torah scroll

The Sefer Torah must be written by hand, and copied letter by letter from an original by a sofer (a scribe). Great care must be taken in its writing, and if the sofer makes a mistake, he has to scratch the ink off the parchment. If, however, the mistake cannot be corrected completely then the whole page must be removed. However, it cannot be destroyed due to the fact that it contains the word of God, and must therefore be buried.

Such care and attention to detail means that it can take a year to complete a new Sefer Torah scroll. The parchment that is used for the scroll must come from the skin of a kosher animal, and each end is stitched to a wooden roller called an etz chaim ('tree of life').

New Torah scrolls are usually commissioned by individuals who pay for their creation. On completion, there will be a special ceremony and the sponsor will be invited to write one of the final letters. It is a great honour to be the one chosen to do this.

Torah reading in the synagogue and home

The Torah scrolls are kept in the Aron Kodesh (the 'Holy Ark' or cabinet) at the synagogue, from which they are taken out for portions to be read in the synagogue three times a week. Small sections are read on Mondays and Thursdays but the main reading is on the morning of Shabbat. The Five Books of Moses are divided into 54 portions, known as parshiot, with at least one being read every week. It takes a year to read through the whole scroll in sequence, and the readers need to be skilled in what they are doing as there are no vowels or punctuation within the text. The portion is also chanted to a tune.

The Sefer Torah is only used in the synagogue, and there is a schedule for the year so that Jews know which portions will be read each week. This means that if they wish, there is an opportunity for preparation and study at home.

Most observant Jews own a printed version of the Torah, which is known as a **Chumash**, which they make use of at home. The Chumash is also highly respected as a sacred text, but does not hold the same level of sacredness as the Sefer Torah. The rituals of Jewish festivals throughout the year also include the reading of passages from the Torah during the celebrations at home.

Reading from the Sefer Torah in a synagogue

Torah study

The most important commandment in the Torah is the commandment to study: 'And you shall teach it to your children.' (Deuteronomy 6:7) It is for this reason, therefore, that education is given very great importance within Judaism. Rabbinic tradition teaches that study of the Torah is equal to all of the other mitzvot combined. It also teaches that the reward for the study of the Torah is equal to the combined rewards of all other commandments:

'These are the things that have no measure ... acts of kindness, and the study of the Torah. These are things the fruits of which a man enjoys in this world ... Honouring one's father and mother, acts of kindness, and bringing peace between a man and his fellow. But the study of Torah is equal to them all.' (Mishnah Peah 1:1)

Study of the Torah is important for two main reasons: firstly, without studying the Torah, one cannot know how to fulfil the mitzvot; secondly, with detailed study, it is possible to gain an insight into the spiritual significance of the mitzvot. Indeed, it is related that when Rabbi Jonathan ben Uzziel sat to learn the Torah, so great was his passion that if a bird flew overhead it would burst into flames.

Key quote

Great is Torah study, for it leads to performance. (Kiddushin 40b)

The tradition for study continues, and for those who wish to continue to a higher Jewish education, there are opportunities to attend a **yeshiva**. A yeshiva is a Jewish institution that focuses on the study of traditional religious texts, primarily the Torah, Tanakh and **Talmud**. Boys attend yeshiva, and they work in pairs, mainly studying parts of the Talmud. A yeshiva study hall is a noisy place, full of animated discussion and debate. The students are assessed by oral examinations, and as they make progress, they move up to higher classes where they study the Talmud in greater detail.

Higher education for Jewish girls is at the **seminary**. There are more structured courses than at a yeshiva as well as a wider range of subjects. Nevertheless, all courses are grounded in Jewish studies.

quickfire

1.18 What is name of the printed version of the Torah which is used in Jewish homes?

quickfire

1.19 Which commandment from the Torah relates to the importance of study?

Key quote

As the child must satisfy its hunger day by day, so must the grown man busy himself with the Torah each hour. (Yerushalmi, Berakhot ch. 9)

Key terms

Chumash: a printed text containing the Five Books of Moses

Seminary: a theological college

Talmud: 'teaching' or 'study': the work of the collected scholars as a running commentary to the Mishnah

Yeshiva: a Jewish academy for Talmudic studies

quickfire

1.20 What was the purpose of the oral Torah?

Key quote

The decisions of the Talmud are words of the living God. (Rabbi Menachem)

Key quote

Midrash is interpretation in the context of covenantal time, the word spoken in the past but still active in the present ... interpreting current events in the light of the Divine word. (Rabbi Sacks)

The role of the oral Torah

Orthodox Jews believe that as well as being given the written Torah on Mount Sinai, Moses also received the oral law that was to be passed down, initially by word of mouth, from one generation to another. The purpose of the oral Torah was to explain in greater detail how to adhere to the commandments of the written Torah when a fuller explanation was needed. For example, the written Torah says that Jews should 'honour the Sabbath', but doesn't explain how this should be done. Therefore, the oral Torah provides the interpretation.

For centuries, the discussions were passed on by word of mouth until eventually being written down in the form of the Mishnah, the Talmud and the Midrash. These continue to provide the basis for further discussion and interpretation by rabbis and yeshiva students. This means that Judaism continues to develop as a lifestyle that is relevant to modern-day society.

The Mishnah

The material that makes up the Mishnah was collected together c.200CE and consists of discussions, lessons and quotations by early rabbis such as Hillel, Shammai and Judah Ha-Nasi. It contains a collection of legal rulings and practices that are still used as the basis for Jewish traditions today. It is organised into sections that are known as the six orders of the Mishnah:

1. Seeds – the laws relating to offerings for priests, gifts for the poor, and laws relating to agriculture.
2. Holidays – laws relating to the Sabbath and other festivals.
3. Women – laws relating to marriage, divorce, incest, adultery and property.
4. Damages – laws regarding civil disputes, rabbinic courts, vows and punishments.
5. Holy things – Temple sacrifices, ritual slaughter and dietary laws.
6. Purity – ritual cleanliness and impurity.

The Talmud

Scholars began to discuss the Mishnah and to add even more information of their own as and when the demands of changes in society became apparent. Rabbis met, discussed issues, and their dialogues were collected together to form another part of the oral Torah which is called the Gemara. The Gemara is a commentary on the various teachings of the Mishnah. Together, the Mishnah and the Gemara form the Talmud, and this book has had a tremendous effect upon the way in which the Jews have lived their lives for centuries.

The Midrash

The Midrash is an ancient commentary consisting of rabbinic teachings and sermons, which seek to read between the lines of things that are found in the Torah. For example, why did Cain kill Abel? There follows a discussion, made up of questions, for which rabbis searched for answers.

AO1 Activity

Research the lives of early rabbis such as Hillel, Shammai and Judah Ha-Nasi. This will help you to gain a greater understanding of the formation of the Mishnah, Talmud and Midrash. Also, being able to quote from their discussions will fuel evidence and examples for both a demonstration of knowledge and understanding (AO1) but also to help sustain an argument (AO2).

The care and respect shown for the Torah – ark, mantle, yad (pointer) and burial

The Sefer Torah is the holiest object in the synagogue, and the way in which it is dressed and treated emphasises this very fact. It is kept in the Holy Ark, a cupboard which is usually built into the East wall of the synagogues in the United Kingdom, as this is the direction of Jerusalem. The Ark represents the golden box which contained the Ten Commandments in the original Temple in that city.

The central feature of the Sabbath morning synagogue service is the opening of the Ark and the removal of the Torah scroll, which is then carried in a ceremonial procession around the synagogue to the **bimah**. All will stand, and prayer shawls will be kissed, before being used to touch the outer cover of the scroll as it passes. During the service, members of the congregation will be called upon to read the portion for the day.

The scroll itself is dressed with a **mantle**, a beautifully decorated cover, which protects it whilst it is being carried from the Ark around the synagogue and which is removed before the reading of the portion. The scrolls are not touched directly when being read because of their sanctity, and therefore a **yad** is used. A yad is a pointer in the shape of a hand with an outstretched finger which is used by the reader in order to keep their place.

When a Torah scroll wears out beyond repair, or is damaged and cannot be used any longer, it cannot be thrown away as doing so would be like discarding the word of God. Instead, it should be placed in a protective container and buried in a Jewish cemetery. The requirement for its encasement can be found in Jeremiah 32:14 which states: 'Thus says the Lord of hosts, the God of Israel: "Take these deeds ... and put them in an earthenware vessel, that they may last for a long time."' It is buried in this way so as to preserve the writing on it for as long as possible.

The prohibition against destroying a damaged scroll can be found in a midrash on Deuteronomy 12:4 which explains that although the Israelites were required to destroy idols and pagan places of worship in Canaan, 'You shall not do so to the Lord your God'. As a result of this, when Jews need to dispose of sacred texts, they bury them rather than destroy them.

A yad

Specification content

Use and treatment of the Torah: The care and respect shown for the Torah – ark, mantle, yad (pointer) and burial.

Key terms

Bimah: a raised reading desk in the synagogue where the Torah is read

Mantle: a decorated cover for the Sefer Torah

Yad: a pointer in the shape of a hand with outstretched finger which is used when reading from the Torah

AO1 Activity

After reading the section on 'The care and respect shown for the Torah', test yourself by making a list of five things which show evidence of the fact that great respect is given to the Torah. This demonstrates that you not only know facts about the use and treatment of the Torah, but can also explain why such actions are significant.

Study tip

When answering a question about the Torah, make sure that you demonstrate to the examiner that you understand that the word 'Torah' has a variety of meanings. Be precise and use specific terms such as written Torah, oral Torah, Sefer Torah in the right context. This shows that you are able to make thorough and accurate use of specialist language and vocabulary.

Key skills

Knowledge involves:

Selection of a range of (thorough) accurate and relevant information that is directly related to the specific demands of the question.

This means you choose the correct information relevant to the question set NOT the topic area. You will have to think and focus on selecting key information and NOT writing everything you know about the topic area.

Understanding involves:

Explanation that is extensive, demonstrating depth and/or breadth with excellent use of evidence and examples including (where appropriate) thorough and accurate supporting use of sacred texts, sources of wisdom and specialist language.

This means that you demonstrate that you understand something by being able to illustrate and expand your points through examples/supporting evidence in a personal way and NOT repeat chunks from a textbook (known as rote learning).

Further application of skills:

Why not explore some examples from the Midrash. Here is a website to get you started: *www.myjewishlearning.com*

AO1 Developing skills

It is now time to reflect upon the information that has been covered so far. It is also important to consider how what you have learned can be focused and used for examination-style answers by practising the skills associated with AO1.

Assessment objective 1 (AO1) involves demonstrating knowledge and understanding. The terms 'knowledge' and 'understanding' are obvious but it is crucial to be familiar with how certain skills demonstrate these terms, and also, how the performance of these skills is measured (see generic band descriptors Band 5 for AS AO1).

▶ **Your new task is this:** you need to develop each of the key points below by adding evidence and examples to fully explain each point. The first one is done for you. This will help you in answering examination questions for AO1 by being able to 'demonstrate extensive depth and/or breadth' with 'excellent use of evidence and examples' (Level 5 AO1 band descriptor).

A focus on examining different ways in which the Torah is treated.

- The mantle is a beautifully decorated cover which is used to protect the Sefer Torah.

DEVELOPMENT: *Its purpose is to protect the scroll whilst it is being carried from the Ark around the synagogue to the reading desk. This indicates the sanctity of the scrolls as containing the word of God.*

- The job of the sofer within a Jewish community is very important because …

- The yad is a … and is used because …

- The two requirements for the burial of a damaged Sefer Torah are … the reasons for these requirements can be found in …

- The purpose of the oral Torah is …

- The Mishnah, Talmud and Midrash are related in the following way: …

Issues for analysis and evaluation

The extent to which the Torah remains the main authority within Judaism today

Orthodox Jews believe that the Torah is the word of God, which was revealed and dictated to Moses on Mount Sinai. As a result of this they continue to accept its authority as the direct revelation of Divine Law. The Torah is therefore always the starting point when a question or issue is raised within Judaism.

Its importance is highlighted by the fact that, in its written form, it is treated with the greatest respect and care. The Sefer Torah must be written by hand, and copied letter by letter from an original by a sofer. It is vital that the original content of the Torah is maintained, thus great care must be taken in its writing. If the sofer makes a mistake, the ink has to be scratched from the parchment. And if it is not possible to rectify the error, then the whole page must be removed. However, it cannot be destroyed due to the fact that it contains the word of God, and must therefore be buried.

The importance and authority of the Torah is further emphasised by the fact that the completed scrolls are housed within the Aron Kodesh at the synagogue which is a representation of the golden box in which the Ten Commandments were stored in the Temple at Jerusalem.

The Torah sets out what God requires of the Jews, and as a result of this, Orthodox Jews continue to live according to the 613 mitzvot that are contained within it, as their guide for everyday life.

Orthodox Jews believe that Moses was also in receipt of the oral Torah; therefore, it too has authority, and acts as a means of explaining further how the commandments are to be interpreted as part of everyday life. For centuries, the discussions were passed on by word of mouth until eventually being written down in the form of the Mishnah, the Talmud and the Midrash. These also act as important sources of authority and continue to provide the basis for further discussion and interpretation.

Another important source of authority within the Jewish faith is that provided by the rabbi. The rabbi, who has studied and understands the Torah, can provide guidance, exemplification, and offer answers to questions about how the Torah is to be interpreted within modern society. This is done by making reference to rabbinic tradition.

Reform Jews also accept the authority of the Torah, believing that its content was revealed by God; however, they attribute its authorship to divinely inspired humans. Nevertheless, the Torah remains the foundation of their religious faith. They consider it to be inspiring and instructional and still a necessary resource, but do not feel the need to adhere to all of the commandments contained within it. This opinion allows for re-interpretation or even a discarding of certain mitzvot if they are not felt to be relevant any longer.

The debate about the extent to which the Torah remains the main authority within Judaism today appears to be open to misunderstanding. In fact, it appears that it will always be the main authority within Judaism today for all adherents of Judaism but the real question – and a much more interesting one – emerges as to 'in what ways' or 'how' the Torah remains an authority within Judaism today. This is where the real focus should be in considering how this authority of the Torah is understood and applied in the modern world.

This section covers AO2 content and skills

Specification content

The extent to which the Torah remains the main authority within Judaism today.

AO2 Activity   *Possible lines of argument*

Listed below are some conclusions that could be drawn from the AO2 reasoning in the accompanying text:

1. There is only one source of authority within the Jewish faith.

2. Reform Jews do not accept the authority of the Torah within modern-day society.

3. Rabbinic tradition is just as important a source of authority as the Torah.

4. The Torah continues to provide guidance for everyday life within the Jewish faith.

5. The Mishnah, Talmud and Midrash serve as important sources of authority.

Consider each of the conclusions drawn above and collect evidence and examples to support each argument from the AO1 and AO2 material studied in this section. Select one conclusion that you think is most convincing and explain why it is so. Now contrast this with the weakest conclusion in the list, justifying your argument with clear reasoning and evidence.

Specification content

Whether the Torah has become a
religious icon.

Key term

Aniconism: opposition to the use
of idols, images and the worship of
objects which are symbolic of a deity

AO2 Activity *Possible lines of argument*

Listed below are some conclusions
that could be drawn from the AO2
reasoning in the accompanying text:

1. Treating a religious object with
great respect does not necessarily
make it an icon.

2. Judaism places greater emphasis
upon the spiritual and moral
guidance that is contained within
the Torah.

3. Veneration of images and objects
is not allowed within Judaism.

4. The emphasis should be given to
the content of the Torah, rather
than the actual physical scroll.

5. The fact that the term 'icon' can be
interpreted in different ways is an
issue that needs to be considered.

Consider each of the conclusions
drawn above and collect evidence and
examples to support each argument
from the AO1 and AO2 material
studied in this section. Select one
conclusion that you think is most
convincing and explain why it is so.
Now contrast this with the weakest
conclusion in the list, justifying
your argument with clear reasoning
and evidence.

Whether the Torah has become a religious icon

The Torah itself, in the Ten Commandments, prohibits the Jews from creating
icons which could lead to idolatrous practices: 'You shall not make for yourself an
image in the form of anything in Heaven above or on the earth beneath or in the
waters below' (Exodus 20:4). This includes representation of God.

The prohibition of idolatry has led to aniconism (opposition to the use of idols,
images and the worship of objects which are symbolic of a deity) within Judaism.

The way in which the Torah is stored and used in the synagogue could lead to the
suggestion that it has become an icon; however, the treatment shows the respect
that Jews have for it as the word of God which has provided guidance for life
throughout the history of the Jewish people. It is therefore not acting as a physical
representation of God.

The fact that for some groups within Judaism its content is open to interpretation
suggests that it is not considered to be iconic.

If the Torah is perceived to have become a representation of God, then it would be
classed as an icon.

The way in which the Torah is treated can lead some onlookers to conclude that
it *has* become a religious icon: the care taken in its writing; the protection of the
mantle and its storage in the Holy Ark; the way in which it is paraded around the
synagogue with congregants touching it with their tallit: all these things can lead to
the conclusion that it is the object rather than what it contains which has become
important.

If veneration of the physical Torah, and the ritual which surrounds its use becomes
the main focus of attention, rather than the spiritual and moral guidance which it
contains, then it could well be classed as no more than a religious icon.

The term 'icon' can be interpreted in different ways, and therefore one's view on
this issue could be dependent upon an individual's understanding of the term. It
might not always have negative overtones.

In conclusion, then, it appears that the Torah as a religious icon needs to be
distinguished from that understanding of an icon as something that leads to a form
of worship. It clearly has 'iconic' status in the way it is used and treated but this
does not necessarily mean that it is worshipped. For some, its use and treatment
reflects its value and is indicative of what it contains in helping a follower of
Judaism live a religious life, serving as a constant reminder of this. For others, the
'iconic' status is nothing more than a tool for aiding focus during worship and
directs one beyond the physical to the metaphysical reality of God's presence in
the synagogue. It could be argued that all followers of Judaism would agree that
anything beyond this understanding is to be avoided.

Study tip

Accurate use of specialist language and vocabulary is vital, therefore make sure
that you study and learn the meanings of key terms as part of your revision. The
inability to understand a term such as 'icon,' for example, could mean that you
do not have a clear understanding of the issue raised by the question set.

Developing skills for AO2

It is now time to reflect upon the information that has been covered so far. It is also important to consider how what you have learned can be focused and used for examination-style answers by practising the skills associated with AO2.

Assessment objective 2 (AO2) involves 'analysis' and 'evaluation'. The terms may be obvious but it is crucial to be familiar with how certain skills demonstrate these terms, and also, how the performance of these skills is measured (see generic band descriptors Band 5 for AS AO2).

Obviously an answer is placed within an appropriate band descriptor depending upon how well the answer performs, ranging from excellent, good, satisfactory, basic/limited to very limited.

▶ **Your next task is this:** develop each of the key points below by adding evidence and examples to fully evaluate the argument presented in the evaluation statement. The first one is done for you. This will help you in answering examination questions for AO2 by being able to ensure that 'sustained and clear views are given, supported by extensive, detailed reasoning and/or evidence' (Level 5 AO2 band descriptor).

A focus on evaluating the Torah as the main source of authority in Judaism today.

- Some argue that the Torah remains the word of God

DEVELOPMENT: *Orthodox Jews believe that the Torah is the word of God, which was revealed and dictated to Moses on Mount Sinai. As a result of this, they continue to accept its authority as the direct revelation of Divine Law. It therefore continues to hold its position as the main source of authority in Judaism today.*

- Jews also believe that Moses was also in receipt of the oral Torah.

- The authority and traditions of the rabbis also have authority within Judaism.

- The Mishnah, Talmud and Midrash have also shaped Jewish belief and lifestyle.

- Reform Jews have a different interpretation of the authorship of the Torah.

- The relevance of a document which was written so many thousands of years ago must surely come under question.

Key skills

Analysis involves identifying issues raised by the materials in the AO1, together with those identified in the AO2 section, and presents sustained and clear views, either of scholars or from a personal perspective ready for evaluation.

This means that it picks out key things to debate and the lines of argument presented by others or a personal point of view.

Evaluation involves considering the various implications of the issues raised based upon the evidence gleaned from analysis and provides an extensive detailed argument with a clear conclusion.

This means that the answer weighs up the various and different lines of argument analysed through individual commentary and response and arrives at a conclusion through a clear process of reasoning.

T2 Religious concepts

Specification content

Absolute monotheism; God as One.

A: Beliefs about the nature of God/concept of God

Absolute monotheism; God as One

Judaism was the first religious tradition to teach **absolute monotheism**, the belief that there is only one God: a God who is **indivisible**, **incomparable** and the ultimate cause of existence.

In his book '*Laws Concerning Idolatry*', Maimonides gives a summary of the process by which he believed humankind came to the recognition of the truth in One God. He proposes that God was known to Adam, but as the generations passed, humanity wrongly came to believe 'that it would be pleasing to God if they were to venerate the forces of nature which serve Him ... Soon they were erecting temples and altars to the sun and the stars, offering sacrifices and hymns of praise to them, believing all this to be the will of God'. Maimonides continues that as the years went by 'the venerable and awesome name of God was forgotten from the lips and minds of humanity'. However, this was to change with the arrival of Abraham.

According to the Talmud, Abraham came to the conclusion that all of existence proceeded from a single source, by a process of elimination. At first, after witnessing how important the sun was to human life, he worshipped it as the supreme deity. By evening, however, he had changed his mind as he saw how the moon and the stars had defeated the power of the sun. In the morning Abraham began to worship the air around him as he perceived it to be the one thing that existed in all parts of creation. This, however, led him to wonder about humankind's superiority to the air: people were able to contain air and breathe, thus having mastery over it. However, Abraham was not about to worship himself or any other person due to the fact that human beings were not flawless. As Rabbi Shmuley Boteach puts it: 'It was only then that he began to understand how all of nature was a veil which masked the presence of the deity, and how man must learn to apprehend the hidden Creator.'

For Jews, the belief in the Oneness of God is the foundation of their faith. The first of the Ten Commandments tells them that they are forbidden to worship any other gods. They are also constantly reminded of the Oneness of God every morning and evening when they recite the prayer known as the Shema: its opening line is 'Hear, O Israel; the Lord our God is One Lord.' (Deuteronomy 6:4)

The belief in absolute monotheism also has consequences for the way in which Jews view the world and everything that is in it. If God, as they believe, is the ultimate cause of existence, then everything that they encounter in nature becomes an encounter with God.

Key quote

... and (Abraham) came to know that there is one God ... who created all, and that in all existence there is none other than Him. (Maimonides)

Key terms

Absolute monotheism: the belief that there is only one God; the ultimate cause of existence

Incomparable: unable to be compared with anything else

Indivisible: unable to be divided or separated

Key quote

You shall have no other gods before me. (Exodus 20:3)

quickfire

2.1 Give two examples which underline the fact that belief in one God is the foundation of the Jewish faith.

AO1 Activity

Design a flow chart that explains the process by which Abraham was brought to a belief in monotheism. This will help you to come to a deeper understanding of the concept.

Introduction

Any discussion about the nature and characteristics of God is bound to be a complex one, since we are dealing with the concept of a supreme being that is an external force which exists beyond human experience. As Nicholas De Lange states: '... there is a general trend to insist that anything we say about God is liable to be false and misleading. All the qualities people attribute to him are **extrapolated** from human experience, which is by its nature fundamentally and categorically different from God.' Further to this, Maimonides writes: 'Those who believe that God is One and that He has many attributes declare the Unity with their lips and assume the **plurality** in their thoughts.' Maimonides famously insisted that only God's actions can be known, and even these only tell us what God is *not* like, not what God *is* like.

Historically, Judaism has tended to be a religion that focuses more on how a person practises their faith, rather than examining the nature of God. Notwithstanding, determining the nature of God within Judaism has been something that has been discussed throughout the centuries. Alan Unterman points out that in order to do this we are bound to use language drawn from the relationship of human beings to each other and to the world to apply to God. Indeed, the Talmudic rabbis would often preface their **anthropomorphisms** with the phrase 'as if it were possible' (i.e. to talk about God in these terms).

God as Creator

The first verse in the Jewish scriptures reads: 'In the beginning God created the heavens and the earth.' (Genesis 1:1). If there is indeed one God as this verse suggests, then it follows that God must be the source of all that is in existence.

Some Jews believe that God created the universe out of nothing, and then stood back and allowed it to develop whilst watching from a distance. Other Jews believe that God continued to be involved in the process of creation by designing the world in such a way as to suit a divine plan.

'It was I who made the earth and created mankind on it.' (Isaiah 45:12)

Specification content

God as Creator; God as incorporeal; God as neither male nor female; God as eternal.

Key quote

If I knew God I would be God. **(Albo)**

Key quote

Anthropomorphism … emphasises the continuity of God's being with man's being … God emerges as personal, caring about man and needing to be placated by him. **(Unterman)**

Key terms

Anthropomorphism: the attribution of human characteristics, feelings or behaviour to a god, animal or inanimate object

Extrapolate: to draw conclusions from known facts

Plurality: a large number or variety

Key quote

If God had started with raw materials, He would not have been able to make the kind of world He wanted. His work would have been hampered by any defects in His materials. By creating the world out of nothing, He made it exactly the way He wanted it. **(Forta)**

quickfire

2.2 Which verse in Jewish scripture states that God was responsible for creation?

The Midrash describes that before creating the world, God opened the Torah scroll and read the beginning of the book of Genesis as though the Torah were an instruction manual. What followed took six days to complete, followed by a day of rest on the seventh day. On Shabbat many Jews imitate God by resting on the seventh day. This is in accordance with one of the Ten Commandments: 'Remember the Sabbath day by keeping it holy' (Exodus 20:8). Throughout the rest of the week Jews may undertake creative activity, but on this day they are to reflect upon their God-given powers, and focus upon the deeper meaning and values in life.

Jews view creation as a continuous event that only exists whilst God pours creative energy into it, and this is known as the doctrine of perpetual creation. If God were to cease, then all would become nothing, and it is for this reason that Jews pray the following lines daily: 'He who in His goodness renews the work of creation each day continually'. As Yanki Tauber explains: 'The doctrine of perpetual creation means that at every point in time, the world is the way it is only because God actively desires to so create it. There can be no "hopeless" situations, no "meaningless" moments, for this very moment, with all its attendant circumstances, was only just now brought into being out of absolute nothingness by a purposeful Creator who is the ultimate source of good.' This does, however, allow for times when God will hold back power to allow people to choose whether they will do good or evil; and at other times when God will step in and perform miracles.

God as incorporeal and is neither male nor female

The belief that God is incorporeal means that God has no physical body or physical substance and therefore has no material existence. This is in contrast to the deities that were worshipped at the time of the Abrahamic covenant, when it was believed that they had a physical presence and could be seen in the world.

The incorporeality of God means that God is not bound by the physical world in any shape or form; this means that the divine being is not restricted to a particular place or time. In the third of 'The Thirteen Principles of Faith', Maimonides states: 'This is the third Principle, as affirmed by the verse "You have not seen any image" (Deuteronomy 4:15), that is to say, you cannot conceive of Him as having any form because, as stated, He is neither a body nor a bodily force.'

Indeed, it has been proposed that if the divine being occupied our world then the consequence would be that humans could be free of God, and could undertake actions and deeds that were not good in the knowledge that God would never find out.

If God is incorporeal, and has no physical existence, then it follows that God can be neither male nor female. It appears to be a contradiction therefore when masculine terms are used in order to write or speak about God. One reason for this is that the only way that we can express our ideas about something that is far beyond our imagination, is by anthropomorphising it. For example, there are many examples of God being described as 'Father', but this is better understood as a way of attributing a fatherly role of protector. Nevertheless, there are also occasions within Judaism when God is referred to in feminine terms. The shekinah, referring to the presence of God in the universe, for example, is a feminine word, and denotes a feminine aspect of God's being.

quickfire

2.3 What does the term 'incorporeal' mean?

Key terms

Deities: gods or goddesses

Incorporeal: without bodily substance

Shekinah: means 'dwelling' or 'settling' and denotes the divine presence of God in the world

quickfire

2.4 What attribute of God is being described by use of the term 'Father'?

God as eternal

One of the designations of God to be found in the Hebrew scriptures is **El Olam** meaning the everlasting or eternal One. Jews believe that God has always existed and always will. This means that God has no beginning and no end. In Genesis 21:33 it tells us that Abraham was aware of this: 'Abraham … called on the name of the LORD, the Eternal God.'

When God was revealed to Moses through the bush which flamed but did not burn, Moses asked for God's name. God replied: 'I Am who I Am' (Exodus 3:14). This is represented by the four Hebrew letters YHWH (or YHVH), and the ambiguity of the phrase is usually interpreted as a reference to God's eternal nature. Likewise Psalm 90:2 tells us: 'Before the mountains were born or you brought forth the whole world, from everlasting to everlasting you are God.'

The characteristics of God: omnipotent

Jews believe that God is **omnipotent**. This implies that God's power has no limits at all. God is totally in control of the universe, and this includes all activities of nature and human beings. This is known as the Sovereignty of God. Jews believe that although God has absolute power and can do anything and everything, this power has been withheld in order to allow people the freedom to live as they choose: this is known as free will. Allowing free will, however, does mean that people can decide whether to choose to be good or evil. Sometimes, however, it is believed that God does use divine power to intervene; and when something incredible or lifesaving happens Jews call such an intervention a miracle.

Moses and the burning bush

Key quote

Wherever you find God's greatness, there you will find His humility.
(Rabbi Jochanan)

The characteristics of God: omniscient

'**Omniscient**' is the term used to describe the belief that God knows all that is happening in creation. The omniscience of God is expressed in two names: the first being found in Genesis 16:13 where God is called 'the Lord Who Sees', meaning that God has the ability to see and know everything. Secondly, 1 Samuel 2:3 tells us that: '… the Lord is a God who knows'. Yet this is not human knowledge, it is a knowledge that covers all things, both present and future, and contains everything within creation.

The characteristics of God: omnibenevolent

On one level, God is seen as a personal God who is aware of human needs. Jews believe that God is there at times of anguish, bringing comfort to the bereaved and the sick. The nature of the covenant that has been made with mankind emphasises the protection that is given to them. However, if this is the case, then how can God be both omnipotent and **omnibenevolent** when there are so many acts of evil and suffering in the world? There is no easy answer to this contradiction, but it has been proposed that God has withdrawn so that people can have free will, but that this withdrawal means that creation lacks full access to the aspect of God's nature that is omnibenevolent.

Specification content

Characteristics: omnipotent, omniscient, omnibenevolent, Holy, Just, Perfect, Merciful.

Key quote

For the Lord your God is God of gods and Lord of lords, the great, the mighty and awe-inspiring God. (Deuteronomy 10:17)

quickfire

2.5 What does the term 'Sovereignty of God' mean?

Key terms

El Olam: a name for God within Judaism, meaning the everlasting or eternal One

Omnibenevolent: having absolute goodness

Omnipotent: all-powerful

Omniscient: all-knowing

Key terms

Adonai: meaning 'Lord'

Pesikta Rabbati: a medieval Midrash

Qodesh: holiness of God

Key quote

You shall not take the name of the Lord your God in vain; for the Lord will not hold him guiltless who takes his name in vain. (Exodus 20:7)

quickfire

2.6 What name for God is used by Jews in order that they do not use God's name in the wrong way?

Key quote

Yet if there is an angel at their side, a messenger, one out of a thousand, sent to tell them how to be upright, and he is gracious to that person and says to God, 'Spare them from going down to the pit; I have found a ransom for them – let their flesh be renewed like a child's; let them be restored as in the days of their youth.' (Job 33:23–25)

Key quote

For you are not a God who delights in wickedness. (Psalm 5:4)

The characteristics of God: Holy and Perfect

The Hebrew word to express the holiness of God is 'qodesh'. To say that God is holy means that God is completely perfect and utterly separate from all evil and deficiency. Such is God's holiness that the third of the Ten Commandments even forbids Jews to use God's name in the wrong way. Jews therefore think the name of God is holy and should not even be spoken. Instead they use the name **Adonai** meaning 'Lord'.

An event that exemplifies the holiness of God can be found in Exodus 19. At Mount Sinai God warned that anyone who touched the mountain would be put to death, and only Moses and Aaron were allowed to ascend. In Exodus 19:23 Moses said to God, 'The people cannot come up Mount Sinai because you yourself warned us, "Put limits around the mountain and set it apart as holy".' The sanctity of the mountain serves as an example of the holiness of God, indicating the huge chasm between God and the people.

The characteristics of God: Just and Merciful

Jews maintain that God's justice and mercy are carefully balanced: God punishes the evil; rewards the good; and is forgiving to those who repent. God also demands that people live moral lives. According to the Talmud, God says, 'All I do, I do in justice. If I sought to pass beyond justice but once, the world could not endure.'

God is also merciful, and the rabbis have made reference to Job 33:23–25 in order to illustrate this particular characteristic. The **Pesikta Rabbati** explains it thus: '... even though there be nine hundred and ninety-nine accusers against a person, and only one who speaks in favour of them, God will be inclined to merit'.

Claude Montefiore writes: 'So far from the ordinary view being accurate that the Jewish God is a God of stern justice, the very opposite would be nearer the truth.' It follows, therefore, that many of the laws that are found in the Torah show concern for doing what is right and treating others fairly. For example, one of the most important commandments for Jews is: 'You shall love your neighbour as yourself.'

AO1 Activity

Using the terms such as 'One', 'Creator', etc., which have been used to describe the nature and characteristics of God, create a mind map which summarises each concept. Make sure that you use examples, where appropriate, from the scriptures and/or rabbinic tradition.

This helps with the ability to select and present the key, relevant features of the material you have read.

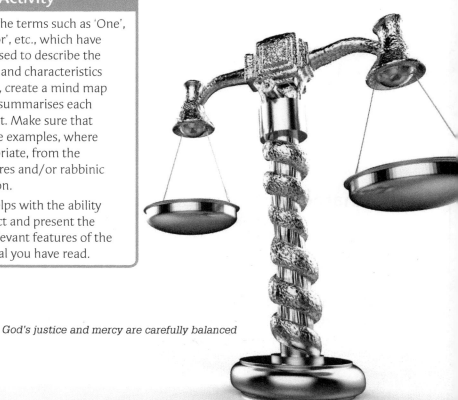

God's justice and mercy are carefully balanced

God's presence as both kavod and shekinah

The terms 'kavod' and 'shekinah' are both used in Judaism when referring to the concept of the presence of God.

Kavod is a word used for the energy that is encountered in moments of awe such as at the revelation on Mount Sinai. It attempts to describe the experience of standing in the presence of God. It literally means 'heavy' or 'weighty', but often denotes honour or glory. Kavod is a means of witnessing the beauty and radiance of God. Maimonides spoke of the kavod in texts such as Exodus 24:16: 'The glory of the Lord settled on Mount Sinai', as 'the created light that God causes to descend in a particular place in order to confer honour on it in a miraculous way.'

The prophets also made many references to visions of the presence of God, particularly connected with the Temple. The prophet Isaiah wrote of just such an experience when he said: 'I saw the Lord sitting upon a throne, high and lifted up; and his train filled the temple' (Isaiah 6:1).

Shekinah means 'dwelling' or 'settling' and denotes the divine presence of God in the world. It is not a word that is used in the Torah but is to be found in the rabbinic tradition. It is essentially a mystical concept, which denotes a profound relationship between God and each individual. It is the feminine aspect of God. Some rabbis teach that the shekinah is the part of God that is in exile along with the Jewish people. Other rabbis say that the shekinah permeates the world in the same way that the soul permeates the body; just as the soul sustains the body, the shekinah sustains the world.

An example of shekinah is evident in the narrative of the Exodus from Egypt, when God's presence was evident in guiding the exiles as a pillar of cloud by day, and pillar of fire by night: 'And the Lord went before them by day in a pillar of cloud to lead them along the way, and by night in a pillar of fire to give them light' (Exodus 13:21). Exodus 33:9 tells us God also spoke to Moses out of a pillar of cloud at the entrance to the tent which was erected as a temporary place of worship in the desert: 'When Moses entered the tent, the pillar of cloud would descend ... and the Lord would speak with Moses.'

The shekinah is also reported as being present in acts of public prayer. In the Mishnah the term can be found twice. Rabbi Hananiah ben Teradion said: 'If two sit together and the words between them are of the Torah, then the shekinah is in their midst.' Likewise Rabbi Halafta ben Dosa claimed: 'If ten men sit together and occupy themselves with the Law, the shekinah rests among them.' Nowadays, the daily prayer known as the Amidah contains a blessing that says: 'Blessed are you, God who returns his presence (shekinah) to Zion.'

Specification content

God's presence as both kavod and shekinah.

Key terms

Exiles: people who have been forced to leave a country

Kavod: literally means 'heavy' or 'weighty', but often denotes honour or glory. It attempts to describe the experience of standing in the presence of God

Key quote

Wheresoever they were exiled, the shekinah went with them. (Talmud)

quickfire

2.7 Which two words are used in Judaism when referring to the concept of the presence of God?

A guiding pillar of cloud by day

A guiding pillar of fire by night

Maimonides (Rabbi Moses ben Maimon)

Maimonides on the attributes of God

Rabbi Moses ben Maimon (1135–1204 CE), better known as Maimonides, was a prominent Jewish philosopher. In *c.* 1160 he composed 'The Thirteen Principles of Faith', which in his view were the essential tenets of the Jewish religion.

Maimonides contested that the study of the Torah is one way of coming to a greater understanding of the characteristics of God. However he was unhappy about describing God using the positive attributes that are to be found within it. The attributes are described in this manner he asserted, because 'The Torah speaks in the language of man' and should not be taken literally. Maimonides insisted that only God's actions can be known, and even these only tell us what God is *not* like, not what God *is* like.

Maimonides writes: 'All we understand is the fact that [God] exists, that [God] is a being to whom none of Adonai's creatures is similar, who has nothing in common with them, who does not include plurality, who is never too feeble to produce other beings and whose relation to the universe is that of a steersman to a boat; and even this is not a real relation, a real simile, but serves only to convey to us the idea that God rules the universe, that it is [God] that gives it duration and preserves its necessary arrangement.'

George Robinson explains that Maimonides came to this conclusion by arguing that God is a perfect unity having no parts, either literally or figuratively: no arms or legs, no back or front, no end or beginning. That also means that one cannot actually say 'God is ...' and proceed to enumerate God's attributes. To describe the Eternal One in such a sentence is to admit of a division between subject and **predicate**, in other words, a plurality. Therefore, Maimonides concludes, one cannot discuss God in terms of positive attributes.

However, on the other hand, one *can* describe what God is *not*. God is not **corporeal**, does not occupy space, experiences neither generation nor corruption. The incorporeality of God means that God is not bound by the physical world in any shape or form; this means that the divine being is not restricted to a particular place or time. In the third of 'The Thirteen Principles of Faith', Maimonides states: 'This is the third Principle, as affirmed by the verse "You have not seen any image" (Deuteronomy 4:15), that is to say, you cannot conceive of Him as having any form because, as stated, He is neither a body nor a bodily force.'

Maimonides concluded that one of the ways in way in which a person can come to know God is through study of the Torah, and by engaging the intellect in the search.

Key quote

Those who believe that God is One and that He has many attributes declare the Unity with their lips and assume the plurality in their thoughts. **(Maimonides)**

Key terms

Corporeal: having a bodily form

Predicate: the part of a sentence which tells us what the subject of the same sentence is or does

AO1 Activity

Explain how a Jew might respond to the following view: 'It is impossible to know what God is like and therefore impossible to have a relationship with God'.

Explain your answer using evidence and examples from what you have read.

Study tip

There are many examples of specialist language and vocabulary in this topic. Make sure that you don't get confused by the different terms that are used to describe the characteristics that Jews ascribe to God. Your ability to use the terms accurately in an examination answer would distinguish a high level answer from one that is simply a general response.

AO1 Developing skills

It is now time to reflect upon the information that has been covered so far. It is also important to consider how what you have learned can be focused and used for examination-style answers by practising the skills associated with AO1.

Assessment objective 1 (AO1) involves demonstrating knowledge and understanding. The terms 'knowledge' and 'understanding' are obvious but it is crucial to be familiar with how certain skills demonstrate these terms, and also, how the performance of these skills is measured (see generic band descriptors Band 5 for AS AO1).

▶ **Your new task is this:** below is a weak answer that has been written in response to a question requiring an examination of the nature of God in Judaism. Using the band level descriptors you need to place this answer in a relevant band that corresponds to the description inside that band. It is obviously a weak answer and so would not be in bands 3–5. In order to do this it will be useful to consider what is missing from the answer and what is inaccurate. The accompanying analysis gives you observations to assist you. In analysing the answer's weaknesses, in a group, think of five ways in which you would improve the answer in order to make it stronger. You may have more than five suggestions but try to negotiate as a group and prioritise the five most important things lacking.

Answer

Jews believe in one God, and they call that god absolute monotheism [1]. Jews believe that their God is good and not evil, and is one of the most important of all the other Jewish gods [2]. The Ten Commandments describe God [3] and tell Jews what he is like. Jews believe that God created the world, and is therefore a nature God [4]. The bible says that only Moses has seen God, and he couldn't say whether God was male or female [5]. The most important thing that Jews know about God is that God rested on the seventh day of the week after finishing creating the world. Jews also rest on the seventh day of the week to obey God.

Jews believe that God has total power on earth and this is called omnipotence [6]. God is also is full of goodness. But there is evil and suffering in the world because God has lost control of the world [7]. God can see everything, and punishes bad people. Jews also believe that God can bring dead people back to life, just like when Jesus did miracles [8]. God wants people to live just lives, and teaches Jews that 'You shall love your neighbour as yourself'. Jews believe that the Torah tells them all about how God wants them to live their lives [9].

Analysis of the answer

1. No clear understanding of the concept of monotheism.
2. This suggests, wrongly, that Jews believe there are other gods.
3. Which one(s)? No quote has been included to support this point.
4. Once again, confusion with polytheism.
5. Confused, and showing a very limited knowledge and understanding of the nature of God in Judaism.
6. Correct use of a key term, but where is the evidence /quotation?
7. Lacks an understanding of the concept of 'free will'.
8. Irrelevant link to a Christian concept.
9. Needs to be linked to a specific characteristic of God.

Key skills

Knowledge involves:

Selection of a range of (thorough) accurate and relevant information that is directly related to the specific demands of the question.

This means you choose the correct information relevant to the question set NOT the topic area. You will have to think and focus on selecting key information and NOT writing everything you know about the topic area.

Understanding involves:

Explanation that is extensive, demonstrating depth and/or breadth with excellent use of evidence and examples including (where appropriate) thorough and accurate supporting use of sacred texts, sources of wisdom and specialist language.

This means that you demonstrate that you understand something by being able to illustrate and expand your points through examples/supporting evidence in a personal way and NOT repeat chunks from a text book (known as rote learning).

Further application of skills:

Go through the topic areas in this section and create some bullet lists of key points from key areas. For each one, provide further elaboration and explanation through the use of evidence and examples.

Specification content

Whether it is possible to know God.

Issues for analysis and evaluation

Whether it is possible to know God

Jews believe that God is transcendent, and therefore cannot be known in the same kind of way in which we know members of our family; or through the relationships that we have with fellow human beings. This does not, however, mean that God cannot be known.

Jews claim that they know God, because God has been revealed to them through the covenants made with Abraham and Moses. They are therefore in possession of knowledge about God, and know what God requires of them. The covenant with Moses, for example, sets out the rules by which the Jewish people are required to live, and they reflect God's purpose for the world.

Study of the Torah is one of the routes by which a Jewish person can know God. It has been revealed through the Torah that God is the creator; is just and merciful; holy and perfect. These are characteristics which can be grasped by human understanding.

A proponent of this view is Maimonides who contested that the study of the Torah is one way of coming to a greater understanding of the characteristics of God. However, he insisted that only God's *actions* can be known and even these only tell us what God is *not* like, not what God *is* like. It follows, therefore, if we follow his line of philosophical argument, that it is possible to know that God is not corporeal, for example; that God is not bound by the physical world in any shape or form, and thus is not restricted to a particular place or time.

The extent of the knowledge is limited as there is such a gap between the holiness of God and the unworthiness of humanity. It has been suggested that it would be impossible to know God in the full sense as the knowledge would be too great for human minds to handle. For instance, fear and terror was the experience of Moses when he encountered God in the burning bush.

Yet, we cannot deny the fact that many people claim that they have experienced God in a spiritual sense, and that this has brought with it a deeper understanding of the divine. The Tenakh contains examples of just such experiences: the writings of the prophets, for example, make many references to visions of the presence of God. The prophet Isaiah wrote of just such an experience when he said: 'I saw the Lord sitting upon a throne, high and lifted up; and his train filled the temple.' (Isaiah 6:1)

If, according to Judaism, God is eternal; is not restricted by space or time; has no limits, then how can humans ever begin to know God when we have an existence in which it is impossible to comprehend infinity with any real understanding?

In conclusion, it appears to be a matter of understanding about the term 'know God' that determines how this debate unfolds. There are clearly different understandings of the type of 'knowledge' or experience that a follower of Judaism can receive, ranging from a shekinah experience to a straightforward knowledge about God. Mystical elements of Judaism would extend the understanding of 'knowing God' that bit further to a more personal level. Despite this, a possible solution would be to accept that in whatever way 'know God' is interpreted or experienced that experience is always in acknowledgement of God as maintaining all the traditional characteristics of monotheism and the inevitable transcendence that this brings with it.

AO2 Activity *Possible lines of argument*

Listed below are some conclusions that could be drawn from AO2 reasoning in the accompanying text:

1. It is impossible to fully understand the nature of something which cannot be known through our human understanding of the world.

2. A person doesn't necessarily need to have a full understanding of something in order to experience it.

3. The Torah can reveal what God is like.

4. A human being's understanding of God will always be limited.

5. A person can come to know God through spiritual awareness.

Consider each of the conclusions drawn above and collect evidence and examples to support each argument from the AO1 and AO2 material studied in this section. Select one conclusion that you think is most convincing and explain why it is so. Now contrast this with the weakest conclusion in the list, justifying your argument with clear reasoning and evidence.

Whether God's characteristics are meaningful today

We live in a world today where there is now a greater scientific understanding of the way in which the universe came into being. The characteristic of God as being omnipotent, for example, was once the only way in the past of explaining how everything came into existence.

Acts of evil and suffering in the world highlight a contradiction between the contention that God is both omnipotent *and* omnibenevolent. If God is all-powerful and possesses absolute goodness, then how can we account for the dreadful things that occur in our world on a daily basis? It is difficult to understand why God, who possesses such characteristics, does not intervene in order to either prevent, or take away such occurrences. And for Jews in particular, one of the biggest questions of all is how could the holocaust have been allowed to happen? If the characteristics of God cannot be comprehended fully, then surely they cannot be meaningful for Jews today.

Some of the characteristics of God are closer to human understanding. A person is generally able to grasp the notions of justice and mercy, for example, as they are evident within society. We expect to be treated fairly, and our legal system punishes those who do not live according to the laws of the land. Justice and mercy provide the premise upon which a fair and equal society is created, and are characteristics that are therefore meaningful. It follows therefore that God demands that people live moral lives.

The holiness of God is still relevant for Jews today, as can be seen in their reverence towards the use of the name of God. The third of the Ten Commandments forbids Jews to use God's name in the wrong way. Jews therefore regard the name of God as being so holy that it should not even be spoken.

Jews still hold on to the belief that God's power has no limits at all. God is still in control of the universe, and this includes all the activities both in nature and also those of humans. God's characteristics set God apart from humankind, and allow Jews to know God in a personal and spiritual way.

Jews believe that God is an eternal God who has remained constant throughout human history; as such they accept fully the characteristics which have been assigned to God.

One conclusion could be that although the characteristics of God could be argued as meaningful or not, these are merely expressions of monotheism and it is, for followers of Judaism, not the 'characteristics' that they put their faith in but, for them, the reality of God in their lives. Whichever way they choose to understand this reality gives meaning to them and so it could be concluded further from this that all characteristics of God are meaningful for the followers of Judaism whether directly relevant today as still having meaning, or indirectly today in that the meaning is related to learning from how their God has been understood in the past.

Specification content
Whether God's characteristics are meaningful today.

Study tip
There are a number of philosophical arguments that aim to explain some of the contradictions which can be found when talking about the characteristics of God. Research the term 'theodicy', for example.

AO2 Activity *Possible lines of argument*

Listed below are some conclusions that could be drawn from the AO2 reasoning in the accompanying text:

1. Scientific discovery means that we can now explain in factual terms how the world came into existence.

2. Only those characteristics of God which are closer to human experiences are meaningful today.

3. We are more likely to question what appear to be contradictions in God's characteristics today.

4. The holiness of God will always be meaningful to practising Jews.

5. God's characteristics are such that they set God apart from humankind; nevertheless, they are still meaningful for Jews today.

Consider each of the conclusions drawn above and collect evidence and examples to support each argument from the AO1 and AO2 material studied in this section. Select one conclusion that you think is most convincing and explain why it is so. Now contrast this with the weakest conclusion in the list, justifying your argument with clear reasoning and evidence.

Key skills

Analysis involves identifying issues raised by the materials in the AO1, together with those identified in the AO2 section, and presents sustained and clear views, either of scholars or from a personal perspective ready for evaluation.

This means that it picks out key things to debate and the lines of argument presented by others or a personal point of view.

Evaluation involves considering the various implications of the issues raised based upon the evidence gleaned from analysis and provides an extensive detailed argument with a clear conclusion.

This means that the answer weighs up the various and different lines of argument analysed through individual commentary and response and arrives at a conclusion through a clear process of reasoning.

AO2 Developing skills

It is now time to reflect upon the information that has been covered so far. It is also important to consider how what you have learned can be focused and used for examination-style answers by practising the skills associated with AO2.

Assessment objective 2 (AO2) involves 'analysis' and 'evaluation'. The terms may be obvious but it is crucial to be familiar with how certain skills demonstrate these terms, and also, how the performance of these skills is measured (see generic band descriptors Band 5 for AS AO2).

Obviously an answer is placed within an appropriate band descriptor depending upon how well the answer performs, ranging from excellent, good, satisfactory, basic/limited to very limited.

▶ **Your task is this:** below is a weak answer that has been written in response to a question requiring evaluation of the relevance of the characteristics of God in today's society. Using the band level descriptors you need to place this answer in a relevant band that corresponds to the description inside that band. It is obviously a weak answer and so would not be in bands 3–5. In order to do this it will be useful to consider what is missing from the answer and what is inaccurate. The accompanying analysis gives you observations to assist you. In analysing the answer's weaknesses, in a group, think of five ways in which you would improve the answer in order to make it stronger. You may have more than five suggestions but try to negotiate as a group and prioritise the five most important things lacking.

Answer

Jews believe that God is the creator, knows everything, and loves everything. They also believe that God judges people and will forgive them if they ask for mercy. Jews believe that God has many characteristics but they are not relevant in today's society [1].

Jews have always believed these things about God and won't stop believing it now [2].

One major problem is evil. If God is all-powerful then why doesn't God stop all the bad things in the world that are going on today? God being all powerful is no longer relevant in today's society. Also, if God is all loving then why does God let people suffer from terrible illnesses? God is not all loving because there is so much illness in the world [3].

In conclusion, I personally think that God must still be relevant for Jews today or else they wouldn't still be going to the synagogue on the Sabbath [4].

Analysis of the answer

1. This is merely a list of some of the characteristics of God within Judaism, concluding with a statement which is not backed up by analysis or evaluation.

2. Why not? Where is the evidence to support this statement?

3. An important point, but in need of greater development.

4. A conclusion that doesn't make reference to the specific focus of the relevance of the characteristics of God in today's society.

B: Beliefs about God and humanity, the meaning and purpose of life

This section covers AO1 content and skills

Specification content

Humanity (the self) created in the divine image.

Humanity (the self) created in the divine image

Judaism's understanding of humanity and its relationship with God is based upon the belief that people were created for a special purpose. This finds expression in the Genesis story of creation: 'So God created mankind in his own image' (Genesis 1:27). But what does it mean to be created in the image of God, and how does this lead to the notion that humans have a special purpose in the world?

If we think about the nature of God then humans are not created in a *physical* image of God as Judaism maintains that God is incorporeal, and therefore has no physical embodiment. Therefore, we must look more closely at the Hebrew word for 'image', which is 'tzelem'. Tzelem does not refer to physical image, but to the nature or essence of a being, therefore suggesting that it is the *essence* of humankind that is like that of God. Rashi (a medieval French rabbi) proposed that the part of human nature that makes us like God lies in the fact that we have been given the power of perception. Maimonides said that by using our intellect, we are able to discern things without the use of our physical senses, and that this particular ability makes us like God, who perceives without having physical senses.

Key quote

... human beings are at the apex of creation, because they alone are made in the image of God. (M. J. Wright)

quickfire

2.8 What is 'tzelem'?

Key quote

We are created in the image of God, if you will, and we are obliged to return the favour. (Rabbi Arthur Green)

Judaism understands this to mean that humans have been given the ability to use their intellect and to be able to perceive what God wants them to do in the world; and it is this ability that makes humankind like God. Furthermore, Judaism maintains that being created in the divine image clearly suggests a difference between humanity and the rest of creation and as a result of this, Jews believe that they have a special role to play within humanity, and that is to live lives which are holy and moral.

Nefesh (life) as a divine gift

The Jewish idea of life as a divine gift is encapsulated in the concept of **nefesh** (meaning 'soul'). Judaism teaches that the body and soul are separate, yet co-exist in human life. God has given humans a body in order to do God's sacred work, and the body needs to be cared for properly in order for this to happen effectively.

There are many examples in Jewish law that emphasise the holiness of human life. For example, the mitzvot cover a range of commandments concerning what to wear; what to eat; how to conduct sexual relationships. The inclusion of such commandments highlights the belief that caring for the body means that one is also caring for the soul. Saadia Gaon, (a rabbi from the late 9th to early 10th century CE) claimed that without the body, the soul would be unable to do the holy, redemptive work of carrying out God's sacred plan.

This belief is further echoed in the **Kabbalah** (a Jewish mystical tradition) which identifies five levels of the soul, of which nefesh is the first. Nefesh represents the **ego** (the consciousness within us) that is responsible for the safety and survival of the body.

Specification content

Nefesh (life) as a divine gift; pikuach nefesh (the sanctity of life); nature of humanity – yetzer hara (evil inclination) and yetzer hatov (good inclination).

Key terms

Ego: the consciousness within us

Kabbalah: Jewish mystical tradition

Nefesh: a term meaning 'soul'

Tzelem: the nature or essence of a being

quickfire

2.9 What does Judaism teach about the relationship between body and soul?

Key quote

It is a religious precept to desecrate the Sabbath for any person afflicted with an illness that may prove dangerous; he who is zealous is praiseworthy while he who asks questions sheds blood.

(Shulchan Aruch)

quickpire

2.10 When is it permissible to break the laws of the Sabbath?

Key terms

Bar mitzvah: 'son of the commandment'; the coming of age ceremony for a Jewish boy at 13 years of age

Pikuach nefesh: the sanctity of life

Vayyitzer: meaning 'formed'

Yetzer hara: evil inclination

Yetzer hatov: good inclination

Key quote

Man is the creature created for the purpose of being drawn to God. He is placed between perfection and deficiency, with the power to earn perfection. Man must earn this perfection, however, through his own free will … Man's inclinations are therefore balanced between yetzer hatov and yetzer hara, and he … has the power of choice and is able to choose either side knowingly and willingly.

(Moshe Chaim Luzzatto)

Key quote

Indeed, there is no one on earth who is righteous, no one who does what is right and never sins.

(Ecclesiastes 7:20)

Pikuach nefesh (the sanctity of life)

Pikuach nefesh is the principle that the saving, protecting and preservation of life is of utmost importance, and it has its basis in the Torah: '… Do not do anything that endangers your neighbour's life.' (Leviticus 19:16). Judaism teaches that all life comes from God; therefore it is considered to be the gift of God, and to do anything which might take away or shorten that life is looked upon as murder.

Pikuach nefesh is such a core precept within Judaism that it overrides any other religious teaching. For example, if the life of a person is in danger, any mitzvot may be ignored in order to save them. The Talmud emphasises this principle by reference to Leviticus 18:5: 'you shall therefore keep my statues … which if a man do, he shall live by them'. The rabbis added to this: 'That he shall live by them, and not that he shall die by them' (Babylonian Talmud).

The Talmud allows for the breaking of the laws of the Sabbath in order to save the life of another person. Indeed, the Jerusalem Talmud states that if a person goes to consult a rabbi first, then they would be considered a murderer if the person died as a result of their delay. Furthermore, the rabbi who is asked would also be in disgrace, as he should have taught his community the right way to act in such a situation.

Nature of humanity – yetzer hara (evil inclination) and yetzer hatov (good inclination)

Genesis 2:7 states that '… the Lord God formed man'. The Hebrew word for 'formed' in this context is 'vayyitzer'. It is an unusual word because it contains two consecutive letters which, in rabbinic tradition, indicates that humanity was created with two impulses: yetzer hara (evil inclination) and yetzer hatov (good inclination).

According to rabbinic tradition, both impulses are present within each individual. Yetzer hatov influences a person to follow the demands of the mitzvot in order to maintain the covenant with God. Yetzer hatov can be described as a conscience, an inner voice that guides the individual into making the right decision when faced with the temptation to do something that is forbidden. It is significant that when a Jewish boy celebrates his bar mitzvah at the age of thirteen, he is at the age at which it is considered that he knows the difference between right and wrong and can take responsibility for his own moral actions.

In contrast to this, yetzer hara, if left unrestricted, can lead to acts of sin. However it is not in itself an evil force that is influencing a person to do immoral things; rather it is perceived to come from the desires within the person themself.

The Talmud declares that yetzer hara is not inherently a bad thing as it was created by God, and that it does have a positive dimension. For example, without the desire to satisfy some personal needs, a person would never aspire to marry, buy a house, have children or be successful in business. However, without the balancing force of yetzer hatov, certain desires can be fulfilled in immoral ways. The Talmud points out that there is nothing wrong with sexual desire, but if it leads to the committing of rape or adultery, for example, then it is wicked.

Jews believe that each individual has been given free will, and as a result of this has a personal choice in which impulse to follow. The Babylonian Talmud states 'All is given into the hands of heaven, except one's fear of heaven' (Niddah 16b). This indicates that a person's decision to be either good or bad is seen as a matter of free choice.

Nevertheless, there is an opportunity for **repentance** for the person who transgresses, and a way in which they can be brought back into the right relationship with God. **Teshuvah** means 'return', and is the word used to describe the concept of repentance in Judaism. Jews are required to reflect upon their misdeeds, and consider how far their actions have fallen short of God's requirements in order to **atone**. Atonement allows Jews to begin again with the right attitudes and actions.

AO1 Activity

Use your knowledge and understanding of the Jewish concepts of yetzer hara (evil inclination) and yetzer hatov (good inclination) to complete the following task:

A Jewish person has been caught stealing from the funds of a local charity. They have confessed to their misdeed and have been punished by the courts. However, they still feel very guilty and sorry for what they have done. Imagine that you are a rabbi: what information and advice would you give to them?

This practises the AO1 skill of being able to show an accurate understanding of religious belief.

The Shema and its content

The **Shema** is a prayer that Jews recite every morning and evening. The word 'Shema' means 'hear' and is the first word of the prayer: 'Hear, O Israel'. It is taken from the Book of Deuteronomy when Moses retells the story of the journey of the Children of Israel through the wilderness: 'Hear, O Israel: The Lord our God, the Lord is One' (Deuteronomy 6:4). This is as close as possible to a declaration of faith in what is central to Judaism: that there is only One God who demands total obedience from the people. The prayer was developed as a way of summarising the whole of the Jewish law and is the central focus of Jewish worship.

The Shema is the first prayer Jewish children learn and it is taught to them by their parents, thus emphasising the responsibility of parents in passing on the faith to their children. The opening line is also recited at the synagogue as the Torah is taken from the ark on the Sabbath and other festivals. Devout Jews hope that if possible, they will be able to make a final confession on their deathbed, before reciting the Shema. If this isn't possible, then those who are present will recite it on their behalf so that they die affirming the Jewish faith.

The Shema is made up of three paragraphs from the Torah: Deuteronomy 6:4–9; 11:13–21; and Numbers 15:37–41.

Part 1: Deuteronomy 6:4–9

'Hear, O Israel: The LORD our God, the LORD is one. Love the LORD your God with all your heart and with all your soul and with all your strength. These commandments that I give you today are to be on your hearts. Impress them on your children. Talk about them when you sit at home and when you walk along the road, when you lie down and when you get up. Tie them as symbols on your hands and bind them on your foreheads. Write them on the doorframes of your houses and on your gates.'

The prayer begins with the declaration that there is only One God. It then expresses the need for the commandments given by God to be the central focus for life. They are to be taught to the children; they are to be discussed; and they are to be reminded of them by wearing **tefillin** and fixing **mezuzot** to the doorpost at home.

Key quote

Exclusive fidelity to God and God's unity are the two major concepts of the Shema. (Alan Mintz)

Part 2: Deuteronomy 11:13–21

'So if you faithfully obey the commands I am giving you today – to love the LORD your God and to serve him with all your heart and with all your soul – then I will send rain on your land in its season, both autumn and spring rains, so that you may gather in your grain, new wine and olive oil. I will provide grass in the fields for your cattle, and you will eat and be satisfied.

Be careful, or you will be enticed to turn away and worship other gods and bow down to them. Then the LORD's anger will burn against you, and he will shut up the heavens so that it will not rain and the ground will yield no produce, and you will soon perish from the good land the LORD is giving you. Fix these words of mine in your hearts and minds; tie them as symbols on your hands and bind them on your foreheads. Teach them to your children, talking about them when you sit at home and when you walk along the road, when you lie down and when you get up. Write them on the doorframes of your houses and on your gates, so that your days and the days of your children may be many in the land the LORD swore to give your ancestors, as many as the days that the heavens are above the earth.'

The second part of the Shema declares the Jews' acceptance of the commandments as well as undertaking to carry them out as evidence of their loyalty to God. It reminds Jews that human actions make a difference in the world. It repeats many of the themes from the first part, but adds promises of rewards and punishments.

Part 3: Numbers 15:37–41

'The LORD said to Moses, "Speak to the Israelites and say to them: Throughout the generations to come you are to make tassels on the corners of your garments, with a blue cord on each tassel. You will have these tassels to look at and so you will remember all the commands of the LORD, that you may obey them and not prostitute yourselves by chasing after the lusts of your own hearts and eyes. Then you will remember to obey all my commands and will be consecrated to your God. I am the LORD your God, who brought you out of Egypt to be your God. I am the LORD your God."'

The third paragraph of the Shema talks about specific things that need to be done, such as the wearing of the tzitzit (fringes) that are worn on the tallit (prayer shawl) during prayer. It also mentions the Exodus from Egypt that Jews are required to remember together with, and as a reminder of, the commandments which God gave to them to 'talk about' and to 'teach' constantly.

> ### AO1 Activity
>
> Write down five key points that you have learned about the Shema.
>
> This will help in selecting relevant information for an answer to a question that expects knowledge and understanding of the Shema and its content.

The nature of Shema as an aid to faith and remembering

The Shema contains many mitzvot or commandments that Jews are required to keep as part of the covenant relationship with God. The words of the prayer are taken literally in the use of the tefillin, mezuzah, tzitzit and tallit, which are all items that act as aids to faith, and reminders of God's commandments.

Tefillin are worn as the result of a direct commandment, which can be found in the first paragraph of the Shema: 'Tie them as symbols on your hands and bind them on your foreheads' (Deuteronomy 6:8).

Key terms

Mezuzah: a small parchment scroll fixed to the right-hand doorpost of every room in a Jewish house (except bathroom and toilet)

Tallit: a woollen or silk shawl worn by Jewish males during morning prayer

Tzitzit: fringes attached to each corner of the tallit

Key quote

The tefillin ... and the mezuzah affixed to the doorpost, are in themselves the source of no totemic powers ... (they are a reminder) that the enjoyment of God's grace ... is absolutely contingent upon obedience to God's will as expressed through the commandments. (Mintz)

quickfire

2.13 How do Jews carry out the commandment to 'Tie them as symbols on your hands and bind them on your foreheads' (Deuteronomy 6:8)?

Tefillin are two small leather boxes with compartments that contain passages from the Torah (the first two paragraphs of the Shema, and also Exodus 13:1–10 and 13:11–16). As Joseph Caro taught, one of the boxes is worn on the head as a reminder to serve God with the mind; the other is wound around the weaker arm (left arm for a right-handed person and vice versa) and points towards the heart as a reminder to serve God with the heart. The wearing of tefillin is therefore a way of reminding the wearer to cultivate holy thoughts and moral actions.

Orthodox Jewish men wear tefillin every morning when they pray (except on Shabbat). They are very sacred objects for a Jew and have to be opened up and checked by a qualified scribe after a few years to check that the writing hasn't faded or cracked. They are always treated with utmost respect.

Wearing tefillin

The mezuzah is a scroll with two passages from the Torah written on it (Deuteronomy 6:4–9 and 11:13–21). These passages declare the Oneness of God and the covenant relationship between God and the Jewish people. It is handwritten by a scribe on kosher parchment and then placed inside a protective case.

A mezuzah is fixed to the doorpost of every room in a Jewish home except for the bathroom and toilet. This is done as a literal response to Deuteronomy 6:9 that states: '... and you shall write them on the doorframes of your houses and on your gates'. It is also the custom to place the mezuzah at an angle, pointing inwards, on the right side of the doorpost as you enter a room. A story from rabbinic tradition says that the rabbis couldn't agree upon whether it should be vertical or horizontal, and so they placed it at an angle to show that compromise is a much valued attribute in the home.

A special blessing will be said on fixing the mezuzah, and once in place a Jew will touch it with their fingertips, then kiss their fingertips as a sign of reverence and remembrance each time they enter the house. Thus the mezuzah acts as a reminder that everything which takes place within the home should be done with respect to God.

Tzitzit are fringes that are worn on the corners of garments as an aid to remembering God and the commandments. The third paragraph of the Shema contains the instruction to wear such an item: 'Throughout the generations to come you are to make tassels on the corners of your garments ... You will have these tassels ... so you will remember all the commands of the Lord, that you may obey them' (Numbers 15:38–39).

Key quote

The rabbis taught, 'Beloved is Israel, since the Holy One ... surrounded them with commandments: on their heads ... and forearms are tefillin, and tzitzit are on their clothes and a mezuzah on their entrances.' **(Talmud)**

A mezuzah

Tallit katan

quickfire

2.14 What is the difference between a tallit gadol and a tallit katan?

The tallit is a shawl which is worn during prayer, and which has evolved as a garment in order that the commandment for tzitzit can be accomplished. There are two types of tallit: the tallit gadol is a large robe which is worn around the shoulders, and the tallit katan is worn at all times by Orthodox Jews under their clothes. The tallit katan is a four-cornered garment with a hole for the head; it fits over the shoulders and drapes over the back and front of the body. Many Orthodox Jews leave the tzitzit hanging out at the waist so that they are visible.

Thus the very act of getting dressed or putting on the prayer shawl becomes a devotional undertaking.

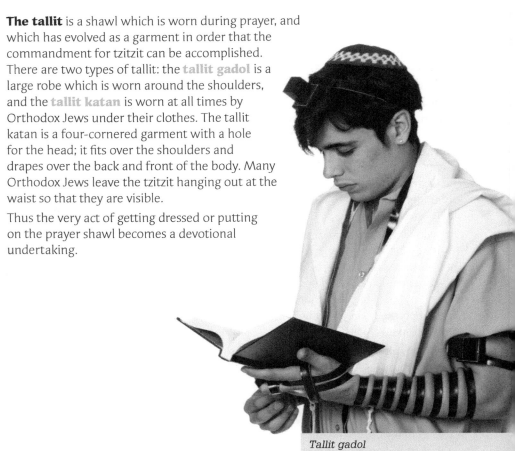

Tallit gadol

AO1 Activity

Prepare a 30-second YouTube video explaining how and why Judaism has taken the words of the Shema literally.

This task will allow you to show that you understand the reason why certain things are done as part of religious worship.

Shema as a reinforcement of covenant relationship and the meaning and purpose of life

Key quote

These commandments that I give you today are to be on your hearts. Impress them on your children. Talk about them when you sit at home and when you walk along the road, when you lie down and when you get up. Tie them as symbols on your hands and bind them on your foreheads. Write them on the doorframes of your houses and on your gates. (Deuteronomy 6:6–9)

The Shema reinforces the covenant relationship on a daily basis by reminding Jews that they are expected to obey God by upholding the laws that God has given to them. Indeed the words of the Torah are so important that Jews continue to follow the instructions given by God in Deuteronomy 6:6–9: to put them in their hearts; to instruct their children; to make them part of daily life and to set the commandments ever before themselves.

Jews today continue to draw upon the traditions of the past so that they carry on being reminded of the covenant established between God and their ancestors. The Shema provides the opportunity for them to acknowledge the sovereignty of the One God whom they believe brought their ancestors out of slavery in Egypt and delivered them into a land of their own. The injunction to carry out physical acts such as tying the words of God onto the forehand and forearm; fixing mezuzot to doorposts are practices that have developed in order to act as a daily reminder that the covenant is always there, in front of each Jew as a guide for everyday life.

Rabbi Jonathan Sacks underlines the importance of the word 'Shema' by pointing out that it is a key word in the book of Deuteronomy, occurring 92 times. It is usually used in the sense of what God wants from humankind. He notes that: 'Shema Israel means something like: "Listen. Concentrate. Give the word of God your most focused attention. Strive to understand. Engage all your faculties, intellectual and emotional. Make His will your own. For what He commands you to do is not irrational or arbitrary but for your welfare, the welfare of your people, and ultimately for the benefit of all humanity."'

As a result of this, Jews are able to achieve a deeper understanding of the purpose of their lives: that they have been sanctified and chosen by God to lead other nations to the same knowledge through obedience and moral behaviour. For Jews, this means that they must live life according to the 613 mitzvot. Obedience to God leads to moral thoughts, which in turn leads to moral actions. Rabbi Dubov speaks of 'making this world an abode for the Divine Presence', which, he says; 'can only be done through a life of Torah and mitzvot'.

Key quote

Human fulfilment is attained when intellect recognises that man, and with him the entire creation, must strive for and achieve acknowledgement of, and attachment to, God, the Creator of the Universe and Master of everything in it. (Rabbi Dubov)

AO1 Activity

An **acrostic** is a form of writing in which the first letter of each line spells out a word. Using the word 'Shema' as set out below, aim to write out **five** facts that you feel sum up its importance/use/ or value within Judaism:

S

H

E

M

A

This practises the skill of demonstrating your depth of understanding, and encourages you to express the ideas in your own words rather than just copying sentences from the text.

Key term

Acrostic: a form of writing in which the first letter of each line spells out a word

Study tip

Being able to make accurate reference to sacred texts, and/or sources of wisdom, where appropriate, is vital if you wish to gain a high level in your answer. However, make sure that the quotations that you use are relevant to the point that you are making in your answer.

Key quote

When Jews proclaim constantly, each day, the Shema, He responds, 'I am the Lord your God, who delivers you from trouble.' (Pirke de Rabbi Eliezer)

Shema Israel

Key skills

Knowledge involves:

Selection of a range of (thorough) accurate and relevant information that is directly related to the specific demands of the question.

This means you choose the correct information relevant to the question set NOT the topic area. You will have to think and focus on selecting key information and NOT writing everything you know about the topic area.

Understanding involves:

Explanation that is extensive, demonstrating depth and/or breadth with excellent use of evidence and examples including (where appropriate) thorough and accurate supporting use of sacred texts, sources of wisdom and specialist language.

This means that you demonstrate that you understand something by being able to illustrate and expand your points through examples/supporting evidence in a personal way and NOT repeat chunks from a text book (known as rote learning).

Further application of skills:

Go through the topic areas in this section and create some bullet lists of key points from key areas. For each one, provide further elaboration and explanation through the use of evidence and examples.

AO1 Developing skills

It is now time to reflect upon the information that has been covered so far. It is also important to consider how what you have learned can be focused and used for examination-style answers by practising the skills associated with AO1.

Assessment objective 1 (AO1) involves demonstrating knowledge and understanding. The terms 'knowledge' and 'understanding' are obvious but it is crucial to be familiar with how certain skills demonstrate these terms, and also, how the performance of these skills is measured (see generic band descriptors Band 5 for AS AO1).

▶ **Your new task is this:** below is a strong answer that has been written in response to a question requiring an examination of the nature of the Shema as an aid to faith and remembering. Using the band level descriptors, you can compare this with the relevant higher bands and the descriptions inside those bands. It is obviously a strong answer and so would not be in bands 1–3. In order to do this it will be useful to consider what is good about the answer and what is accurate. The accompanying analysis gives you clues and prompts to assist you. In analysing the answer's strengths, in a group, think of five things that make this answer a good one. You may have more than five observations and indeed suggestions to make it a perfect answer!

Answer

The Shema is a prayer that has a central focus within the Jewish faith. Such is its importance that it is the first prayer that a Jewish child will learn. It is taught to them by their parents, thus allowing the parents to pass on the Jewish faith to their children. The name 'Shema' means 'hear' and is followed by 'Hear, O Israel: the Lord our God, the Lord is One'. These words are taken from the book of Deuteronomy in the Torah and are like a declaration of faith in one God who demands obedience from the people [1].

The Shema is made up of three paragraphs from the Torah: Deuteronomy 6:4–9; 11:13–21; and Numbers 15:37–41, and its contents act as an important aid to faith and remembering. The Shema reminds Jews that there is only one God, and it also emphasises the requirement to follow the commandments that God gave them as part of daily life. The Shema provides particular instructions for aids to worship, and many Jews take the words of the prayer literally [2].

For example, Deuteronomy 6:8 states: 'Tie them as symbols on your hands and bind them on your foreheads.' Tefillin are worn as a direct result of this commandment. They are two leather boxes with compartments that contain passages from the Torah. One is worn on the head, reminding the wearer to serve God with their mind; the other is wound around the arm, with the box next to the heart as a reminder to serve God with love [3].

Orthodox Jews also have a small box called a mezuzah fixed to the doorpost of every room in their houses except for the bathroom and toilet. This is done because Deuteronomy 6:9 says: '… and you shall write them on the doorframes of your houses and on your gates'. The mezuzah acts as a reminder that everything that takes place within the home should be done with respect to God [4].

The Shema also commands Jewish men to wear a garment with fringes. The fringes are called tzitzit: '… you are to make tassels on the corners of your garments … so you will remember all the commands of the Lord, that you may obey them.' The fringes are attached to a shawl which is worn during prayer, and is known as a tallit. There are two types of tallit: a tallit gadol is worn around the shoulders, and a tallit katan is worn at all times by Orthodox Jews under their everyday clothes.

The tallit katan is like a small vest that is put on over the head and drapes over the back and front of the body. The tzitzit are sometimes left hanging out. The reason for this is that even when Jews are getting dressed, the putting on of the prayer shawl reminds them of their duty to devote themselves to God [5].

Thus the Shema continues to provide an invaluable aid to Jewish faith and its commandments act as reminders of devotion and duty to God [6].

Hints

1 Identifies?
2 Evidence and scriptural links?
3 References?
4 Expansion?
5 Further development of link to religious practice?
6 Conclusion?

Completed hints

1 Good introduction with supporting quote, as well as examples that underline the significance of the Shema for Jews.
2 Clearly shows the scriptural basis for the Shema.
3 Good use of relevant and accurate quotation as exemplification.
4 A further relevant example is used, thus maintaining the focus of the question.
5 Clearly demonstrates the relationship between the Shema and religious practice.
6 Good, if brief, summary to conclude the answer.

Tefillin, tallit and tzitzit

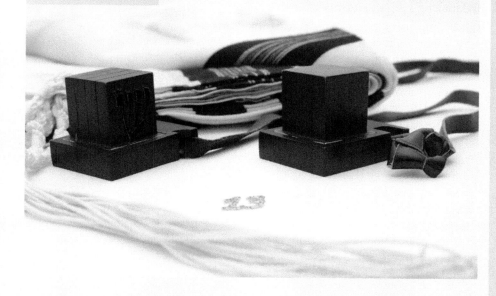

Key quote

Hear, O Israel: The LORD our God, the LORD is one. Love the LORD your God with all your heart and with all your soul and with all your strength. These commandments that I give you today are to be on your hearts. Impress them on your children. Talk about them when you sit at home and when you walk along the road, when you lie down and when you get up. Tie them as symbols on your hands and bind them on your foreheads. Write them on the doorframes of your houses and on your gates. (Deuteronomy 6:4–9)

Specification content

Whether the Shema contains the
most important beliefs within
Judaism.

Issues for analysis and evaluation

Whether the Shema contains the most important beliefs within Judaism

The Shema was developed as a way of summarising the whole of the Jewish law and is the central focus of Jewish worship. Its opening line 'Hear, O Israel: The Lord our God, the Lord is One' is as close as possible to a declaration of faith in what is central to Judaism: that there is One God who demands total obedience from the people. Alan Mintz sums up this contention when he states: 'Exclusive fidelity to God and God's unity are the two major concepts of the Shema.'

The Shema sums up the very essence of the covenant relationship between God and the Jewish people: for example, the second part of the Shema declares the Jews' acceptance of the commandments as well as undertaking to carry them out as evidence of their loyalty to God.

The Exodus from Egypt, which Jews are required to remember every day as a reminder of the commands which God gave to them, is also contained within the Shema.

The fact that it is recited every morning and evening and, as such, is the central focus for Jewish worship reminding Jews of their responsibilities to God, indicates its importance as containing the most important beliefs within Judaism.

Furthermore, such is its importance as a summary of the most important beliefs that it is the first prayer a Jewish child will learn. It is taught to them by their parents, thus emphasising the responsibility of parents in passing on the faith to their children. Devout Jews also hope, if possible, that it will be the last prayer they will recite on their deathbed.

It also reminds Jews to put their beliefs into action by obeying God's commands and making a positive difference in the world.

The Talmud also adds weight to the argument that the Shema contains the most important beliefs within Judaism: 'Beloved is Israel, since the Holy One ... surrounded them with commandments: on their heads ... and forearms are tefillin, and tzitzit are on their clothes and a mezuzah on their entrances.' Such is its importance that the commandments contained within it have developed into actual objects that Jews are required to wear or display as aids to faith and reminders of God's demands. Alan Mintz claims that the use of such items do not, in themselves, contain 'totemic powers' but are important as a reminder that 'the enjoyment of God's grace ... is absolutely contingent upon obedience to God's will as expressed through the commandments'.

However, it all depends upon what a Jew determines to be the most important beliefs within their religion. The Shema contains many mitzvot which Jews are required to keep as part of their covenant relationship with God. Reform Jews, however, have different views from Orthodox Jews on the carrying out of the mitzvot. Therefore, some Reform Jews would not wear the tzitzit which act as aids to faith and reminders of God's commandments.

AO2 Activity *Possible lines of argument*

Listed below are some conclusions that could be drawn from the AO2 reasoning in the accompanying text:

1. The Shema affirms the Jewish belief in one God.

2. The Shema contains the essence of the covenant relationship upon which Jewish faith and beliefs are built.

3. The Shema contains reminders of how to follow the commandments on a daily basis.

4. It is important at all stages of a Jewish person's life: from childhood to death.

5. It is open to interpretation.

Consider each of the conclusions drawn above and collect evidence and examples to support each argument from the AO1 and AO2 material studied in this section. Select one conclusion that you think is most convincing and explain why it is so. Now contrast this with the weakest conclusion in the list, justifying your argument with clear reasoning and evidence.

The extent to which the Shema is precise enough to guide Jewish belief and practice

Judaism is a way of life that is based upon a set of practices. These practices, or mitzvot, serve as the way in which an individual connects with God, and carries out God's commandments. Keeping the mitzvot is a requirement of the covenant relationship between God and humanity. The Shema reinforces the covenant relationship on a daily basis by reminding Jews of their responsibility to obey God by upholding the laws which God has given to them; however, on its own, it does not provide a precise guide to Jewish practice.

It is the Torah, containing as it does the mitzvot, that acts as the principal guide to Jewish belief and practice. The Ten Commandments serve as the central categories for the remaining 603 mitzvot.

It must be remembered that the religious practices of the Jewish faith have developed, through a process of evolution, over the centuries. And it is the oral Torah that has been the basis upon which this development has taken place. Rabbinic discussion, commentary and interpretation have followed, providing fuller explanations as to how to adhere to the commandments.

Notwithstanding, the Shema *does* contain a number of mitzvot that Jews are required to keep. The words of the prayer are taken literally in the use of the tefillin, mezuzah, tallit and tzitzit, which are all items that act as aids to faith and reminders of God's commandments. However, even in this case, the Shema is not precise about what particular form each of these must take, and current Jewish practice has evolved over many thousands of years of rabbinic interpretation.

The Shema is important within all branches of the Jewish faith, and yet its content is not always followed in the same precise way across the different groups. In Reform Judaism, for example, certain sections of the prayer are often omitted because this group has different views from Orthodox Jews on carrying out the mitzvot. For example, Reform Jews do not accept the commandment requiring the wearing of fringes on garments, therefore the end of the third section (from Numbers 15:40) is omitted. Some Reform Jews also leave out the second paragraph of the Shema (Deuteronomy 11:13–21) as their view of God's actions in taking retribution is different from that of the more Orthodox groups.

Nevertheless, wherever Jews have found themselves in the world, it has been the Shema that has united them and has been a constant reminder of God's love for them, and their commitment to God in return. God will provide protection in return for loyalty and obedience to the commandments. It has always played an integral part in the faith, and is perhaps better seen as having been developed for the purpose of summing up the very essence of Jewish belief: that there is One God who demands total obedience from the people.

In conclusion, it could be suggested that the Shema is certainly precise in that it focuses on the essentials of Jewish belief but that its precision in directing and guiding followers of Judaism in belief and practice can be found in not what it contains but in what it points one to and provides access to; that is, the wider understanding and application of the Torah. In this understanding it is certainly a precise guide to Jewish belief and practice.

Specification content

The extent to which the Shema is precise enough to guide Jewish belief and practice.

AO2 Activity *Possible lines of argument*

Listed below are some conclusions that could be drawn from the AO2 reasoning in the accompanying text:

1. The Shema acts as a reminder to Jews on a daily basis of their responsibility to obey God.

2. The Torah, containing as it does the mitzvot, is the most important guide to Jewish belief and practice.

3. There are other sources of information within the Jewish religion that offer more detailed guidance to belief and practice.

4. Certain aspects of the Shema have become part of Jewish practice, but even these have evolved over the centuries.

5. The Shema plays a more important role as a declaration of faith.

Consider each of the conclusions drawn above and collect evidence and examples to support each argument from the AO1 and AO2 material studied in this section. Select one conclusion that you think is most convincing and explain why it is so. Now contrast this with the weakest conclusion in the list, justifying your argument with clear reasoning and evidence.

Key skills

Analysis involves identifying issues raised by the materials in the AO1, together with those identified in the AO2 section, and presents sustained and clear views, either of scholars or from a personal perspective ready for evaluation.

This means that it picks out key things to debate and the lines of argument presented by others or a personal point of view.

Evaluation involves considering the various implications of the issues raised based upon the evidence gleaned from analysis and provides an extensive detailed argument with a clear conclusion.

This means that the answer weighs up the various and different lines of argument analysed through individual commentary and response and arrives at a conclusion through a clear process of reasoning.

AO2 Developing skills

It is now time to reflect upon the information that has been covered so far. It is also important to consider how what you have learned can be focused and used for examination-style answers by practising the skills associated with AO2.

Assessment objective 2 (AO2) involves 'analysis' and 'evaluation'. The terms may be obvious but it is crucial to be familiar with how certain skills demonstrate these terms, and also, how the performance of these skills is measured (see generic band descriptors Band 5 for AS AO2).

Obviously an answer is placed within an appropriate band descriptor depending upon how well the answer performs, ranging from excellent, good, satisfactory, basic/limited to very limited.

▶ **Your task is this:** below is a strong answer that has been written in response to a question requiring evaluation of the Shema as providing a detailed guide to Jewish belief and practice. Using the band level descriptors, you can compare this with the relevant higher bands and the descriptions inside those bands. It is obviously a strong answer and so would not be in bands 1–3. In order to do this it will be useful to consider what is good about the answer and what is accurate. The accompanying analysis gives you clues and prompts to assist you. In analysing the answer's strengths, in a group, think of five things that make this answer a good one. You may have more than five observations and indeed suggestions to make it a perfect answer!

Answer

The issue for debate here is whether or not the Shema, on its own, is able to provide a detailed guide to Jewish belief and practice [1].

In the first instance, I would suggest that it is highly unlikely that a prayer that is made up of three paragraphs would be able to sum up the full extent of the Jewish religion as well as outlining all of its beliefs and practices. That is not to say, however, that the Shema does not have an important part to play in Jewish worship. The very fact that it is taught to every Jewish child, and that devout Jews wish it to be the last words that they speak before death, underlines its importance within the Jewish faith [2].

We have to remember that Jewish beliefs and religious practices have evolved over the centuries. Both the written and the oral Torah provide the basis for the development of the principles of Jewish belief and practice. Generations of rabbis have interpreted the mitzvot that are contained in the Torah, and it is from this tradition that Jews have been able to formulate their practices [3].

Nevertheless, we should not ignore the Shema as a form of guidance, as the words of the prayer are taken literally in the use of the tefillin, mezuzah, tallit and tzitzit, which are all items that act as aids to faith and reminders of God's commandments. However, even in this case, the Shema is not precise about what particular form each of these must take, and current Jewish practice has evolved over many thousands of years of rabbinic interpretation [4].

Even if the Shema is not able to provide a detailed guide to Jewish belief and practice then we should not forget its purpose. Rather than acting as a guide to Jewish practice, it is perhaps better seen as having been developed for the purpose of summing up the very essence of Jewish belief: that there is One God who demands total obedience from the people [5].

Hints

1. Identifies?
2. Evidence and link?
3. Alternative?
4. Expansion?
5. Original?

Completed hints

1. Sets out the issue for debate both clearly and concisely.
2. States reason for not supporting the contention that the Shema is capable of providing a detailed guide to Jewish belief and practice, notwithstanding its significance.
3. Makes accurate reference to alternative sources within Judaism that provide the basis for the development of Jewish beliefs and practices.
4. Introduces another alternative argument with relevant examples.
5. The conclusion is appropriate, and sums up by using a suggestion as to how the Shema could best be viewed.

C: Beliefs about judgement – the Messiah and the afterlife

This section covers AO1 content and skills

Specification content

The Messiah in Judaism – The Anointed One and Judge who brings peace and goodwill to humanity (Isaiah 2:1–4); the establishment of a new world order.

The Messiah in Judaism – The Anointed One and Judge who brings peace and goodwill to humanity (Isaiah 2:1–4)

The word Messiah ('Mashiah' in Hebrew) literally means 'anointed one', referring to the ritual practice of anointing and consecrating kings and high priests at their investiture in ancient times. However, it is usually understood as a term that refers specifically to a future leader of the Jewish people who will bring in a new age of freedom, justice, peace and goodwill, which will be established under the rule of God.

The idea of the Messiah is not explicitly mentioned in the Torah, and the concept was probably introduced during the time of the prophets. Nevertheless, Nicholas De Lange describes the doctrine of the Messiah as being 'one of the most distinctive ideas of classical Judaism'. And Hermann Cohen called it 'the most significant and original product of the Jewish spirit'.

According to the writings of the prophets, there will be a time in the future when the Jewish people will be free from subjugation to other nations. This new age for the Jewish people is referred to in Isaiah 2:1–4 where we read that they will return to Israel, and the Temple will be restored in Jerusalem: 'the mountain of the LORD's temple will be established as the highest of the mountains' (Isaiah 2:2). God's presence will be felt by everyone, both Jews and gentiles, and the rule of God will be established upon the earth: 'He will teach us his ways, so that we may walk in his paths' (Isaiah 2:3).

Some of the prophets go further in claiming that this future age will be associated with a human leader, sent by God, who will create a peaceful society as Isaiah 2:4 states, 'Nation will not take up sword against nation, nor will they train for war anymore.' This concept of a Messiah, as Judge, who will bring peace and goodwill to the world can also be found in Isaiah 11:2–5.

'The Spirit of the LORD will rest on him—
the Spirit of wisdom and of understanding,
the Spirit of counsel and of might,
the Spirit of the knowledge and fear of the LORD—
and he will delight in the fear of the LORD.

He will not judge by what he sees with his eyes,
or decide by what he hears with his ears;
but with righteousness he will judge the needy,
with justice he will give decisions for the poor of the earth.
He will strike the earth with the rod of his mouth;
with the breath of his lips he will slay the wicked.
Righteousness will be his belt
and faithfulness the sash around his waist.'

(Isaiah 11:2–5)

This passage describes a time when justice and righteousness will be established under the rule of God. It will be a period when God's presence will be evident to everyone.

Key quote

Anyone who does not believe in him (the Messiah) or does not await his coming not only denies the rest of the prophets, he denies Torah and (the prophecy) of Moshe Rabbeinu. (Maimonides)

Key terms

Anointing: to put oil on someone's head, usually as part of a religious ceremony

Consecrating: making someone/something sacred; setting them apart for holy use

Gentiles: the general term for people who are not Jewish

Investiture: a formal ceremony giving a special role to someone

Messiah: the 'anointed one'; one who will usher in a new era for humanity, which will be established under the rule of God

Subjugation: to be in a state of domination by another nation

Key quote

All prophets prophesy only for the days of the Messiah. (Talmud)

Key quote

The world was created only for the Messiah. (Talmud)

quickfire

2.15 What are the names of two of the prophets who make reference to the Messiah?

Key quote

… the king of Israel must come from the House of David and the seed of Solomon. Anyone who opposes this dynasty defies the Almighty and the words of His prophets. (Maimonides)

quickfire

2.16 What did Maimonides predict about the Messiah?

Key terms

Ani Ma'amin: a poetic form of Maimonides' Thirteen Articles of Faith which is recited every day after morning prayers at the synagogue

Resurrected: to bring back to life

Tarry: to be slow or late in coming; to linger

The prophet Jeremiah says that the Messiah will be a political leader, a descendant of King David. He will be well versed in Jewish law and observant of the commandments of God. Above all, he will be a great judge who will make decisions based upon righteousness: 'In those days and at that time I will make a righteous Branch sprout from David's line; he will do what is just and right in the land' (Jeremiah 33:15).

The establishment of a new world order

Jews refer to the world after the Messiah has come as the Messianic Age; however, there is no single, unified concept of exactly what the future Messianic Age will be like. Indeed, De Lange points out that 'one rabbi, for example, states that it is vain to hope for a future Messiah, because the Messiah mentioned in the Bible came in the time of Hezekiah, at the beginning of the seventh century BCE'. Neither does the Babylonian Talmud subscribe to the fact that the Messianic Age will be a supernatural disturbance in history. Rather, it will be 'no different from the present except that Israel will no longer be in subjection to the kingdoms of the world'.

During the Middle Ages there was agreement that there would be a personal Messiah, and yet disagreement about whether the Messianic Age would be a natural or supernatural event. Maimonides warned against the expectation that the course of nature would be changed with the arrival of the Messiah. Nevertheless, he predicts that the Messiah will restore the kingdom of David to its former glory; restore the Temple; and gather the Jews together as a nation once more. The Messiah will also be a ruler who will reign according to the commandments contained in the Torah.

For Maimonides, the purpose of the Messianic Age is not that the Jews should claim superiority over the other nations of the world, but that they would be free to study the Torah and to prepare for the Coming Age, or 'World to Come' (the afterlife).

Orthodox Jews believe in a personal Messiah who will come at the time of God's choosing, and who will lead all humanity back to God. The Messiah will be descended from the line of King David, and preceded by the return of the prophet Elijah. After a period of decline and catastrophe, the Messiah will establish a new world order based upon the laws of God and characterised by peace upon the earth: 'He will judge between the nations and will settle disputes for many peoples … nor will they train for war anymore' (Isaiah 2:4). Jerusalem will be rebuilt and at the close of this era, the dead will be **resurrected**, re-joined with their souls and a final judgement will be made. All this will be achieved as a result of the influence of the Messiah.

Nevertheless, there has been much scholarly debate about when the Messiah will come, and this has led to a variety of opinions; but generally it is believed that the conduct of humankind will determine the time. Either the Messiah will come at a time when most needed, that is, when the world is in a sinful state; or at a time when most deserving, as a result of good conduct.

The **Ani Ma'amin** states 'I believe with complete faith in the coming of the Messiah, and even if he should **tarry**, I nevertheless will wait every day for his coming.'

Reform Jews, too, believe in the Messianic era; a period of peace. However, they do not subscribe to the belief in the restoration of a Jewish state. The fifth clause of the Pittsburgh Platform states: 'We recognise in the modern era of universal culture of heart and intellect the approaching of the realisation of Israel's great Messianic hope for the establishment of the kingdom of truth, justice and peace among all men.' Reform Jews reject the notion that the Jews are in exile from their God-given land. Instead, they see their dispersion as a necessary thing, and that they have been chosen to spread the monotheistic truth and morality all over the earth by being an example to others.

Death and the resurrection of the dead (Daniel 12:2); the final judgement

There is no real theological significance to death in Judaism other than it is part of God's plan for human beings. Mourning and funeral practices within Judaism express more about remembering the deceased and comforting the living than they do about what will happen to the deceased in the afterlife. The doctrine of the resurrection of the dead appears in Jewish eschatology, and is associated with events that will happen in the Messianic Age when the dead will rise to live again.

There are only two biblical references to the resurrection of the dead in the Hebrew Bible: 'But your dead will live, Lord; their bodies will rise – let those who dwell in the dust wake up and shout for joy – your dew is like the dew of the morning; the earth will give birth to her dead' (Isaiah 26:19); and 'Multitudes who sleep in the dust of the earth will awake: some to everlasting life, others to shame and everlasting contempt' (Daniel 12:2). Scholars have pointed out that both of these passages come from a later date within the scriptures, and have therefore suggested that the passages have been influenced by Persian thought.

If we study the book of the prophet Daniel in more detail, we see that it doesn't mention the term 'Messiah'; however, the title 'son of man' is evident within the text that, it has been claimed, has the same connotations. 'Son of man' refers to a future figure whose coming will signal the end of history and bring about the time of God's judgement. The goal of history is thus portrayed as the coming of *God's Kingdom*, rather than a human kingdom, which will present itself in God's own time, and as a result of God's power.

According to the book of Daniel, the arrival of God's Kingdom will be preceded by a time of great trouble. Nevertheless, those who have been faithful to God will be rescued from the hardship. Furthermore, there will be a Day of Judgement on which there will be a resurrection of the dead, when God will judge each soul and determine where each will spend eternity: 'Multitudes who sleep in the dust of the earth will awake: some to everlasting life, others to shame and everlasting contempt' (Daniel 12:2).

The doctrine of resurrection is one that has been a subject for debate within Judaism throughout its history. In the final statement of his 'Thirteen Principles of the Jewish Faith', Maimonides claims that the resurrection of the dead is one of the foundations of belief. However, references to resurrection in other of his writings appear to show that he believed in the resurrection of the immortal soul and not of the body. This is in contrast to statements found in rabbinic literature that the dead will be resurrected wearing their clothes: 'The just in the time to come will rise in their own clothes' (Babylonian Talmud). Further, Hasdai Crescas, a medieval philosopher, proposed that since in our lifetime body and soul co-exist, it is fitting that there be an ultimate reward and punishment for both as well. Hence, in his conclusion, there is a need for a bodily resurrection.

Another aspect of the debate about resurrection endeavours to set out a timeline for the event with the Midrash claiming that the humble will be raised first. There is also a belief amongst some in Judaism that those who are buried in Israel will be the first to rise.

Specification content

Death and the resurrection of the dead (Daniel 12:2); the final judgement.

Key quote

In the world which He will create anew, where He will revive the dead … may He bring forth His redemption and hasten the coming of His Messiah. **(Kaddish)**

quickfire

2.17 What does the term 'eschatology' mean?

Key term

Eschatology: the branch of theology dealing with death, divine judgement, and life after death

Orthodox Jews still maintain a belief in the resurrection, and make reference to it in daily prayers and at funerals, especially the Kaddish that is recited by a son at the funeral of a parent. Furthermore, it is the resurrection of the body that is accepted, and as a result of this many Jews object to cremation. Reform Jews on the other hand, reject the doctrine of the resurrection of the body in favour of the immortality of the soul.

Modern-day Jewish scholars tend not to discuss the matter of the resurrection in any great detail, perhaps for the same reason as Joseph Albo, a sixteenth-century Jewish philosopher, who quoted the Talmudic saying: 'We will consider the matter when they come to life again'.

Olam ha-ba (the afterlife)

Specification content
Olam ha-ba (the afterlife).

Olam ha-ba is a Hebrew term that means 'the world to come', and which is used to denote the concept of the afterlife. This suggests that Jews believe that death is not the end of human existence. However, there is very little to be found in the Torah relating to what they actually believe happens after a person dies. This means that there is no accepted agreement amongst different groups within Judaism about olam ha-ba, apart from the fundamental emphasis of living now and forever in the ways in which God intends.

A portion of the Mishnah says: 'Be not like servants who serve their master for the sake of receiving a reward; instead, be like servants who serve their master not for the sake of receiving a reward, and let the awe of Heaven (meaning God, not the afterlife) be upon you.' In other words, one should serve God out of love of truth.

Key terms

El male rachamim: a funeral prayer

Gehinnom: a place of spiritual punishment and/or purification

Kaddish: a prayer said by a mourner

Olam ha-ba: literally 'the world to come'; the afterlife

Key quote

This world is like the eve of Shabbat, and the olam ha-ba is like Shabbat. He who prepares on the eve of Shabbat will have food to eat on Shabbat. (Talmud)

Nicholas De Lange contends that the concept of rewards and punishments being meted out in the afterlife comes from the post-biblical era of Judaism. Furthermore, it was a view that could not have been introduced until Jews had adopted the idea of the survival of the soul after the death of the body. This idea seems to have been borrowed from Greek thought, and thus assimilated into Jewish belief.

The Talmudic rabbis speak of the repose of souls of the righteous departed in the Garden of Eden, and this idea is mentioned in the memorial prayer for the dead, the El male rachamim: 'O God … grant perfect peace to the soul of (name) … who has gone to his/her eternity, may he/she rest in the Garden of Eden ….'

It seems from texts such as this that the souls of those who have led a good life, will live on forever in tranquillity whilst the souls of the wicked go down to Gehinnom, where, according to some views, they suffer torment. There is also a suggestion that the souls of the dead wait in the Garden of Eden until the coming of the Messiah and the general resurrection of the dead. It is at this point that they will be reunited with their bodies. This in turn will be followed by the olam ha-ba.

Key quote

Even Orthodox Jews would probably agree that given the inherent difficulties of the subject, the lack of clear guidance in the sources, and the absence of empirical evidence, it is difficult if not impossible for the finite human mind to find a clear path among the various possibilities. (De Lange)

Key quote

In the Coming Age there is no eating or drinking or reproduction or business activity or envy or hatred or competition, but the righteous sit with crowns on their heads feasting on the radiance of the shekinah. (Talmud)

However, uncertainty persists about the afterlife, as can be seen in the variety of beliefs that are to be found within Judaism. For example, many Jews believe that God rewards the good and punishes sinners both in this life and the next; the soul is immortal, and everyone will be judged at death; those who have lived a good life will be close to God and those who have done wrong will need purification in hell.

Some Orthodox Jews believe that there will be a resurrection of the body and soul; however, many others stress that the essence of Judaism is about how a person lives in this world. It is therefore probably true to say that Jews generally believe that it is far more important to focus on what is happening during life rather than being concerned about what might happen in the afterlife; thus leaving the details of the olam ha-ba to God.

Key quotes

The prophets ... were all agreed upon this: that the reward for a person's behaviour is not meted out in this world but is only given in that which comes after it. (Saadia Gaon)

I believe in resurrection when the body and soul will arise and the bones will come to life again. (Meshullam ben Solomon)

AO1 Activity

After reading the sections on the resurrection of the dead, the final judgement and olam ha-ba, select six quotations from across the following sources, and explain how each one can be used as evidence for particular beliefs.

The sources are: Isaiah; Daniel; Talmud; Jospeh Albo, Kaddish, El male rachamim.

This practises the AO1 skill of making thorough and accurate reference to sacred texts and sources of wisdom.

The Pittsburgh Platform (paragraph 7) and Reform views about the afterlife

Paragraph 7 of the Pittsburgh Platform states that: 'Reform Judaism rejects the idea of bodily resurrection but accepts the view that the soul is immortal and that the spirit is divine.'

Reform Jews therefore do not believe that there will be a resurrection of the dead. As a result of this, passages that contained references to the resurrection in Reform prayer books have been either deleted or interpreted as an allusion to the immortality of the soul. Reform theology now concerns itself solely with the belief in a *spiritual* life after death.

The belief in the immortality of the soul is a concept that Reform Jews consider to be deeply rooted in the scriptures. Each person has been created in the image of God: 'So God created mankind in his own image' (Genesis 1:27). It is the divine element within each of us which makes us unique, and which is, like God, immortal. For Reform Jews, this God-given dimension of existence brings with it the particular responsibility to live in accordance with God's wishes, in the hope that it will serve as an example to others and ultimately make the world a better place for the whole of humanity.

Rabbi Howard Berman sums it up in the following way: 'But the distinctive nature of this concept is that we achieve immortality primarily through the goodness we bring to other lives – while we ourselves are alive ... and we continue to live – primarily through the lasting blessings we impart ... and through the memories we leave behind.'

Specification content

The Pittsburgh Platform (paragraph 7) and Reform views about the afterlife.

quickfire

2.18 What does paragraph 7 of the Pittsburgh Platform state?

Study tip

Make sure that you have a confident understanding of the variety of views that are to be found within Judaism on the subject of the Messiah, Messianic Age, Judgement, and the afterlife. A common mistake is to suggest in an exam answer that 'all' Jews believe one thing, and then to contradict that by stating that 'other' Jews believe something else.

Key skills

Knowledge involves:

Selection of a range of (thorough) accurate and relevant information that is directly related to the specific demands of the question.

This means you choose the correct information relevant to the question set NOT the topic area. You will have to think and focus on selecting key information and NOT writing everything you know about the topic area.

Understanding involves:

Explanation that is extensive, demonstrating depth and/or breadth with excellent use of evidence and examples including (where appropriate) thorough and accurate supporting use of sacred texts, sources of wisdom and specialist language.

This means that you demonstrate that you understand something by being able to illustrate and expand your points through examples/supporting evidence in a personal way and NOT repeat chunks from a text book (known as rote learning).

Further application of skills:

Go through the topic areas in this section and create some bullet lists of key points from key areas. For each one, provide further elaboration and explanation through the use of evidence and examples.

AO1 Developing skills

It is now time to reflect upon the information that has been covered so far. It is also important to consider how what you have learned can be focused and used for examination-style answers by practising the skills associated with AO1.

Assessment objective 1 (AO1) involves demonstrating knowledge and understanding. The terms 'knowledge' and 'understanding' are obvious but it is crucial to be familiar with how certain skills demonstrate these terms, and also, how the performance of these skills is measured (see generic band descriptors Band 5 for AS AO1).

▶ **Your new task is this:** below is a fairly strong answer, although not perfect, that has been written in response to a question requiring an examination of the concept of the Messiah in Judaism. Using the band level descriptors, you can compare this with the relevant higher bands and the descriptions inside those bands. It is obviously a fairly strong answer and so would not be in bands 5, 1 or 2. In order to do this it will be useful to consider what is both strong and weak about the answer and therefore what needs developing.

In analysing the answer, in a group, identify three ways to make this answer a better one. You may have more than three observations and indeed suggestions to make it a perfect answer!

Answer

Jews believe in a Messiah. The Messiah is a person who will lead the Jews at some time in the future and will bring the entire world to a time of peace. We do not really know where the idea of the Messiah comes from because it's not in the Torah, but the prophets started to mention a time of peace when God would be in charge. For example, the prophet Isaiah says that the Messiah will come to earth and bring in a new age for the Jewish people: 'He will teach us his ways, so that we may walk in his paths'. The Messiah will return them to Israel, and they will be able to rebuild the Temple in its rightful place in Jerusalem. Also, the rule of God will cover the whole of the world and include everyone, even people who are not Jews.

Even though Orthodox Jews do not know when the Messiah will come, they believe that they must wait for God to decide when the time is right. However, they believe that they will be able to recognise him when he comes as he will be a descendant of King David, and that the prophet Elijah will return before him.

Unfortunately, before the Messiah comes there will be a time of war and catastrophes in the world, but then peace will come and a new world order will be established.

Another prophet, called Daniel, also talks about a time in the future when God will establish a kingdom on earth. Daniel seems to be talking about the same type of figure as the Messiah although he uses the term 'son of man'. Daniel says that there will be times of great trouble, but that there will be a day of judgement, and all the people who have been faithful to God will be rescued from hardship. Daniel goes a bit further than Isaiah, and in chapter 12 verse 2 mentions that on the day of judgement, all the people who have died will be resurrected. It is called the day of judgement because God will look at each person's life and will give them a place in either Heaven or Hell depending on how good or bad they have been with 'some to everlasting life' and others 'to shame and everlasting contempt'.

Reform Jews also believe in the Messiah, and that the covenant with God will be finally fulfilled and the world will be at peace. God will be in charge, and God's power will be experienced.

Issues for analysis and evaluation

Whether Jewish beliefs about judgement and the afterlife are relevant for Jews today

Ideas about Heaven and hell, the resurrection of the body and the immortality of the soul have been assimilated into Jewish thought from Hebrew and Greek doctrines. This means that there is no accepted agreement amongst different groups within Judaism, and thus there is a wide range of opinions amongst present-day Jews about what actually happens after death. Nicholas De Lange contends that the concept of judgement, followed by the awarding of reward or punishment actually comes from the post-biblical era of Judaism.

Jews generally believe that it is far more important to focus on what is happening during life rather than being concerned about what might happen in the afterlife. Most Jews are content to leave the details of the afterlife to God. A portion of the Mishnah says: 'Be not like servants who serve their master for the sake of receiving a reward; instead, be like servants who serve their master not for the sake of receiving a reward, and let the awe of Heaven (meaning God, not the afterlife) be upon you.' In other words, one should serve God out of love of truth.

The concept of judgement and the afterlife can be found in the Hebrew Scriptures. The book of Daniel predicts a Day of Judgement when there will be a resurrection of the dead, and God will judge each soul and determine where each will spend eternity. More importantly, the Torah presents Jews with the notion of a God who punishes the bad and rewards the good according to the way in which each has responded to the commandments given to Moses. One would think that this would mean that both judgement and the afterlife would be of great importance to Jews today.

There is very little to be found in the Torah relating to what Jews actually believe happens after a person dies. However, the Talmudic rabbis speak of the repose of souls of the righteous departed in the Garden of Eden, and this idea is mentioned in the memorial prayer for the dead, the El male rachamim: 'O God ... grant perfect peace to the soul of (name) who has gone to his/her eternity, may he/she rest in the Garden of Eden ...' This seems to suggest that the souls of those who have led a good life will live on forever in peace, whilst the wicked will suffer torment in Gehinnom.

Perhaps it is the concept of judgement that is of more relevance for Jews today rather than what happens in the afterlife, as many believe that God will reward the good and punish sinners *in this life* as well as the next. This is evident during the festival of Yom Kippur when the people stand before God and confess their sins before God makes a final judgement on each individual's fate for the coming year. It is a festival at which many Jews who do not normally go to the synagogue throughout the year are present, which shows its relevance for Jews today.

Another conclusion could possibly be that it is not the specific details of belief about judgement and the afterlife that are critical for followers of Judaism but the general view of hope for the future establishment of God's kingdom through the Messianic Age and, as Maimonides argues, that this is the real focus of attention. It is therefore only when the Messianic Age is upon Jewish believers that they are then free to study the Torah and truly prepare for the afterlife.

This section covers AO2 content and skills

Specification content
Whether Jewish beliefs about judgement and the afterlife are relevant for Jews today.

AO2 Activity *Possible lines of argument*

Listed below are some conclusions that could be drawn from the AO2 reasoning in the accompanying text:

1. There is a lack of agreement between different Jewish groups about these issues.

2. It's more important to focus on living a good life than to worry about what might happen in the afterlife.

3. If the concepts of judgement and the afterlife are to be found in the Jewish scriptures then they must still be relevant for Jews today.

4. Perhaps judgement has more relevance than a belief in the afterlife.

5. The festival of Yom Kippur places great emphasis upon reward and punishment in the present life as opposed to the afterlife.

Consider each of the conclusions drawn above and collect evidence and examples to support each argument from the AO1 and AO2 material studied in this section. Select one conclusion that you think is most convincing and explain why it is so. Now contrast this with the weakest conclusion in the list, justifying your argument with clear reasoning and evidence.

Specification content

Whether the concept of 'Messiah' is
a serious religious belief for all Jews
today.

Whether the concept of 'Messiah' is a serious religious belief for all Jews today

The concept of the 'Messiah' has been an issue for debate throughout Jewish history. However, there is no single, unified notion of exactly what the future Messianic Age will be like. In the Middle Ages there was agreement that there would be a personal Messiah, and yet disagreement about whether the Messianic Age would be a natural or supernatural event. Maimonides warned against the expectation that the course of nature would be changed with the arrival of the Messiah. Nevertheless, he predicted that the Messiah would restore the kingdom of David to its former glory; restore the Temple; and gather the Jews together as a nation once more. The Messiah would also be a ruler who would reign according to the commandments contained in the Torah.

The debate continues, with the Babylonian Talmud denying that the Messianic Age will be a supernatural disturbance in history. Rather, it will be 'no different from the present except that Israel will no longer be in subjection to the kingdoms of the world'. Nicholas De Lange also points out that 'one rabbi, for example, states that it is vain to hope for a future Messiah, because the Messiah mentioned in the Bible came in the time of Hezekiah, at the beginning of the seventh century BCE'.

For Orthodox Jews, the concept of a personal Messiah who will come at the time of God's choosing, and who will lead all humanity back to God, is a fundamental part of Jewish tradition and belief. This is because the Jewish religion is built upon the covenant relationship, with the promise that the Jewish people will once again take possession of a land of their own. Only when God has sent the long-promised 'anointed one' will the exiles of Israel return to the Holy Land and all nations will turn to Jerusalem to learn of the One God.

Reform Judaism, however, denies that there will be an individual Messiah who will appear and create a perfect world. Instead, Reform Jews believe that *they* have been chosen to spread the monotheistic truth and morality over all the earth, and to be an example to others. God's Kingdom will come about as a result of human effort, and living according to God's rules rather than by waiting for a messenger sent by God.

Furthermore, the idea of the Messiah is not explicitly mentioned in the Torah, but appears to have been introduced at a later period probably during the time of the prophets. As the Torah alone contains God-given instructions to the Jewish people then it could be claimed that the content and the beliefs which have evolved from it have a higher value and should be taken more seriously than the traditions of the Messiah, which came later in Jewish history.

This suggests rather that Jews should be focused upon what they can do in the here and now by living in accordance with the mitzvot which God gave to Moses on Mount Sinai, rather than waiting for deliverance at an undefined future event.

Overall, one conclusion could be that there is clearly uncertainty and debate about the Messianic Age today but this does not mean that this makes the concept any less 'serious' as a religious belief. It appears the debate is more to do with clarity and focus in relation to wider aspects of Judaism. This line of argument further concludes that it is definitely a serious belief but that it is one that in not yet fully revealed and also has to be viewed within the broader context of Jewish belief and practice.

AO2 Activity Possible lines of argument

Listed below are some conclusions that could be drawn from the AO2 reasoning in the accompanying text:

1. Orthodox Jews hold a fundamental belief in the concept of a personal Messiah.

2. The concept of the 'Messiah' is linked to the promises of the covenant relationship.

3. Reform Jews believe that God's Kingdom will be established as a result of human efforts.

4. The concept of the Messiah is not explicit in the Torah.

5. It's more important to live life according to the mitzvot which God gave to Moses.

Consider each of the conclusions drawn above and collect evidence and examples to support each argument from the AO1 and AO2 material studied in this section. Select one conclusion that you think is most convincing and explain why it is so. Now contrast this with the weakest conclusion in the list, justifying your argument with clear reasoning and evidence.

AO2 Developing skills

It is now time to reflect upon the information that has been covered so far. It is also important to consider how what you have learned can be focused and used for examination-style answers by practising the skills associated with AO2.

Assessment objective 2 (AO2) involves 'analysis' and 'evaluation'. The terms may be obvious but it is crucial to be familiar with how certain skills demonstrate these terms, and also, how the performance of these skills is measured (see generic band descriptors Band 5 for AS AO2).

Obviously, an answer is placed within an appropriate band descriptor depending upon how well the answer performs, ranging from excellent, good, satisfactory, basic/limited to very limited.

▶ **Your task is this:** below is a reasonable answer, although not perfect, that has been written in response to a question requiring an examination of the relevance of a belief in the afterlife for all Jews today. Using the band level descriptors you can compare this with the relevant higher bands and the descriptions inside those bands. It is obviously a reasonable answer and so would not be in bands 5, 1 or 2. In order to do this it will be useful to consider what is both strong and weak about the answer and therefore what needs developing.

In analysing the answer, in a group, identify three ways to make this answer a better one. You may have more than three observations and indeed suggestions to make it a perfect answer!

Answer

When discussing this issue we need to realise that not all Jews have the same beliefs about the afterlife. It is also important to note that even though there is a term for the afterlife in Hebrew that means 'the world to come', there isn't much in the Torah about what happens after a person dies. As the Torah is believed to have been given to Moses by God then perhaps it is more important to concentrate on living according to the mitzvot rather than worrying about an afterlife.

Some people might wonder what the purpose of life is if not to prepare you for an afterlife with God. A belief in an afterlife can be relevant as it can bring comfort to the dying as well as to the mourners at a funeral.

Reform Jews do not place much emphasis upon the concept of an afterlife, and this can be seen in paragraph 7 of the Pittsburgh Platform. However, this doesn't stop Reform Jews from living a life that they hope will be pleasing to God. Their purpose is more about making the world a better place for all in their current lives.

Orthodox Jews, however, believe that the afterlife is relevant to them. Their belief in the immortality of the soul means that they are aware that God punishes sinners and rewards the good people in this life and the next. They believe in a day of judgement when God will decide, and therefore a belief in the afterlife is relevant to them because they would hope of a place in heaven.

When we look at where the ideas of an afterlife come from we see that they have evolved from areas outside the Torah. Perhaps it is because of this that not all Jews are in agreement about the doctrine of the afterlife and that is why it is not relevant to all of them. And anyway, as long as each Jew aims to live according to the mitzvot as set out by God then perhaps it doesn't matter.

Key skills

Analysis involves identifying issues raised by the materials in the AO1, together with those identified in the AO2 section, and presents sustained and clear views, either of scholars or from a personal perspective ready for evaluation.

This means that it picks out key things to debate and the lines of argument presented by others or a personal point of view.

Evaluation involves considering the various implications of the issues raised based upon the evidence gleaned from analysis and provides an extensive detailed argument with a clear conclusion.

This means that the answer weighs up the various and different lines of argument analysed through individual commentary and response and arrives at a conclusion through a clear process of reasoning.

T3 Religious life

This section covers AO1 content and skills

Specification content

The role of the Jewish community of believers (Orthodox, Reform, Hasidic) in understanding the relevance of the 613 mitzvot with reference to: their interpretation today, literal or otherwise; their application today; their importance today.

A: The diversity of views within Judaism with regards to mitzvot (commandments)

Introduction

Mitzvot (singular **mitzvah**) means 'commandments' and the mitzvot are the laws relating to Jewish life based on the Torah and the Talmud. Jews use this term when speaking of the rules that God wants them to keep: 'And now, Israel, what does the Lord your God ask of you? ... to walk in obedience to him ... and to observe the Lord's commands and decrees that I am giving you today for your own good.' (Deuteronomy 10:12–13)

The mitzvot remain a vital part of the Jewish faith, and the idea of obedience to the commandments of God is still accepted by almost all of the traditional and Orthodox groups within Judaism. However, we need to take account of the diversity that can be found within Judaism regarding the perceived relevance and role of the mitzvot in modern-day society.

The mitzvot within Orthodox Judaism

Orthodox Judaism is the traditional branch within the Jewish faith whose members accept literally that the Torah is the direct revelation of God. As a result of this belief, Orthodox Jews consider it their duty to continue to obey the mitzvot which are contained within it. As Nicholas De Lange explains: 'The rabbis maintained firmly that all rules of the halakhah, whether specifically mentioned in the Torah or deduced by the rabbis themselves and mentioned in the Talmud ... all originated with God at Sinai and are to be observed.'

The mitzvot are a complex set of rules that have developed over many years, with their purpose being to discipline the Jewish people towards the holiness of a covenant people. Therefore, the observance of the mitzvot is of paramount importance in Orthodox Judaism. The mitzvot set the Jewish people apart, and through their observance, Jews demonstrate their belief in God and the acceptance of the demands of the covenant. Keeping the mitzvot is a religious duty, and observing them is humanity's means of communicating with God.

There are 613 mitzvot, which cover every area of life, and each mitzvah has something to teach. There are 248 positive commandments, i.e. things that Jews *must* do, and 365 negative commandments or prohibitions. The Torah describes how God gave these commandments to Moses, who taught them to the Israelites in the desert. Several Jewish scholars have compiled a complete list of the mitzvot over the centuries, with the Mishneh Torah composed by Maimonides being amongst the most notable.

Judaism has been described as a way of life, and indeed, the mitzvot cover activities which are outside those which are usually regarded as being religious: business activities; court and **judicial** procedures; property rights are all included. Keeping the mitzvot in the ordinary everyday things leads to a disciplined life. However, over 200 mitzvot can no longer be observed as they are linked to ritual that must take place in the Temple, which was destroyed in 70 CE.

Key quote

When God gives commandments, they are universally applicable in every age and at every time.
(Rabbi Shmuley Boteach)

quickfire

3.1 How many mitzvot are there?

Key terms

Judicial: referring to the decisions of a judge

Mitzvah: commandment (singular)

Furthermore, generations of rabbis have continued to discuss the original mitzvot and adapt them in order to meet the needs of a changing world. Each modification, however, retains a link to the original 613. Modern-day interpretations might deal with medical ethical issues such as organ donation and fertility treatment. For example, organ donation is an opportunity to fulfil the positive commandment of pikuach nefesh in order to preserve life. The Talmud emphasises this commandment by reference to Leviticus 18:5: 'You shall therefore keep my statutes ... which if a man do, he shall live by them.' The rabbis added to this: 'That he shall live by them, and not that he shall die by them' (Babylonian Talmud).

Mitzvot consist of **ritual** and ethical acts, and examples of the difference between these two types of mitzvot can be found in the Ten Commandments: 'Remember the Sabbath day by keeping it holy ... On it you shall not do any work' (Exodus 20:8–10) is a ritual mitzvah, and 'You shall not steal' (Exodus 20:15), is an ethical act.

A further distinction can be made between the mitzvot, as there is one class of commandment known as **chukim** (statutes). The chukim are distinctive because no particular reason is given for having to keep them, and they are regarded as a test of a Jew's faith. The commandments about eating only certain kinds of food for example are chukim.

In order to discover the mitzvot, Jews refer to the halakhah. Halakhah means Jewish law, although its literal meaning is 'the path that one walks'. It is a term that refers to the complete body of rules and practices that Orthodox Jews are bound to follow: the rules and regulations by which a Jew 'walks' through life. Halakhah is a means of regulating the mitzvot, and it has its source in the Torah, rabbinic thought and long-standing traditions.

Brian Close explains that sometimes the traditions, decisions and judgements of earlier generations could find no obvious authorisation in the Torah; nevertheless, they could be justified as forming 'a fence round the Torah', that is, they safeguarded the Torah laws from being unintentionally broken. Close gives an example related to the prohibition of work on the Sabbath, for which the halakhah states that even the handling of work tools is forbidden.

The halakhah has therefore enabled Orthodox Jews to practise their religion according to the mitzvot right up to the 21st century, as the religion has adapted to survive new challenges. Bearing in mind that the mitzvot are over 4,000 years old, it must be acknowledged that an attempt to make some relevant to the present day was inevitable. This was the purpose of the oral law from the start: an attempt to enable Jews to continue practising their faith in the face of new challenges; to try and overcome difficulties and to make rules relevant and clear.

It is very important for Orthodox Jews that they continue to live according to the mitzvot, as they believe that they will be judged eventually on the way in which they have, or have not, kept the covenant: being true to the Torah links them to the past with the Patriarchs such as Abraham.

Key quote

... there could be no area of life which did not come under the umbrella of religion ... if situations arose for which the Law did not seem to provide, then the Law had to be interpreted and related to cover the particular difficulty. The Law of God thus remained relevant and real in the lives of the people. (Close)

quickfire

3.2 Which two types of acts make up the mitzvot?

Key terms

Chukim: commandments for which no particular reason has been given for having to keep them

Ritual: an often repeated procedure or set of actions

Key quote

In speaking of 'the halakhah', Jews indicate a notional body of rules, roughly comparable to the English phrase 'the law'. One can say, for example, 'What does the halakhah say about ...? or 'That would be against the halakhah.' (De Lange)

The mitzvot within Reform Judaism

One of the defining characteristics of Reform Judaism is its attitude to the revelation of the Law on Mount Sinai as set out in clauses 3 and 4 of the Pittsburgh Platform:

'We recognise in the Mosaic legislation a system of training the Jewish people for its mission during its national life in Palestine, and today we accept as binding only the moral laws, and maintain only such ceremonies as elevate and sanctify our lives ... We hold that all such Mosaic and rabbinical laws as regulate diet, priestly purity, and dress originated in ages and under the influence of ideas altogether foreign to our present mental and spiritual state ... Their observance in our days is apt rather to obstruct than to further modern spiritual elevation ... We consider ourselves no longer a nation, but a religious community, and therefore expect neither a return to Palestine, nor a sacrificial worship under the sons of Aaron, nor the restoration of any of the laws concerning the Jewish state.'

Although Reform Jews believe the Torah contains many divine truths, and that it remains the foundation of their religion, they consider it to be a product of human minds. In other words, they believe that God *did* reveal the Law to Moses, but that this revelation was not dictated word for word to him. Rather that the revelation from God inspired others to write.

It follows that if the Torah is the word of God as interpreted by human beings, then humans can make mistakes. It is therefore important to re-evaluate the mitzvot in the light of each new situation in which the Jews find themselves. As society changes, Reform Jews view their religion as something that does not remain static, but that also develops and changes constantly. It is therefore possible to adjust the mitzvot according to the needs and situation of the individual.

The emphasis upon individual choice in itself means that there is diversity within Reform Judaism. For example, some Reform Jews keep the kosher food laws, and others do not. Some Reform families light Shabbat candles on a Friday night, and some do not. It is considered to be up to each family or individual to make a considered choice about which rules to follow at home, work, and in the synagogue.

The original Laws of the Torah gave instructions for a particular period in history, but are now no longer applicable in modern society where new ethical, moral and spiritual values have been revealed. Therefore, in order to keep Judaism relevant, Reform Jews also consider it to be acceptable to discard practices that no longer serve any useful purpose. For example, according to the halakhah, Jews are allowed to divorce as long as they have gone through the correct Jewish court procedure. Reform Jews, however, accept that civil divorce is acceptable.

This does not mean, however, that Reform Jews disregard the mitzvot entirely; neither do they abandon some of the requirements for the sake of convenience. They still believe that they are obliged to live ethical and moral lives. Keeping the Sabbath and attending the synagogue allows them to continue to maintain their Jewish identity.

Lighting the Shabbat candles

Key quote

The Biblical writers were men inspired by God, but they were not super-human and there can be no guarantee that they were equally inspired in everything they wrote. Indeed, how can one be sure that they always recorded correctly what God had said to them?
(Close)

Key term

Civil divorce: divorce according to the laws of the country

The mitzvot within Hasidic Judaism

The Hasidim (the pious ones) are part of an ultra-orthodox wing of the Jewish religion. They came about as the result of a spiritual revival within the religion that was developed in the eighteenth century by a man who came to be known as the Baal Shem Tov (1698–1760).

Key quote

(The Baal Shem Tov) was a mystic ... he emphasised the hidden truths over the revealed aspects of Torah. (Weiner)

Like all Orthodox groups, the Hasidim believe that the rules for life were presented by God to Moses on Mount Sinai in the form of the written and the oral Torah. Hasidic Jews hold that all of the mitzvot are relevant, and their understanding of them is that they should never lose the opportunity to keep a mitzvah. This even extends to personal appearance: for example, Hasidic men are instantly recognisable by their long beard and ear locks. This is in obedience to the mitzvah that states, 'Do not cut the hair at the sides of your head or clip off the edges of your beard' (Leviticus 19:27).

Rigid obedience to the mitzvah is required at all times, and allows Hasidic Jews to fulfil their duty to God through personal religious devotion. Through this, the Hasid achieves Jewish identity, clear direction in religious life and the fulfilment of their sense of duty; all of which are a cause for great joy. As the Kotzker Rebbe said: 'Joyfulness is the outcome of holiness'. Hasidic synagogues are lively places in which worship is accompanied by joyous singing, music and dance.

Key quote

Everything must be done for the sake of Heaven. (The Kotzker Rebbe)

In addition, the role of rebbe or tzaddik (meaning 'righteous man') is granted great importance within the Hasidic tradition. The rebbe is the religious leader within the community, and this position was first held by the Baal Shem Tov, the founder of Hasidism. The rebbe has great status and authority, and is believed to possess spiritual power beyond the range of ordinary people. The most important function of the rebbe is to teach the Torah and to interpret Jewish law. His decisions and rulings are accepted as absolute.

There is a greater emphasis on religious experience in Hasidism as compared to other Jewish groups; and this is considered to hold equal importance with observation of the mitzvot. This has led to the development of a mystical tradition known as the Kabbalah. Its teachings are believed to have been transmitted through the generations back to Moses, and teach, in a philosophical way, how God relates to the world.

The classical text of Kabbalah is the Zohar. The Zohar explains the Torah by use of mystical insights. Brian Close explains that: 'Its thought rests on a complex view of the creation and continued existence of the universe and humankind through the mediation of the Torah and the commandments.' He goes on to say that the notion is that every mitzvah reveals a truth about the upper world, and every Jewish practice has cosmic significance 'since human thoughts and actions communicate themselves to the heavenly realms for evil or for good. Thus humankind is given its own part in the process of spiritual perfection.'

The obligation of a Hasidic Jew is the continual practice of devekut (devotion to God). God must be kept constantly in the mind, and every thought and action should be an expression of attachment to the Creator. Hasidic Jews place great emphasis upon the belief that God is everywhere in the universe, and that every human activity is considered to be a holy act, thus allowing a person to worship God continuously as they go about their daily life.

An Hasidic Jew

quickfire

3.4 How do Hasidic Jews ensure that they follow the commandment as set out in Leviticus 19:27?

Key terms

Baal Shem Tov: literally means 'Master of the Good Name' (i.e. the name of God)

Devekut: devotion to God; having God permanently in the mind

Hasidim: literally means 'the pious ones'; an ultra-orthodox wing of Judaism

Rebbe: the title given to the spiritual leader of Hasidic Jewish communities

Tzaddik: meaning 'righteous man'

Zohar: the classical text of Kabbalah; a mystical interpretation of the Torah

quickfire

3.5 What is the relationship between the Zohar and the Torah?

quickfire

3.6 What is 'devekut'?

It follows therefore that Hasidism places a very high value upon ethical and pious behaviour as set out in the mitzvot. This is a means of allowing the individual to achieve closeness to God, but also to set an example to the world of that which is required by the God who entered into a covenant relationship with the Jewish people at Mount Sinai.

Examples of the diversity of views within Judaism with regards to mitzvot

Keeping kashrut – In general, Orthodox Jews follow the rules governing kashrut as found in Leviticus 11 and Deuteronomy 14. For example, they prescribe that certain fish, poultry and meat are forbidden, and that meat and dairy products must not be eaten in the same meal. They should also be prepared separately. Orthodox Jews therefore have to maintain a kosher home, and can only eat out in kosher restaurants.

Many Reform Jews do not keep kashrut at all, whilst others have chosen to keep a degree of kashrut by avoiding some of the prohibited foods such as pork or shellfish. Some Reform Jews observe the food laws at home, but are quite comfortable in eating out in non-kosher restaurants and non-kosher homes.

Shabbat – On Shabbat, Orthodox Jews refrain from work by not carrying out any of the 39 melachot which are forbidden. For example, one of them prohibits the lighting of fire. In modern society, this extends to not producing electricity by the turning on of a light or electrical appliance. Orthodox Jews are also forbidden to drive on the Sabbath which means that they live within walking distance of the synagogue. Shabbat is also considered to begin just before sunset on Friday evening; thus the time changes every week as the seasons progress.

The celebration of Shabbat remains an important element of Reform Judaism, however, unlike Orthodox Jews, the Friday evening service at the synagogue might well start at the same time every week regardless of the time at which the sun sets. Also, many Reform Jews regard the prohibition regarding work as relating to the job that they do throughout the week. They therefore see nothing wrong with driving on the Sabbath, for example.

Key quote

These are the animals which you may eat ... anything which has a completely split hoof and chews the cud, this you may eat ... (Leviticus 11:2–3)

Key quote

(Shabbat is an opportunity) to achieve rest from the abundance of one's toil so that one might acquire a little knowledge and pray a little more, and so that people might meet one another and discuss matters of Torah. (Saadia Gaon)

Key terms

Kashrut: religious dietary laws

Kosher: food which a Jew is permitted to eat; food prepared in accordance with dietary laws

Melachot: the 39 types of work forbidden on Shabbat

AO1 Activity

You are interviewing some representatives from (a) the Orthodox (b) the Reform and (c) the Hasidic communities. Write out the responses that each might give to the following questions:

(1) How do you interpret the mitzvot?

(2) How do you apply the mitzvot in everyday life?

(3) How important are the mitzvot?

Study tip

There are many opportunities in this topic to show that you can make thorough and accurate use of specialist language. Rather than just learning the definitions of each key word, however, test yourself further by including them in paragraphs, thereby showing that you can use them confidently in context.

AO1 Developing skills

It is now time to reflect upon the information that has been covered so far. It is also important to consider how what you have learned can be focused and used for examination-style answers by practising the skills associated with AO1.

Assessment objective 1 (AO1) involves demonstrating knowledge and understanding. The terms 'knowledge' and 'understanding' are obvious but it is crucial to be familiar with how certain skills demonstrate these terms, and also, how the performance of these skills is measured (see generic band descriptors Band 5 for AS AO1).

▶ **Your new task is this:** below is a below average answer that has been written in response to a question requiring an examination of the relevance of the mitzvot for Orthodox and Reform Judaism. It is obviously a below average answer and so would be about band 2. It will be useful, initially, to consider what is missing from the answer and what is inaccurate. The accompanying list gives you some possible observations to assist you. Be aware, as not all points may be relevant! In analysing the answer's weaknesses, in a group, choose five points from the list that you would use to improve the answer in order to make it stronger. Then write out your additions, each one in a clear paragraph, remembering the principles of explaining with evidence and/or examples. You may add more of your own suggestions, but try to negotiate as a group and prioritise the most important things to add.

Answer

Jews believe in the mitzvot and think that they are very important. The mitzvot can be found in the Ten Commandments although these are the most important of all. The Torah tells all Jews how they should live, therefore being a good Jew means following all of the mitzvot all of the time.

Orthodox Jews say that the mitzvot came from God to Moses, but Reform Jews do not agree, and this is why they don't think that they are all relevant. Reform Jews believe that the mitzvot need to be updated.

Because they believe that the mitzvot came from God, Orthodox Jews are more religious than Reform Jews, and they are the only ones who believe that a person must keep all of the mitzvot. They don't work on the Sabbath, for example, because God told them to rest. Reform Jews, however, will work on the Sabbath and eat non-kosher food.

Observations

1. An introduction is needed that explains what the mitzvot are.

2. Explain the purpose of the mitzvot.

3. A list of the Ten Commandments is needed to serve as examples of the different kinds of mitzvot.

4. Include a detailed description of the giving of the Law to Moses at Mount Sinai.

5. Needs to explain that the mitzvot are important to both Orthodox and Reform Jews, but that they have a different understanding of them.

6. Explain that Orthodox Jews accept literally that the Torah is the word of God.

7. Explain the concept of halakhah.

8. Include examples that show how Orthodox Jews have adapted the mitzvot to suit modern-day issues.

9. Needs to explain the Reform attitude to the revelation of the Law on Mount Sinai, showing an understanding of the impact of the Pittsburgh Platform upon belief and practice.

10. Give examples of the way in which Reform Jews interpret the mitzvot today.

11. It would be helpful to refer to Hasidic beliefs as well in order to explain clearly just how the mitzvot are interpreted within Judaism.

12. Needs a summary at the end that relates to the question.

Key skills

Knowledge involves:

Selection of a range of (thorough) accurate and relevant information that is directly related to the specific demands of the question.

This means you choose the correct information relevant to the question set NOT the topic area. You will have to think and focus on selecting key information and NOT writing everything you know about the topic area.

Understanding involves:

Explanation that is extensive, demonstrating depth and/or breadth with excellent use of evidence and examples including (where appropriate) thorough and accurate supporting use of sacred texts, sources of wisdom and specialist language.

This means that you demonstrate that you understand something by being able to illustrate and expand your points through examples/supporting evidence in a personal way and NOT repeat chunks from a textbook (known as rote learning).

Further application of skills:

Go through the topic areas in this section and create some bullet lists of key points from key areas. For each one, provide further elaboration and explanation through the use of evidence and examples.

Specification content

The extent to which the concept of mitzvot is divisive within Judaism.

AO2 Activity *Possible lines of argument*

Listed below are some conclusions that could be drawn from the AO2 reasoning in the accompanying text:

1. It is acceptable to reinterpret the mitzvot for modern-day life.

2. It is the maintenance of the essence of the mitzvot which is important.

3. The oral Torah is the means by which the mitzvot can be relevant in the modern world.

4. Some Jewish groups have gone so far away from the original mitzvot in some cases that it has caused division.

5. Observance of the mitzvot does not make a person Jewish.

Consider each of the conclusions drawn above and collect evidence and examples to support each argument from the AO1 and AO2 material studied in this section. Select one conclusion that you think is most convincing and explain why it is so. Now contrast this with the weakest conclusion in the list, justifying your argument with clear reasoning and evidence.

Issues for analysis and evaluation

The extent to which the concept of mitzvot is divisive within Judaism

Not all groups within Judaism have a unified view of the mitzvot. For Reform Jews, the Torah is the foundation of their faith, and they believe that it contains many divine truths. However, they consider it to be a product of human minds, in that God revealed the Law to Moses, but it was not dictated word for word to him. Rather, the revelation from God inspired others to write. This then, has had an impact upon the way in which Reform Jews interpret the mitzvot. However, Reform Jews do not accept that their practice of reinterpreting the mitzvot has led to a dilution of the faith. Their justification for this is that in order to continue to live moral and ethical lives within the covenant relationship, it is acceptable to reinterpret the commandments for present-day situations, and even to discard some which are no longer relevant.

Reform Jews also argue that it is important to be assimilated into secular society, and as some of the mitzvot would prevent this from occurring, there needs to be compromise. Only in this way can Judaism survive in the modern world. As long as the essence of the covenant relationship is maintained, then the reinterpretation of the mitzvot is not a negative thing. Take, for example, the practice of keeping kashrut. This can be problematic in the United Kingdom where Jews are in the minority, and where there is a shortage of shops and restaurants that cater for the needs of a kosher diet. The requirement to be at home before Shabbat starts on a Friday evening can also cause problems, especially in the winter. Reform Jews believe that to discard these requirements does not take anything away from their faith.

Orthodox Jews disagree with the Reform viewpoint as they believe that it is still possible to live according to the mitzvot even though they are over 4000 years old. They see the giving of the oral Torah as the means by which this can be achieved, and which has allowed the religion to adapt and survive into the 21st century.

Hasidic Jews view the mitzvot as the way in which they can show their devotion to God at all times, and their practices mark them out as different from other Jewish groups. Within this group, rigid obedience is required at all times, and even extends to personal appearance with the men wearing long beards and ear locks in obedience to the mitzvah that states: 'Do not cut the hair at the sides of your head or clip off the edges of your beard.' (Leviticus 19:27)

It could be claimed that Reform and Hasidic Jews have distorted the purpose of the mitzvot. However, the fact that the mitzvot are still a focus, in whichever sense, means that they have not invalidated them.

It could also be argued that Jewish identity is not entirely dependent upon keeping the mitzvot in their entirety. Their observance marks one out as being a Jew, and shows devotion to God, but Jewish identity comes from being born to a Jewish mother, therefore this is what makes a person a Jew in the first place.

Perhaps the safest conclusion could be to argue that 'divisive' is quite a harsh word and that it is best to see the concept of mitzvot (commandment) as one raising meaningful discussion and a division of views rather than one that leads to aggressive divisions between communities. In this way, mitzvot is seen to be a useful concept and not a divisive one because it guides and instructs according to the needs of both individuals and communities.

Whether mitzvot contribute effectively to spirituality in Judaism

Specification content
Whether mitzvot contribute effectively to spirituality in Judaism.

The purpose of the mitzvot is to give moral and ethical guidance on the way in which God wants a Jew to live. They allow a Jew to cultivate their relationship with God at all levels of daily life: in their relationships with other people; what they eat; how they conduct their business affairs. If life is lived with God as the focus then it is likely that this will lead, ultimately, to a greater understanding of the purpose of life. However, we need to take account of the diversity that can be found within Judaism regarding the perceived relevance of the mitzvot in modern-day society.

Hasidic Jews gain great spiritual joy from their observance of the mitzvot, as they believe that this allows them to fulfil their duty to God through the practice of devekut, with the mitzvot acting as a means of focusing the mind on God through daily human activity. Indeed, the Baal Shem Tov emphasised the hidden truths over the revealed aspects of Torah. The fact that Hasidic Jews gain great spiritual joy from this bears witness to the fact that, for them, their spiritual lives are enhanced by keeping the mitzvot. Brian Close explains that every mitzvah reveals a truth about the upper world, and every Jewish practice has cosmic significance 'since human thoughts and actions communicate themselves to the heavenly realms for evil or for good. Thus humankind is given its own part in the process of spiritual perfection.'

Having to keep so many mitzvot on a daily basis can be seen as a restriction, which in turn can become a burden. This can quell spirituality. For instance, the requirement to buy, prepare, and eat only kosher food can become a burden for Jews who do not live in an area that caters for their needs.

Questioning the relevance of some of the mitzvot in 21st-century secular society can lead to dissatisfaction, which has a negative impact upon spiritual development.

If carrying out the mitzvot becomes merely routine, then even though they have been followed according to God's instructions, there is a danger that they are not being enacted in a spiritual way.

Even though Reform Jews have discarded many of the mitzvot as outdated for the modern world, this does not mean that they lack spirituality as a religious group. They can focus on carrying out the mitzvot that *are* relevant within modern society, living as examples of the way in which God wants others to live. This can bring spiritual benefits.

There are other ways to grow spiritually within Judaism: an important aspect of the Jewish faith is prayer (tefillah), and regular opportunities are provided for this on a daily basis in the synagogue. Prayer and meditation can also take place whenever or wherever a person wishes. Regular devotion helps to keep a person conscious of the bigger context in which they live.

Perhaps the best conclusion, therefore, in the light of this debate would be to see mitvot as used invariably to effectively aid spiritual development. In this way, it is not the idea of a commandment that is useful but how it is understood and applied both within the life of an individual or community but also in conjunction with other pertinent Jewish beliefs and practices. Together, these collective beliefs and practices work in different ways to effectively aid spiritual development.

AO2 Activity *Possible lines of argument*

Listed below are some conclusions that could be drawn from the AO2 reasoning in the accompanying text:

1. The main purpose of the mitzvot is to act as a moral and ethical guide.

2. The fulfilment of one's duty to God through keeping the mitzvot can bring spiritual joy.

3. The mitzvot are so restrictive that they have a negative impact upon spiritual development.

4. The mitzvot can easily become merely a part of daily routine.

5. Prayer and meditation is a better way in which to achieve spiritual development within Judaism.

Consider each of the conclusions drawn above and collect evidence and examples to support each argument from the AO1 and AO2 material studied in this section. Select one conclusion that you think is most convincing and explain why it is so. Now contrast this with the weakest conclusion in the list, justifying your argument with clear reasoning and evidence.

Key skills

Analysis involves identifying issues raised by the materials in the AO1, together with those identified in the AO2 section, and presents sustained and clear views, either of scholars or from a personal perspective ready for evaluation.

This means that it picks out key things to debate and the lines of argument presented by others or a personal point of view.

Evaluation involves considering the various implications of the issues raised based upon the evidence gleaned from analysis and provides an extensive detailed argument with a clear conclusion.

This means that the answer weighs up the various and different lines of argument analysed through individual commentary and response and arrives at a conclusion through a clear process of reasoning.

AO2 Developing skills

It is now time to reflect upon the information that has been covered so far. It is also important to consider how what you have learned can be focused and used for examination-style answers by practising the skills associated with AO2.

Assessment objective 2 (AO2) involves 'analysis' and 'evaluation'. The terms may be obvious but it is crucial to be familiar with how certain skills demonstrate these terms, and also, how the performance of these skills is measured (see generic band descriptors Band 5 for AS AO2).

Obviously, an answer is placed within an appropriate band descriptor depending upon how well the answer performs, ranging from excellent, good, satisfactory, basic/limited to very limited.

▶ **Your new task is this:** below is a below average answer that has been written in response to a question requiring an evaluation of whether mitzvot contribute effectively to spirituality in Judaism. It is obviously a below average answer and so would be about lower band 2. It will be useful, initially, to consider what is missing from the answer and what is inaccurate. The accompanying list gives you some possible observations to assist you. Be aware, as not all points may be relevant! In analysing the answer's weaknesses, in a group, choose five points from the list that you would use to improve the answer in order to make it stronger. Then write out your additions, each one in a clear paragraph. Remember, it is how you use the points that is the most important factor. Apply the principles of evaluation by making sure that you: identify issues clearly; present accurate views of others making sure that you comment on the views presented; reach an overall personal judgement. You may add more of your own suggestions, but try to negotiate as a group and prioritise the most important things to add.

Answer

All Jews live according to the mitzvot, as they believe that God gave mitzvot as a guide to life; however, they are not as important as prayer and meditation, which are more obvious spiritual activities.

Reform Jews do not get spiritual development from keeping the mitzvot because they do not believe that they come directly from God. They have lost the connection with God by changing some of the mitzvot.

It is very difficult to keep things like the food laws, and so a Jew could get very frustrated by this and get angry with God. Getting angry isn't good for spiritual development.

Overall, I think that only Orthodox Jews get spiritual development from keeping the mitzvot as they try to carry out each and every one of them every day of their lives.

Observations

1. A big introduction giving specific examples from the 613 mitzvot.

2. Include a detailed description of the giving of the mitzvot to Moses on Mount Sinai.

3. Needs to identify the purpose of the mitzvot.

4. Show how Hasidic Jews gain spiritual joy from keeping the mitzvot.

5. Show how the mitzvot can be restrictive to life within modern-day society, thus having a negative effect on spiritual development.

6. Give examples of mitzvot that are no longer relevant today, and discuss how that can prevent spiritual development.

7. Need to mention how Reform Jews are able to benefit spiritually even though they have discarded many of the mitzvot which they regard as being outdated.

8. Make reference to other means of gaining spiritual development within Judaism.

9. Mention that true spiritual development can only be gained by becoming a rabbi.

10. A conclusion that is balanced, reflective of the argument presented and that clearly links to question is needed.

B: Jewish teachings about tefillah (prayer) with reference to the Amidah and teachings about tzedakah (charity)

Tefillah (prayer)

An important aspect of the Jewish faith is the belief that God communicates with human beings. The Torah is the primary source of communication, but Jews also place great emphasis upon **tefillah**, or prayer, and consider it to be an important part of their relationship with God. Prayer provides an opportunity for a Jewish believer to reflect upon the nature of God, thereby coming to a greater understanding of the path that God wants them to take in life.

There are many instances in the Bible of individual prayer, such as when Abraham prayed to God for an heir (Genesis 15:2–3); and when Moses prayed for Israel to be spared (Deuteronomy 9:20 & 26). However, there is no explicit commandment to pray. This could be because prayer is accepted as being a normal, human activity for one who is in a relationship with God.

Deuteronomy 11:13 says that a person is: '... to love the Lord your God, and to serve him with all your heart and with all your soul.' As a result of this, the Talmud refers to prayer as '**avodah shebalev**', meaning 'service of the heart'. Prayer is thus seen as service to God on a personal basis; a reaching out to connect with the source of all life.

A Jewish prayer book

Jews believe that a person can pray to God whenever or wherever they wish, although regular opportunities are provided through daily communal prayer services at the synagogue. There is also a **siddur** (prayer book) that contains set prayers. Praying at regular times can be helpful as it provides a timetable in which a person can set aside time for devotion. Such regular prayers keep a person conscious of the bigger context in which they live. However, Judaism acknowledges that repeating the words of set prayers on a regular basis can sometimes mean that the inner meaning is lost. This can be a problem, and that is why the concept of **kavvanah** (intention) is so important. Kavvanah means that prayer requires inner commitment that comes from the heart rather than just from the lips. Kavvanah can be found in all aspects of life, yet in prayer, particularly, there is an opportunity for spiritual self-reflection, and a mystical encounter with God.

There are many levels of kavvanah, starting from the basic sense of being able to understand the significance of the words that are being said; moving to the awareness of being in the presence of God. Prayer in this sense is an outpouring of the soul: 'Out of the depths I cry to you, Lord' (Psalm 130:1). Maimonides emphasised the importance attached to kavvanah in the Talmud. He said that a person 'should empty his mind of all other thoughts and regard himself as if he were standing before the Divine Presence'. He further maintained that prayer without kavvanah was no prayer at all and should be done again with kavvanah.

Kavvanah also entails an awareness of the full meaning of the words chosen for prayer. The **Shulchan Arukh** states: 'Better a little supplication with kavvanah, than a great deal without it.'

This section covers AO1 content and skills

Specification content

Tefillah as spiritual self-reflection in relation to God; reasons for tefillah; the structure and content of the Amidah; the use of the Amidah in daily prayers; minyan (congregation) and the diversity of practice of prayer within Judaism.

Key quote

(Prayer) is the foundation of the whole Torah. This means that man knows God, recognising His greatness and His splendour with a serene and whole mind, and an understanding heart. Man should reflect on these ideas until his rational soul is awakened to love God, to cleave to Him and His Torah, and to desire His commandments. **(Rabbi Zalman)**

quickfire

3.7 Why is tefillah an important part of a Jew's relationship with God?

Key terms

Avodah shebalev: meaning 'service of the heart'

Kavvanah: literal meaning is 'intention'; used to denote a state of mental concentration and devotion at prayer

Shulchan Arukh the Code of Jewish Law

Siddur: prayer book

Tefillah: prayer

quickfire

3.8 Identify two levels of kavvanah.

Key quote

Prayer is a mystery, directed in its essence towards changing the order of the world. Every star and sphere is fixed in its order, yet man wants to change the order of nature; he asks for miracles. (Rabbi Nahman)

Key terms

Amidah: literally means 'standing'; one of the principal prayers of the Jewish liturgy

Arvit: evening prayer

Bakashah: section 2 of the Amidah

Baruch atah Adonai, melech ha'olam: Blessed are you, Lord, our God, sovereign of the universe

Berakah: blessing (singular)

Berakot: blessings (plural)

Matriarch: the female head of a community or tribe

Minchah: afternoon prayer

Petition: to request; to make an appeal, usually to a higher authority

Shacharit: morning prayer

Shemonah Esray: meaning 'the eighteen', and referring to the 18 original benedictions of the Amidah

Shevach: section 1 of the Amidah

quickfire

3.9 What are the names of the three daily synagogue services that offer opportunities for prayer?

Judaism recognises that prayer, as well as keeping the mitzvot, helps to keep life focused upon God's wishes. Rabbi Nissan Mindel points out that God 'has commanded us to pray to Him for our sake. God does not need our prayer; He can do without our prayers, but we cannot do without prayer. It is good for us to acknowledge our dependence on God for our very life, our health, our daily bread, and our general welfare.'

Maimonides said: 'We are told to offer up prayers to God, in order to establish firmly the true principle that God takes notice of our ways, that He can make them successful if we serve Him, or disastrous if we disobey Him; that success and failure are not the result of chance or accident.' Consequently there are a number of different reasons for tefillah. These include: asking God for help for oneself or others; praising God; thanksgiving; confession; asking for forgiveness; even questioning God about a difficult issue in life.

One of the most common kinds of prayer within Judaism is a **berakah** (blessing) which is an expression of praise directed to God. **Berakot** (blessings) are recited on a variety of occasions: as part of the synagogue service; during private prayer; before performing a commandment; as grace before eating. In fact, virtually every aspect of life can be marked by a blessing. Perhaps one of the most recited blessings is said in the Jewish home every week when Shabbat is welcomed with the lighting of candles, and the woman of the household reciting '**Baruch atah Adonai, melech ha'olam**' ('Blessed are you, Lord, our God, sovereign of the universe').

AO1 Activity

Refer to the quotes from Rabbi Zalman, Rabbi Mindel and Maimonides. Read each carefully, and write out what you consider to be the significant point(s) that each one is making. This will help you to develop the skill of being able to make accurate and relevant references to sources of wisdom in your answers.

The Amidah

On each day at the synagogue a Jew can attend one of three services that offer an opportunity for communal prayer. There is **arvit** (evening prayer), **shacharit** (morning prayer) and **minchah** (afternoon prayer). According to the Talmud, the three daily services are intended to correspond with the times when sacrifices were offered at the Temple in Jerusalem.

The **Amidah** (the standing prayer), is the central prayer of each of the three daily services, and, as its name suggests, the congregation stands to recite it. It is often also known as the Tefillah or **Shemonah Esray**, meaning 'the eighteen', and referring to the 18 benedictions it originally contained, even though a 19th was added some time ago. It is traditional, before reciting the Amidah, to take three steps backward and then forward again to symbolise entering into God's presence. The Amidah is first said quietly, with feet together, hands folded over heart and facing Jerusalem, and at four points one bows slightly.

The 19 blessings of the Amidah are divided up into three sections that reflect the way in which a worshipper should approach God: first there should be words of praise; secondly bringing one's **petitions**; thirdly, concluding with thanksgiving.

Section 1: **Shevach** – the first three blessings express praise for the patriarchs, the wonders of God, and God's holiness. In Liberal synagogues, the **matriarchs**, Sarah, Rebecca, Leah and Rachel are also mentioned alongside the patriarchs. This first blessing praises God for remembering their good actions, and by implication, asks God to hear the prayers of the worshipper favourably because of their merit.

Section 2: **Bakashah** – the bulk of the prayer is petitionary, and this section contains requests that both spiritual and physical needs are met. Things such as knowledge, repentance, forgiveness, redemption, healing, prosperity, freedom, justice, and final salvation by the Messiah are all requested. There are 13 blessings in all. This section is prayed silently as individuals pray by, and for, themselves.

Section 3: Hoda'ah – The prayer concludes with three blessings of thanksgiving concerning acceptance of the worship, gratitude, and blessings of peace.

Melanie J. Wright presents the prayer as follows:

'Fathers', praising God for choosing and remembering the patriarchs (Abraham, Isaac and Jacob)

Acknowledgement of God's power to sustain life and revive the dead

Acknowledgement of God's holiness

Prayer for wisdom and knowledge

Prayer for repentance

Request for pardon from sin

Prayer for release from trouble

Prayer for healing

Prayer for 'blessing of the years' (sustenance)

Prayer for the ingathering of the exiles

Prayer for true justice administered by good leaders

Prayer against the minim

Prayer for the righteous and pious

Prayer for the rebuilding of Jerusalem

Prayer for the coming of the Messiah, a descendant of David

Prayer for God to accept prayers

Prayer for the return of the divine presence to Zion

Thanksgiving

Prayer for the people of Israel.

On Shabbat and other Jewish festivals there is an amendment to the central section of the Amidah, whereby a single blessing, which focuses on the holiness of that particular day, is said instead of the usual 13. On Shabbat morning, therefore, the central section of the Amidah describes Moses receiving the Ten Commandments, followed by the verses from Exodus that describe the observance of Shabbat as a sign of the covenant between God and the Jewish people. Shabbat is summarised as a gift given to the Jews as a sign of God's love for them. It concludes with a blessing thanking God for making Shabbat holy.

Following the conclusion of the Amidah, the worshipper recites the words 'May God who brings peace to the universe, bring peace to us and all of the people, Israel. Amen.' This is said while taking three steps backward, bowing to both sides, and taking three steps forward again, formally retreating from God's presence.

The Amidah has an important status within Jewish worship; however, its origins are uncertain. Wright indicates that it has been a subject for debate amongst scholars across the years. Some have suggested it was introduced to identify heretics (the 'minim' of the prayer) who would be unwilling to recite a blessing that called for their own downfall. Moreover, it has been suggested that the heretics were early Jewish Christians. This is based upon evidence from an early version of the prayer that refers to 'the Nazoraeans who are the minim'. However, Wright concludes, there is no widespread evidence of this.

Key quotes

Blessed are you, O Lord our God and God of our fathers, God of Abraham, God of Isaac, God of Jacob, the great, mighty and revered God, God most high, generous and kind, owner of all things. **(Extract from first section of the Amidah)**

A man should never petition for his needs either in the first three blessings or in the last three, but in the middle ones, for Rabbi Hanina said: 'In the first three blessings he is like a servant who addresses a tribute to his master; in the middle ones he resembles a servant who requests generosity from his master; and in the last ones he resembles a servant who has received generosity from his master and takes his leave.' **(Babylonian Talmud)**

Key terms

Heretic: someone whose religious views are in conflict with the majority

Hoda'ah: section 3 of the Amidah

Minim: relating to those who belong to a sect, whose views differ from the mainstream

Nazoraeans: early Jewish Christians

AO1 Activity

Create a mind map that focuses on the structure, content and status of the Amidah.

The minyan (congregation) and the diversity of practice of prayer within Judaism

Prayer as a means of private communication between an individual and God can take place anywhere, and as and when the need arises. However, Judaism also places value on praying as a community. Praying with other like-minded worshippers adds another dimension of spirituality, for the shekinah (presence of God) is present at the gathering of the faithful.

A minyan, which is a group of ten men over the age of 13, is needed before an act of communal prayer at the synagogue can take place, and this requirement finds its source in the Book of Numbers when Moses sent out spies to the land of Canaan. Ten returned and stated that it was not a land that they would be able to conquer. The account tells us that God, on hearing this, was disappointed that they lacked faith and asked Moses and Aaron, 'How long will this wicked assembly grumble against me?' (Numbers 14:27). It is from this event that the term 'assembly' became connected with the requirement for ten men. Non-Orthodox communities now count women as part of the minyan.

There is no halakhic obligation to pray in a minyan, yet rabbinic tradition has always encouraged it. The Shulchan Arukh says: 'A person should make every effort to attend services in a synagogue with a minyan; if circumstances prevent him from doing so, he should pray, wherever he is, at the same time that the synagogue service takes place.'

Apart from regular worship at the synagogue, the minyan may gather in any suitable place for public prayers. An important example of this is when they gather at a house where there has been a bereavement in order to offer prayers for the dead. Other significant events include the recitation of the seven blessings at dinner on one of the seven days following a wedding.

De Lange says that a group of people who happen to be together for whatever purpose, 'for example for a meeting, or because they work nearby, may decide to constitute a minyan to say their prayers together. This minyan may sometimes develop into a fixed gathering that becomes in a sense an alternative to the regular synagogue worship.'

At prayer

De Lange further analyses the role that the minyan has to play within the traditional Jewish community. He says that the worshippers do not always arrive at the synagogue at the same time, and therefore it is convenient to have a definition of when enough people have arrived to allow public worship to begin. To make up a minyan is also particularly important in small worshipping communities, where public prayer may be suspended if the crucial number of ten is not reached.

Not all Jewish communities share the same practices concerning the minyan.

Reform Judaism has done away with the requirement completely: thus prayers may be said with any number present, and services all begin at published times.

Conservative rabbis, seeking to redress the lack of gender equality, have included adult women to be counted within the minyan.

Key quote

The prayer of the community is always heard … hence a person must join himself with the community … (Maimonides)

Key term

Minyan: congregation or assembly; a group of ten males over the age of 13 required before an act of communal prayer can take place at the synagogue

quickfire

3.10 What is a minyan?

Study tip

When answering a question on prayer make sure that you make precise use of relevant key terms. This will ensure that you are making 'thorough and accurate use of specialist language and vocabulary in context' (L5 band descriptor AO1).

The importance of tzedakah within Judaism

The Hebrew word tzedakah is usually translated as 'charity'; however its literal meaning is 'justice' or 'righteousness'. When a Jewish person carries out a charitable act, they are undertaking one of the most basic requirements of the mitzvot: that of providing for those who are unable to provide for themselves. Thus, for Jews, charitable acts are more than just showing a kindness by making a donation to a worthy cause; they are considered to be right actions which are just as important as any other mitzvot. The Torah says 'There will always be poor people in the land. Therefore I command you to be open-handed toward your fellow Israelites who are poor and needy.' (Deuteronomy 15:11)

One of the ways in which a Jewish person can give to charity on a regular basis is through a tithe (which is the giving of a tenth of their income, after taxes have been taken, to charity). Judaism sees this act as moving some way towards redressing the balance between those who are fortunate and those who are not.

The Jewish religion teaches that every person has an obligation to avoid becoming in need of tzedakah, and should take any opportunity to work in order to be able to support themselves. However, Jews are also realistic, and know that hardship does occur. In such circumstances then it is considered wrong to refuse help when it is offered.

However, the giving of tzedakah is not only about giving money to worthy causes. The Talmud says, 'Just as God visits the sick, feeds the hungry and clothes the naked, so you do the same.' It is important to show kindness and mercy to those who are in difficulties and who need support. This can be done best by giving up one's time to help someone.

Moreover, Jews are not only commanded to provide help where there is need, but also to ensure that they respect the dignity of those they help. This requirement is set out in Leviticus 19:9–10: 'When you reap the harvest of your land, you shall not reap your field to its very border, neither shall you gather the gleanings after your harvest. And you shall not strip your vineyard bare, neither shall you gather the fallen grapes of your vineyard; you shall leave them for the poor and for the stranger: I am the Lord your God.'

Thus the corners of the field are left for those who are unable to harvest for themselves; the fallen grain and fruit for those who are unable to harvest but still able to pick up from the ground. This approach offers a dignified way in which to help others.

Giving of one's own time and effort is called gemilut hasadim, which literally means 'the giving of loving kindness', and is all about doing good deeds. In Jewish communities, one finds gemilut hasadim being carried out in the form of friends and neighbours helping out; for example, when there is illness in a family. It can take many forms such as helping to look after children if a parent is ill, or providing a meal. An important aspect of gemilut hasadim is that it is something that anyone can do; both rich and poor alike, and it is done without expecting anything in return. It has been said that the highest level of gemilut hasadim is to attend a funeral service in order to show your respect. This is because the person who has died has no future opportunity to repay the kindness.

Giving to charity is also an important part of Jewish festivals. At Purim for instance, there is a special feast, and to make sure that all members of the Jewish community have enough food for the celebration, everyone sends gifts of food to friends and acquaintances. In this way, both rich and poor can give and receive, and everyone can accept without embarrassment.

Specification content

The importance of tzedakah within Judaism; Maimonides and the 'ladder of tzedakah'.

Key quote

To do what is right and just is more acceptable to the Lord than sacrifice. (Proverbs 21:3)

quickfire

3.11 What does Deuteronomy 15:11 say about charity?

Key quote

Whoever is kind to the poor lends to the Lord, and he will reward them for what they have done. (Proverbs 19:17)

Key quote

Whosoever has not pity upon his fellow man is no child of Abraham. (Talmud)

Key terms

Gemilut hasadim: 'the giving of loving kindness'; doing good deeds

Tithe: the giving of a tenth of one's income, after taxes have been taken, to charity

Tzedakah: 'charity'; literal meaning is 'justice' or 'righteousness

quickfire

3.12 Give an example of gemilut hasadim in a Jewish community.

quickfire

3.13 How are pushkes used in a Jewish home?

A pushke

Key terms

Alms: donations of food, money, etc., to the poor

Pushkes: collection boxes for charity

quickfire

3.14 According to Maimonides, what is the highest level of the 'ladder of tzedakah'?

Study tip

It is important to make 'thorough and accurate reference to sacred texts and sources of wisdom, where appropriate' in your answers (L5 band descriptor AO1). Make sure, therefore, that you are able to use relevant quotes from sources such the Torah, Talmud, and/or rabbinic tradition with confidence.

Such is the importance of charitable giving that it is also evident in the home where many families keep **pushkes**, collection boxes, for charity. Family members will use them by depositing their small change after shopping, for example.

In the 19th century, Rabbi Israel Salanter promoted the idea that Talmud study had to be accompanied by ethical good works in everyday life. He wrote: 'Normally we worry about our own material well-being and our neighbours' souls; let us rather worry about our neighbours' material well-being and our own souls.'

Maimonides and the 'ladder of tzedakah'

Maimonides identified eight different stages of tzedakah with each one being higher than the one before. This has become known as the 'ladder of tzedakah', and, beginning with the lowest level, each step climbed brings one closer to the ideal:

1. Help the poor to rehabilitate themselves by lending them money, employing them, or giving them work, for in this way the end is achieved without any loss of self-respect at all.

2. Give so that neither the donor nor recipient knows the identity of the other

3. Give so that the recipient doesn't know who the donor is

4. Give so that the donor doesn't know who the recipient is

5. Give before being asked

6. Give only after being asked

7. Give willingly, but less than is appropriate

8. Give only grudgingly

Maimonides pointed out that it is far better to lend someone money to start their own business than it is to give **alms**. This is reflected in Deuteronomy 15:8 that says, '... and freely lend them whatever they need'. In order to avoid awkwardness or embarrassment it can be regarded as an indefinite, interest-free loan. In some cases, the giver does not seriously expect the loan to be repaid, but the borrower always has the option of intending to repay at some time in the future.

Maimonides claimed that by this partnership, the poor person is really being strengthened, and refers to Leviticus 25:35 that says, 'If any of your fellow Israelites become poor and are unable to support themselves among you, help them as you would a foreigner and stranger, so they can continue to live among you.'

Maimonides highlights the fact that, not only are Jews commanded to provide help when it is needed, but also that the dignity of the recipient should be considered. We can make reference once more to Leviticus 19:9–10, that commands that when harvesting crops, the corners of the field should be left for those unable to harvest but still able to pick up from the ground: ' ... leave them for the poor and for the stranger'. In modern society, this can be carried out by the donor remaining anonymous, as in the third step of the ladder, or even when neither the donor or recipient are aware of the identity of the other as in step 2.

A lesser form of charity is when one gives without being asked. An example of this can be found in an episode from the life of Abraham. Genesis 18:2–5 tells of the arrival of three strangers, and describes Abraham's reaction, which was to go out unasked, and urge them to come into his tent where he could provide them with food, water and shade.

AO1 Activity

Explain, in a paragraph, why Jews believe that some ways of giving to charity are more beneficial than others.

AO1 Developing skills

It is now time to reflect upon the information that has been covered so far. It is also important to consider how what you have learned can be focused and used for examination-style answers by practising the skills associated with AO1.

Assessment objective 1 (AO1) involves demonstrating knowledge and understanding. The terms 'knowledge' and 'understanding' are obvious but it is crucial to be familiar with how certain skills demonstrate these terms, and also, how the performance of these skills is measured (see generic band descriptors Band 5 for AS AO1).

▶ **Your new task is this:** below is a below average answer that has been written in response to a question requiring an examination of the importance of tzedakah in Judaism. It is obviously a below average answer and so would be about band 2. It will be useful, initially, to consider what is missing from the answer and what is inaccurate. This time there is no accompanying list to assist you. In analysing the answer's weaknesses, in a group, decide upon five points that you would use to improve the answer in order to make it stronger. Then write out your additions, each one in a clear paragraph, remembering the principles of explaining with evidence and/or examples.

Answer

The Torah makes it very clear to Jews that charity is very important, and they give money regularly from their wages. Giving to charity is a way of bringing justice to the world and is just as important as following the mitzvot.

Jews believe that if you are a farmer you are to allow poor people to come into your fields and take the crop that is left over.

If you haven't got any spare money, you should do kind things to help other people who are in need. This is called gemilut hasadim. This is something which anyone can do, and therefore encourages equality. Jewish homes also have collection boxes where you put your spare change, and when they are full the money goes to charity.

Maimonides said that giving to charity is like going up a ladder, and the closer you get to the top, the better you are at giving to others. He said that the best way to help someone is to do it without them knowing so that they are not embarrassed or feel that they should do something in return.

In my opinion, I agree that giving to charity is very important, and if no one gave to charity then the world would be a much worse place, therefore I agree with the importance of giving to charity in the Jewish religion.

Key skills

Knowledge involves:

Selection of a range of (thorough) accurate and relevant information that is directly related to the specific demands of the question.

This means you choose the correct information relevant to the question set NOT the topic area. You will have to think and focus on selecting key information and NOT writing everything you know about the topic area.

Understanding involves:

Explanation that is extensive, demonstrating depth and/or breadth with excellent use of evidence and examples including (where appropriate) thorough and accurate supporting use of sacred texts, sources of wisdom and specialist language.

This means that you demonstrate that you understand something by being able to illustrate and expand your points through examples/supporting evidence in a personal way and NOT repeat chunks from a text book (known as rote learning).

Further application of skills:

Go through the topic areas in this section and create some bullet lists of key points from key areas. For each one, provide further elaboration and explanation through the use of evidence and examples.

Specification content

The extent to which the Amidah
is an encapsulation of the most
important beliefs, values and
teachings of Judaism.

AO2 Activity *Possible lines of argument*

Listed below are some conclusions
that could be drawn from the AO2
reasoning in the accompanying text:

1. The Amidah provides an
    opportunity for communicating
    with God rather than as a
    statement of belief.

2. Its content underlines the many
    characteristics of God, and can
    act as a reminder of the covenant
    relationship.

3. There are different versions of the
    Amidah, that reflect the diversity
    of beliefs within particular Jewish
    groups.

4. The content of the Torah reflects
    the most important beliefs, values
    and teachings of Judaism.

5. The Shema was developed as a
    way of summarising the most
    important beliefs and teachings of
    the Jewish religion.

Consider each of the conclusions
drawn above and collect evidence and
examples to support each argument
from the AO1 and AO2 material
studied in this section. Select one
conclusion that you think is most
convincing and explain why it is so.
Now contrast this with the weakest
conclusion in the list, justifying
your argument with clear reasoning
and evidence.

Issues for analysis and evaluation

The extent to which the Amidah is an encapsulation of the most important beliefs, values and teachings of Judaism

An important aspect of the Jewish faith is tefillah, and regular opportunities
are provided for this on a daily basis in the synagogue. The main purpose of the
Amidah is that it provides an important opportunity to approach God for private
prayer rather than act as a statement of belief, values and teachings. It focuses the
worshipper's mind on the fact that God should always be at the centre of one's
life as a Jew. This can be seen in the format of the prayer: God is praised, God is
petitioned; God is thanked.

Reciting the Amidah provides the opportunity for a Jewish believer to reflect upon
the nature of God, thereby coming to a greater understanding of the path that God
wants them to take in life. As Rabbi Zalman said: '(Prayer) is the foundation of the
whole Torah. This means that man knows God, recognising His greatness and His
splendour with a serene and whole mind, and an understanding heart. Man should
reflect on these ideas until his rational soul is awakened to love God, to cleave to
Him and His Torah, and to desire His commandments.'

Such is the Amidah's fundamental importance as an opportunity to commune with
God on a private and personal level that it is forbidden to interrupt a person when
they are engaged in it.

Notwithstanding, the format of the Amidah can provide the opportunity for the
worshipper to reflect upon fundamental Jewish beliefs; for example, the first
section underlines the manifold characteristics of God, and reminds the Jews of the
covenant relationship.

The different versions of the Amidah indicate to some extent that it demonstrates
the important beliefs, values and teachings of particular Jewish groups. Within
Reform Judaism, references to a personal messiah and a resurrection of the dead,
for example, have all been rephrased.

The most important beliefs, values and teachings of Judaism are to be found in the
Torah, with the 613 mitzvot providing the template for living a moral and ethical
life in accordance with God's wishes. However, it could be said that the Amidah
complements the requirements of the mitzvot with its emphasis upon maintaining
a sound relationship with God.

There is no question that the Amidah has an important status within Jewish
worship; however, its origins and initial purpose are uncertain. Wright indicates
that it has been a subject for debate amongst scholars across the years. Some have
suggested it was introduced to identify heretics (the 'minim' of the prayer) who
would be unwilling to recite a blessing that called for their own downfall.

It is the Shema, rather than the Amidah, which encapsulates the most important
beliefs within Judaism, and which was developed as a way of summarising the
whole of the Jewish law. Its opening line 'Hear, O Israel: The Lord our God,
the Lord is One' is as close as possible to a declaration of faith in what is central to
Judaism: that there is One God who demands total obedience from the people.
The Amidah is one encapsulation of the most important beliefs, values and
teachings of Judaism but it is not the only one, nor arguably the best form.

Whether prayer has become a spiritually ineffective ritual

Prayer is an important aspect of the Jewish faith due to the belief that it is the means by which God communicates with human beings. Even though the Torah is perceived to be the primary source of communication, Jews also place great emphasis upon prayer as the means by which they can reflect upon the nature of God, thereby coming to a greater understanding of the path that God wants them to take in life. Taking the opportunity to pray with others at the synagogue on a daily basis can enhance the spiritual life of a Jewish worshipper. Knowing that they are in the presence of other like-minded believers can give them a sense of strength and unity in their spiritual lives.

Furthermore, having specific opportunities for prayer at the synagogue on a daily basis can ensure that the worshipper makes a regular time for personal communion with God, allowing them to step aside from the busyness of everyday family and work pressures in order to be refreshed, and ready to face the rest of the day.

Judaism acknowledges that repeating the words of set prayers, such as the Shema and Amidah, on a regular basis can sometimes mean that the inner meaning is lost, and in such a situation it can become spiritually ineffective. The concept of kavvanah is therefore very important as it emphasises the fact that prayer requires inner commitment which comes from the heart rather than just from the lips. Maimonides emphasised the importance attached to kavvanah in the Talmud. He said that a person 'should empty his mind of all other thoughts and regard himself as if he were standing before the Divine Presence'. He further maintained that prayer without kavvanah was no prayer at all and should be done again with kavvanah.

There is a danger that the mind can wander during prayer, especially when there are other matters going on in life which seem to demand greater attention. Repeating the words of a set prayer on a regular basis can also lead to it becoming merely a ritualistic action if it lacks any accompanying meaningful purpose. For an Orthodox Jew, the ritual of putting on the tefillin can focus the mind and the heart on the prayers which are to follow, and create a space in which meaningful prayer can take place.

Jews also accept that a person can pray to God whenever or wherever they wish. Private, spontaneous prayer could perhaps therefore be seen as more spiritually effective since it is usually done in direct response to a particular need or observation in life, and could therefore be considered to be of greater relevance to the worshipper.

Feeling that prayers have not been answered can lead some to the conclusion that praying is a spiritually ineffective ritual.

Judaism recognises that prayer, as well as keeping the mitzvot, helps to keep life focused upon God's wishes.

One possible conclusion, then, is that despite the obvious dangers of prayer becoming simply an action or 'ritual', if it is practised in accordance with the teachings of Judaism then it is by no means spiritually ineffective.

Specification content
Whether prayer has become a spiritually ineffective ritual.

AO2 Activity *Possible lines of argument*

Listed below are some conclusions that could be drawn from the AO2 reasoning in the accompanying text:

1. Praying with other like-minded believers can bring a sense of spiritual strength and unity.

2. Regular daily prayer times allow for time to be taken out of the busy schedule of each day in order to focus upon God. Also, accompanying rituals such as putting on tefillin can act as a focus for the mind in preparation for the prayers which are to follow.

3. The repeating of set prayers can become routine, meaning that the inner commitment is lost.

4. Dealing with disappointment when prayers have not been answered can detract from spiritual development.

5. Prayer, in addition to keeping the mitzvot, can enhance a Jew's spiritual life.

Consider each of the conclusions drawn above and collect evidence and examples to support each argument from the AO1 and AO2 material studied in this section. Select one conclusion that you think is most convincing and explain why it is so. Now contrast this with the weakest conclusion in the list, justifying your argument with clear reasoning and evidence.

Key skills

Analysis involves identifying issues raised by the materials in the AO1, together with those identified in the AO2 section, and presents sustained and clear views, either of scholars or from a personal perspective ready for evaluation.

This means that it picks out key things to debate and the lines of argument presented by others or a personal point of view.

Evaluation involves considering the various implications of the issues raised based upon the evidence gleaned from analysis and provides an extensive detailed argument with a clear conclusion.

This means that the answer weighs up the various and different lines of argument analysed through individual commentary and response and arrives at a conclusion through a clear process of reasoning.

AO2 Developing skills

It is now time to reflect upon the information that has been covered so far. It is also important to consider how what you have learned can be focused and used for examination-style answers by practising the skills associated with AO2.

Assessment objective 2 (AO2) involves 'analysis' and 'evaluation'. The terms may be obvious but it is crucial to be familiar with how certain skills demonstrate these terms, and also, how the performance of these skills is measured (see generic band descriptors Band 5 for AS AO2).

Obviously, an answer is placed within an appropriate band descriptor depending upon how well the answer performs, ranging from excellent, good, satisfactory, basic/limited to very limited.

▶ **Your new task is this:** below is a below average answer that has been written in response to a question requiring an evaluation of whether prayer has become a spiritually ineffective ritual in Judaism. It is obviously a below average answer and so would be about band 2. It will be useful, initially, to consider what is missing from the answer and what is inaccurate. This time there is no accompanying list to assist you. In analysing the answer's weaknesses, in a group, decide upon five points that you would use to improve the answer in order to make it stronger. Then write out your additions, each one in a clear paragraph. Remember, it is how you use the points that is the most important factor. Apply the principles of evaluation by making sure that you: identify issues clearly; present accurate views of others, making sure that you comment on the views presented; reach an overall personal judgement. You may add more of your own suggestions, but try to negotiate as a group and prioritise the most important things to add.

Answer

You could argue that prayer is important, but also that keeping the mitzvot is just as important for spirituality.

When Jews pray with others at the synagogue, you could say that it is very spiritual as they are all saying the same things to the same God at the same time.

However, repeating the words of the same prayers all the time can become boring, and you might just be saying them but thinking of something else.

If a Jew wants to get something spiritual from prayer then they should become a rabbi because rabbis are closer to God, and God listens to them first.

Also, God doesn't always answer prayers, and that would make someone give up going to the synagogue.

In conclusion, I think that all Jews should put on their tefillin so that God knows they are going to pray and will be able to listen to them more carefully. This will make the prayer a lot more spiritual when you know that God is actually listening at that time.

C: Key moral principles – the importance of the Ten Sayings (Aseret ha-D'ibrot) or Ten Commandments for Judaism

This section covers AO1 content and skills

Specification content

The Ten Sayings in the context of the 613 mitzvot; the Ten Sayings as a basis for religious and ethical life.

The Ten Sayings in the context of the 613 mitzvot

The Ten Commandments or Ten Sayings are the first of the 613 commandments that Jews believe God gave to the Jewish people through Moses on Mount Sinai. In Judaism they are called either Aseret ha-D'ibrot (the Ten Sayings) or Aseret ha-D'varim (the Ten Principles). They are to be found in Exodus 20:2–14 and are repeated in Deuteronomy 5:7–21. According to Jewish tradition they are numbered in the following way:

1. I am the Eternal God who brought you out of the land of Egypt.
2. You shall have no other gods before me. You shall not make a graven image.
3. You shall not use the name of God in vain.
4. Remember the Sabbath day by keeping it holy.
5. Honour your father and your mother.
6. You shall not kill.
7. You shall not commit adultery.
8. You shall not steal.
9. You shall not bear false witness.
10. You shall not covet.

Key terms

Aseret ha-D'ibrot: the Ten Sayings

Aseret ha-D'varim: the Ten Principles

Covet: the desire to possess something (especially something which belongs to someone else)

The Tablets of stone

These are the principles that serve as the foundation for all of the other 603 mitzvot that God gave to the Jews.

The Torah recounts that the Ten Statements were carved on two stone tablets, and it is clear that they can be divided into two categories: the first four setting out what is expected regarding a person's relationship with God; and the rest setting out the expectations regarding a person's relationship with others.

Both categories are considered to hold equal status with duties to God being just as important as duties to other people. However, if a Jew has to make a choice between serving God or helping another person, then the obligation to the person should take precedence. The Talmud gives an example by way of a story of a man who ignored the cries for help of a drowning man because he did not want to interrupt his prayers. The moral of this story is that it is much more important to help other people when they call upon us, as God will never need our help.

quickfire

3.15 What is the Jewish term for the Ten Sayings?

Key quote

Elsewhere in the ancient Near East the laws were believed to be the product of human minds, particularly the king. (Tigay)

Key quote

Implicit in this biblical view is that God is Israel's king, hence its legislator. This elevated the status of law … and endowed it with sanctity. Obedience to law … became a religious duty; obedience made one holy and crimes were sins, a flouting of God's authority. (Tigay)

Key term

Immutable: unable to be changed

The Ten Sayings as a basis for religious and ethical life

The two versions of the Ten Sayings from Exodus and Deuteronomy are known as the 'Ethical Decalogue' (in contrast to the 'Ritual Decalogue' of Exodus 34:12–16, which G. W. Anderson calls the 'short code'). Scholars have proposed that the Ritual Decalogue was composed first, and that the Ethical Decalogue reflects a later change of emphasis from ritual practice to ethical behaviour: '… the Ethical Decalogue reflects and is derived from the moral teaching of the 8th-century prophets'. (Anderson)

Key quote

(The) Ten Commandments are an effective expression of fundamental religious and moral standards in ancient Israel and of their relation to Yahweh's saving acts. (G.W. Anderson)

Rabbi Shmuley Boteach writes that the essence of the Ten Commandments lies in their introduction of an **immutable**, divine law as the operating force in the universe: they 'illustrate the majestic scope of his mission on earth. They soar from the most basic "I am the Lord your God" to embrace the whole gamut of human existence. Even thoughts are included, "Do not covet your neighbour's wife or possessions".'

Furthermore, when God gives laws, they are universally applicable in every age and in every time: they are not subject to interpretation or modification. Thus the commandment not to steal is as relevant today as it was in ancient times.

Key quote

The profundity of the Ten Commandments does not lie in the substance – indeed the human mind might dictate these commandments itself. Rather the uniqueness of the Ten Commandments lies in the fact that it was God who commanded them. (Rabbi Shmuley Boteach)

Neither rewards nor punishments are provided for in the commandments; neither is there a justification of each one in the sense that they do not say 'Do not kill because …' The general nature of the Ten Commandments, and the lack of reference to sanctions means that they are more aptly characterised as ethical or moral exhortations than as laws. Their aim is to bring the world, through Judaism, to ethical monotheism, with the primary demand being to treat fellow human beings decently. The Ten Sayings thus serve as the foundation for all the other mitzvot of Jewish religious life, and provide the template for religious practice.

AO1 Activity

A Jew would say that the Ten Sayings are just as relevant today as they were when they were first given to Moses. Work with a partner, and search for news stories/examples from social media which can be used to illustrate that the same kinds of issues are present in today's world. Present your findings to the rest of the group.

The Aseret ha-D'ibrot in rabbinical understanding as the ten categories of mitzvot

Specification content
The Aseret ha-D'ibrot in rabbinical understanding as the ten categories of mitzvot.

According to rabbinic tradition, the Aseret ha-D'ibrot are not individual commandments, but are categories into which each of the 613 mitzvot can be placed under one of the ten classifications. Indeed, it has been suggested that the Ten Sayings serve as an outline for the Torah. In this context it is perhaps easier to think of each one as a subject heading, since many other mitzvot can be listed under them.

Bernhard W Anderson asserts that: 'With the exception of commandments 4 and 5, the Decalogue is a series of prohibitions, each beginning with a verb in the second person singular, indicating that each member of the covenant community is addressed ... The Decalogue merely stakes out general limitations which are defined by the covenant relationship; but within these limitations there is wide latitude for freedom of action or for interpretation of obligation to God and to one's fellow human beings.'

(1) Belief in God: The first of the Ten Sayings comes from the declaration in Exodus 20:2 which says 'I am the Lord your God.' For Jews, the belief in the Oneness of God is the foundation of their faith. The first of the Ten Sayings tells them that they are forbidden to worship any other gods.

(2) Prohibition against improper worship: Exodus 20:3–6 begins 'You shall have no other gods before me ...' In addition to prohibiting the worship of other gods, Jews are told that they should not take part in any improper forms of worship to God, such as worshipping through idols: 'You shall not make for yourself a graven image ...' (Exodus 20:4).

(3) Prohibition against the taking of oaths: Exodus 20:7 says 'You shall not take the name of the Lord in vain.' This is a commandment against **blasphemy** and refers to the abuse of God's name in oaths, for example. One of the first commandments listed by Maimonides in the Mishneh Torah was this one, and he considered that it was forbidden to speak God's name at any time. Jewish scholars refer to this as 'uttering the Name of Heaven uselessly'.

Jews nowadays refrain from using God's name either in speech or in writing: when speaking, they use the name 'Adonai' which means 'Lord'; and when writing the name of God, they substitute letters such as 'G-d'.

(4) The observation of sacred times: Exodus 20:8–11 categorises the mitzvot that are related to the observance of Shabbat, and other sacred times: 'Remember the Sabbath day, to keep it holy ...'

(5) Respect for parents and teachers: this is derived from Exodus 20:12, which states 'Honour your father and your mother ...' The Talmud compares the keeping of this commandment to honouring God, and the Mishneh Torah underlines the requirement to honour both parents equally. However, a child is not bound to obey their parent if asked to do something that would fall outside the requirements of Jewish law. The Midrash says 'Everything that your father says to you, you are obliged to obey. But if he says to you "Let us bow down to idols" you must not obey him lest you become an **apostate**.'

Jews are also required to continue to honour their parents even after their mother and father have passed away. This is done by reciting the Kaddish for 11 months after their decease.

Key terms

Apostate: someone who rejects a belief

Blasphemy: an act that insults God

quickfire

3.16 Which of the Aseret ha-D'ibrot prohibits blasphemy?

Key quote

God commanded us to abstain from work on the Sabbath, and to rest, for two purposes, namely (1) that we might confirm the true theory, that of the Creation, which at once and clearly leads us to the theory of the existence of God. (2) That we might remember how kind God had been in freeing us from the burden of the Egyptians. The Sabbath is therefore a double blessing: it gives correct notions, and also promotes the well-being of our bodies. (Maimonides)

quickfire

3.17 How do Jewish children continue to keep the commandment to honour their parents even after their mother and father have passed away?

Key terms

Lashon hara: literally means 'evil tongue'; derogatory speech about another person

Noachide Laws: the minimal moral duties required by all people (not just Jews)

(6) Prohibition against harming another person: 'You shall not kill' (Exodus 20:13) emphasises the sacredness of human life. This particular prohibition can also be found in the Noachide Laws, comprising seven laws considered by rabbinic tradition to set out the basic moral duties of humankind. For example, Genesis 9:6 states 'Whoever sheds the blood of man, by man shall his blood be shed; for God made man in his own image.'

Key quote

1. Do not deny God
2. Do not blaspheme
3. Do not murder
4. Do not engage in improper sexual relationships
5. Do not steal
6. Do not eat of a live animal
7. Establish courts/legal system to ensure obedience to the law.

(Noachide Laws)

(7) Prohibition against sexual immorality: 'You shall not commit adultery' (Exodus 20:14) is a requirement which supports the sanctity of marriage, and which is upheld to this day within the wider Jewish community.

(8) Prohibition against theft: Exodus 20:15 states: 'You shall not steal.' The term 'steal' covers a variety of categories such as robbery, deception, fraud and unethical business practices. In ancient Jewish tradition, it referred to kidnapping.

(9) Prohibition against harming another person through speech: Exodus 20:16 states 'You shall not bear false witness against your neighbour.' The power of speech is greatly acknowledged within Judaism, for they believe that the universe itself was created through the voice of God. Sins relating to speech are known as 'lashon hara' (literally 'evil tongue'). The Talmud warns that the tongue is such a dangerous weapon that it must be kept hidden from view behind the mouth and the teeth, in order to prevent it from being misused.

quickfire

3.18 What type of sin does the term 'lashon hara' relate to?

Lashon hara covers many types of harmful speech such as slander; evil reports about another person; rumours; and the relating of unpleasant facts. Indeed, both the teller and the listener are guilty of breaking this prohibition. The Babylonian Talmud warns that if a person indulges in lashon hara, then they are effectively denying the existence of God, and that '... the Almighty, declares "I and he cannot live in the same world".'

A tale from the Hasidic branch of the Jewish religion illustrates the danger of improper speech: A member of the Jewish community had been going about telling malicious lies about his rabbi. He later came to the realisation that he had done wrong and went to ask forgiveness from the rabbi, claiming that he would do anything in order to make amends. The rabbi told him to take a feather pillow, cut it open and scatter the feathers in the wind. The man thought that this was a simple enough thing to do, although rather strange, and so he carried it out. On returning to the rabbi to report that the task had been done, the rabbi said 'Now go and collect back in all of the feathers'. The moral of this tale is that evil speech, just like the feathers, once released cannot be fully recalled.

Key quotes

Keep your tongue from evil and your lips from telling lies. (Psalm 34:13)

I will watch my ways and keep my tongue from sin. (Psalm 39:1)

(10) Prohibition against coveting: 'You shall not covet your neighbour's house ... wife ... manservant ...maidservant ...ox ... ass ... or anything that is your neighbour's' (Exodus 20:17). Unlike the other prohibitions, this particular commandment focuses upon inward thoughts rather than outward actions.

Maimonides described this prohibition as a fence or boundary that keeps us a safe distance from the serious sins of theft, adultery, and even murder, which may result from covetousness. He wrote, 'Desire leads to coveting, and coveting leads to stealing. For if the owner does not wish to sell, even though he is offered a good price ... the person (who covets the object) will come and steal it, as it is written in "They covet fields and (then) steal them". And if the owner approaches him with a view to reclaiming his money or preventing the theft, then he will come to murder.'

However, Maimonides concluded that one isn't guilty until one takes action in order to take possession of the coveted object. This suggests that the feeling of envy is not critical until there is some action that results from it.

AO1 Activity

Draw or source ten images that will give you a visual hint for each of the Ten Sayings. Underneath each image, write out the relevant quote from the book of Exodus that goes with it.

Study tip

When answering a question on the Aseret ha-D'ibrot in rabbinical understanding as the ten categories of mitzvot, make sure that you don't merely write a list. Your response needs to demonstrate depth and/or breadth with a detailed discussion of each category.

Aseret ha-D'ibrot (Exodus chapter 20)

Key skills

Knowledge involves:

Selection of a range of (thorough) accurate and relevant information that is directly related to the specific demands of the question.

This means you choose the correct information relevant to the question set NOT the topic area. You will have to think and focus on selecting key information and NOT writing everything you know about the topic area.

Understanding involves:

Explanation that is extensive, demonstrating depth and/or breadth with excellent use of evidence and examples including (where appropriate) thorough and accurate supporting use of sacred texts, sources of wisdom and specialist language.

This means that you demonstrate that you understand something by being able to illustrate and expand your points through examples/supporting evidence in a personal way and NOT repeat chunks from a textbook (known as rote learning).

Further application of skills:

Go through the topic areas in this section and create some bullet lists of key points from key areas. For each one, provide further elaboration and explanation through the use of evidence and examples.

AO1 Developing skills

It is now time to reflect upon the information that has been covered so far. It is also important to consider how what you have learned can be focused and used for examination-style answers by practising the skills associated with AO1.

Assessment objective 1 (AO1) involves demonstrating knowledge and understanding. The terms 'knowledge' and 'understanding' are obvious but it is crucial to be familiar with how certain skills demonstrate these terms, and also, how the performance of these skills is measured (see generic band descriptors Band 5 for AS AO1).

▶ **Your new task is this:** below is a list of several key points bulleted in response to a question that has been written requiring an examination of the Ten Sayings as a basis for religious and ethical life in Judaism. It is obviously a very full list. It will be useful, initially, to consider what you think are the most important points to use in planning an answer. This exercise, in essence, is like writing your own set of possible answers that are listed in a typical mark scheme as indicative content. In a group, select the most important points you feel should be included in a list of indicative content for this question. You will need to decide upon two things: which points to select; and then, in which order to put them in an answer.

List of indicative content:

- Belief in the Oneness of God; prohibition against improper worship and the taking of oaths; observing sacred times, provide the basis for Jewish religious life.
- Ethical and moral behaviour in relation to: honouring one's father and mother; not killing; committing adultery; stealing; bearing false witness or coveting.
- The Ten Sayings are just as applicable today as they were when first given by God to the ancient Israelites.
- Furthermore, God's laws are universally applicable in every age.
- The Ten Sayings can be divided into two categories: firstly, setting out the religious expectations between a person and God; and secondly the expectations of a person in their relationships with other people.
- The two versions of the Ten Sayings from Exodus and Deuteronomy are known as the 'Ethical Decalogue', which scholars believe is derived from the moral teaching of the 8th-century prophets.
- They are general in nature, and do not contain sanctions, and are therefore perhaps better categorised as ethical and moral advice rather than as laws.
- Their aim is to show how to treat fellow humans decently.
- Their aim, through Judaism, is to bring the world to ethical monotheism.
- Rabbinic tradition views the Ten Sayings as categories into which each of the mitzvot can be placed.
- They serve as an outline for the Torah.
- Examples of how the Ten Sayings as categories can serve as a foundation for religious and ethical life: refer to numbers 1–4.
- The Ten Sayings are known as Aseret ha-D'ibrot in Judaism, and are the first of the 613 mitzvot that God gave to Moses on Mount Sinai.
- They represent the fundamental religious and moral standards expected of the Jewish people by God.
- The essence of the Ten Sayings lies in their ability to cover the whole range of human experience: even thoughts are included as in 'Do not covet your neighbour's wife or possessions'.
- Perhaps they should be seen as subject headings.

Issues for analysis and evaluation

Whether the Ten Sayings are an effective guide for ethical living

The Ten Sayings aren't the first principles in the Torah that set out regulations for ethical living. Indeed the Ten Sayings are based upon the Noachide Laws that provide the basis of the universal covenant God established with Noah, his descendants, and the whole of humanity. As such, therefore, they are not unique.

Perhaps we can better understand the need for the Ten Sayings if we were to look at them in the context in which they were given. It could be argued that they were originally introduced in order to bring stability to the community of Israelites during the time when they were wandering in the wilderness after the escape from slavery in Egypt. As such, therefore, perhaps they should not be considered as a guide for modern-day society that has so many more complicated ethical issues as compared with those from the early days of the Jewish religion.

Orthodox Jews would argue that they continue to provide an effective guide for ethical living as they believe that when God gives laws they are universally applicable in every age and in every time: they are not subject to interpretation or modification. Thus the commandment not to steal, for example, is as relevant today as it was in ancient times.

It cannot be denied that the Ten Sayings cover a wide sweep of issues, but maybe it would be better to consider them as ten 'categories' rather than sayings for the purpose of guidance for ethical living. They might be better understood as the foundation for all of the other 603 mitzvot that God gave to the Jews; a framework that requires further analysis and explanation.

The Ten Sayings can be clearly divided into two categories, with the first four setting out what is expected regarding a person's relationship with God; and the rest setting out the expectations regarding a person's relationship with others. Non-religious people would undoubtedly question the relevance of the commandments relating to the relationship with God. Nevertheless, from a Jewish point of view, if one's relationship with God is right then it is to be expected that appropriate ethical behaviour is sure to follow.

The Ten Sayings are still acceptable as a guide for ethical living in the modern world as they cover all of the things that still affect humanity: from outward actions through to inner actions such as thoughts. Even within a non-religious context they are still to be found as the basis for the rules of every civilised society in the world.

One possible conclusion could be that although it could be argued that the Ten Sayings do not in themselves provide a comprehensive guide for ethical living, they are an effective guide and certainly have formed the basis for living in a similar way that key commandments or precepts have done so for other religions. However, their effectiveness does have limitations in that first of all they are a guide in the sense they are a brief overview of essentials, and, secondly, they are – in rabbinic understanding – a springboard for ethical deliberation as an outline and summary for further ethical instruction found within the religious laws of Judaism as a whole.

This section covers AO2 content and skills

Specification content

Whether the Ten Sayings are an effective guide for ethical living.

AO2 Activity *Possible lines of argument*

Listed below are some conclusions that could be drawn from the AO2 reasoning in the accompanying text:

1. They were not the first set of regulations that set out guidance for ethical living.

2. They should be considered within their historical context.

3. They continue to provide an effective guide, as God's laws are applicable in every age and at every time.

4. They might better be considered as 'categories' rather than 'sayings'.

5. The issues that can be found within the Ten Sayings deal with ethical issues that are still relevant in modern-day society.

Consider each of the conclusions drawn above and collect evidence and examples to support each argument from the AO1 and AO2 material studied in this section. Select one conclusion that you think is most convincing and explain why it is so. Now contrast this with the weakest conclusion in the list, justifying your argument with clear reasoning and evidence.

Specification content

The extent to which the Ten Sayings adequately summarise religious belief.

The extent to which the Ten Sayings adequately summarise religious belief

The Ten Sayings should perhaps be seen more as a guide for ethical living rather than as a summary of religious belief: their aim being to bring the world, through Judaism, to ethical monotheism.

Perhaps we can come to a better understanding of their purpose if we look at them in the context in which they were given. It could be argued that they were originally introduced in order to bring stability to the community of Israelites during the time when they were wandering in the wilderness after the escape from slavery in Egypt. As such, they were more of a guide to ethical and moral living rather than a summary of the core religious beliefs of the faith. As an ethical guide, they cover all of the things that still affect humanity within modern society. These range from outward actions such as the prohibition against stealing, for example, to inner thoughts such not coveting the possessions of one's neighbour.

Within the rabbinic tradition, they are not perceived to be individual commandments, but rather as categories into which each of the mitzvot can be placed. The Ten Sayings are therefore regarded as the foundation for all the other mitzvot of Jewish life, and provide the template for religious practice.

The content of the Ten Sayings, nevertheless, can be said to reflect the essence of Jewish religious beliefs: that there is One God who demands total obedience from the people: 'I am the Eternal God who brought you out of the land of Egypt' (Exodus 20:2). Judaism is a way of life which is based upon a set of practices. These practices, or mitzvot, serve as the way in which an individual can connect with God, and carry out God's commandments. Keeping the mitzvot is a requirement of the covenant relationship between God and humanity. The Ten Sayings reinforce the covenant relationship on a daily basis by reminding Jews of their responsibility to obey God by upholding the divine laws which have been given to them.

There are other sources within Judaism that offer a more adequate summary of religious beliefs: the Shema, for example, was developed as a way of summarising the whole of the Jewish law and is the central focus of Jewish worship. Its opening line 'Hear, O Israel: The Lord our God, the Lord is One' is as close as possible to a declaration of faith in what is central to Judaism: that there is One God who demands total obedience from the people. Alan Mintz sums up this contention when he states: 'Exclusive fidelity to God and God's unity are the two major concepts of the Shema.' Furthermore, the Shema sums up the very essence of the covenant relationship between God and the Jewish people: for example, the second part of the Shema declares the Jews' acceptance of the commandments as well as undertaking to carry them out as evidence of their loyalty to God.

One possible conclusion could be to see the Ten Sayings as not primarily meant to be an adequate summary of religious belief but more a statement of essential beliefs. Their adequacy, according to this reasoning, can be judged in relation to what they point to in terms of further religious beliefs and, more importantly, how they are used as a basis for these beliefs and in relation to them.

AO2 Developing skills

It is now time to reflect upon the information that has been covered so far. It is also important to consider how what you have learned can be focused and used for examination-style answers by practising the skills associated with AO2.

Assessment objective 2 (AO2) involves 'analysis' and 'evaluation'. The terms may be obvious but it is crucial to be familiar with how certain skills demonstrate these terms, and also, how the performance of these skills is measured (see generic band descriptors Band 5 for AS AO2).

Obviously an answer is placed within an appropriate band descriptor depending upon how well the answer performs, ranging from excellent, good, satisfactory, basic/limited to very limited.

▶ **Your new task is this:** below is a list of several key points bulleted in response to a question requiring an evaluation of the importance of the Ten Sayings as a guide to ethical living in Judaism. It is obviously a very full list. It will be useful, initially, to consider what you think are the most important points to use in planning an answer. This exercise, in essence, is like writing your own set of possible answers that are listed in a typical mark scheme as indicative content. In a group, select the most important points you feel should be included in a list of indicative content for this question. You will need to decide upon two things: which points to select; and then, in which order to put them in an answer.

List of indicative content:

- They are considered to be universally applicable in every age and time.
- They are not unique and are based upon an earlier set of laws: the Noachide Laws that provided the basis of the universal covenant God established with Noah.
- Perhaps they are better seen as a guide for the community of Israelites when they were wandering in the wilderness after the Exodus from Egypt.
- They are perhaps better understood as categories, with the purpose of guidance for ethical living.
- One might question the relevance of the particular commandments which relate to a person's relationship with God.
- The prohibition against killing is as relevant today as it was in ancient times.
- Nevertheless, if a person's relationship with God is right, then one would expect them to strive for a lifestyle which is ethically sound.
- The Ten Sayings remain relevant even in modern-day society as they cover issues that still affect humanity.
- Even in a secular context they are still to be found as the basis for the rules of civilized societies.
- We need to look at them within the context they were given.

Key skills

Analysis involves identifying issues raised by the materials in the AO1, together with those identified in the AO2 section, and presents sustained and clear views, either of scholars or from a personal perspective ready for evaluation.

This means that it picks out key things to debate and the lines of argument presented by others or a personal point of view.

Evaluation involves considering the various implications of the issues raised based upon the evidence gleaned from analysis and provides an extensive detailed argument with a clear conclusion.

This means that the answer weighs up the various and different lines of argument analysed through individual commentary and response and arrives at a conclusion through a clear process of reasoning.

This section covers AO1 content and skills

Specification content

The origins of the synagogue as a permanent institution in Babylonian captivity.

quickfire

4.1 What is the meaning of the word 'synagogue'?

quickfire

4.2 When, and by whom, was the Temple in Jerusalem destroyed?

Key terms

Exile: enforced absence from one's country of origin

Synagogue: comes from a Greek word meaning 'to gather together'; the name given to the Jewish place of worship

Tabernacled: relating to the sanctuary for the Ark of the Covenant

A: The role of the synagogue in Judaism

The origins of the synagogue as a permanent institution in Babylonian captivity

The Jewish place of worship is called a **synagogue**. The word synagogue comes from a Greek word meaning 'to gather together', and refers to the place where Jewish people meet to worship God; study religious texts; and gather as a community for a variety of events.

Jews have been meeting in synagogues for over 2500 years. Before this, the most important place of worship was at the Temple in Jerusalem that had been built by King Solomon. However, the Temple was destroyed by the Babylonians in 586 BCE, and the Jewish people were forced to leave their historic homeland and were taken into **exile**.

' ... Nebuzaradan commander of the imperial guard, an official of the king of Babylon, came to Jerusalem. He set fire to the temple of the Lord ... (and) carried into exile the people who remained in the city ...' (2 Kings 25:8–12)

The Temple in Jerusalem had been at the very centre of Jewish religious life as Jewish law specified that certain important religious rituals, such as animal sacrifices, could only take place there. With the destruction of the Temple, it would seem that the linchpin of Jewish worship had been destroyed. Bernhard W. Anderson notes that: 'The most serious adjustment that the Jews of Babylonia had to make was a religious one. Their faith had been oriented to the land of Palestine, the inheritance Yahweh had given to them, and to the Temple of Jerusalem, the place where Yahweh "**tabernacled**" in the midst of the worshipping people, according to Priestly theology. The greatest danger was that in time the Jewish faith, torn from these historical moorings, would be drowned in the sea of Babylonian culture.'

A synagogue

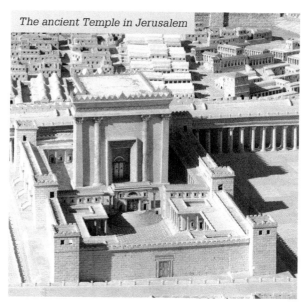

The ancient Temple in Jerusalem

Anderson likens the problem faced by the Jews in exile in Babylon to the one faced by the early Israelites in their transition from the wilderness to the new land of Canaan: could Yahweh be worshipped in a strange land where other gods seemed to be in control? This mood is reflected in Psalm 137:

'By the waters of Babylon, there we sat down and wept, when we remembered Zion … How shall we sing the Lord's song in a foreign land?'

Many Jews, no doubt, became assimilated into Babylonian culture; but others looked for ways in which to preserve their Jewish cultural and religious identity. Anderson indicates that the great prophets had 'paved the way for the new expression of Israel's faith by proclaiming that Yahweh was not bound to the Temple in Jerusalem'. In a letter to the exiles, the prophet Jeremiah insisted that even in a faraway land, where there was no Temple, the people could have access to God through prayer.

The prophet Ezekiel described a vision of Yahweh's 'glory' going to the people in exile, just as the ancient ark had moved from place to place during the years in the wilderness. Also, in a passage from Deuteronomy 4:27–29, which scholars believe was written either during the period of exile or shortly before it, we read:

'The Lord will scatter you among the peoples … But if from there you seek the Lord your God, you will find him if you seek him with all your heart and with all your soul.'

These assurances that God could be worshipped anywhere gave heart to the faithful, and they undoubtedly started to meet together in small groups. They first met in each other's homes for worship and study of the Torah, and later, in an attempt to make sure that the faith did not die out, built temporary places for worship. These building became known as synagogues: they were never meant to replace the Temple, but to act as temporary places of worship until the Temple in Jerusalem could be rebuilt.

Although synagogues today differ from one another, their layout is based upon the original Temple. This has resulted in them containing features that are reminders of its structure. For example, they are always built facing Jerusalem and the contents, such as the ark, remind Jews of the original temple in Jerusalem and the importance of their history.

Key quote

Then you will call on me and come and pray to me, and I will listen to you … I will be found by you … and will bring you back from captivity. (Jeremiah 29:12–14)

quickfire

4.3 Which of the prophets claimed that people could have access to God even where there was no Temple?

Key quote

Therefore say, this is what the Sovereign Lord says: 'Although I sent them far away among the nations and scattered them among the countries, yet for a little while I have been a sanctuary for them in the countries where they have gone.' (Ezekiel 11:16)

Key quote

The synagogue proved itself a most effective preserver of the ancient sanctities in the national memory of the Jewish people. During the millennia of exile, the Jews gathered daily in their synagogues and prayed for the restoration of the Temple. They symbolically performed the Temple rites … thus (keeping) themselves in constant readiness for the resumption of the sacerdotal rituals in the rebuilt Temple. (Millgram)

Specification content
The role of the ark in reminding Jews
of the Jerusalem temple.

Key terms

Aron Kodesh: originally the name
given to the wooden box, covered in
gold, in which were stored the two
tablets of stone given to Moses at Sinai

Parochet: curtain

Sanctuary: a holy or sacred place

quickfire

4.4 What was the purpose of the Aron
Kodesh in the Sanctuary?

Key quote

The ... religion of Israel differed
radically from the religions of other
ancient peoples, who represented
the deity's presence by setting up
the image of a god or goddess in a
temple .... (B. W. Anderson)

quickfire

4.5 Who built the first permanent Temple
building in Jerusalem?

The role of the ark in reminding Jews of the Jerusalem temple

According to Exodus 25:10–22 and 37:1–9, the Israelites built a **Sanctuary** made
of posts, boards and curtains which housed the two tablets of stone given to Moses
at Sinai. These were contained in a wooden box covered with gold, known as the
Aron Kodesh (Holy Ark). It was a temporary structure that would be assembled
wherever the Israelites made camp. The Sanctuary contained an inner chamber
known as the Holy of Holies, which was separated by a **parochet** (curtain), and it
contained the Holy Ark. The instructions for the use of a parochet can be found in
Exodus 40:21: 'Then he (Moses) brought the ark into the tabernacle and hung the
shielding curtain and shielded the ark of the covenant law, as the Lord commanded
him.' (Exodus 40:21)

The Holy Ark

G.W. Anderson suggests that if we ask what the religious significance of the Ark
was, we must consider the possibility that it was understood in different ways
at different times. In 1 Samuel 4 it is brought into camp in the hope of ensuring
victory, which suggests that it represented the mighty presence of Yahweh with the
people in what were regarded as holy wars against their enemies:

'Now the Israelites went out to fight against the Philistines ... Israel was defeated
... the elders of Israel asked, "Why did the Lord bring defeat on us today before the
Philistines? Let us bring the ark of the Lord's covenant from Shiloh, so that he may
go with us and save us from the hand of our enemies."' (1 Samuel 4:1–3)

Later it came to be thought of as the throne of the invisible Yahweh. This is in
accordance with the Ten Commandments, which strictly forbids the making of an
image of God. It was firmly believed that God's presence travelled with the people,
and went before them as their leader, enthroned upon the Ark.

In Deuteronomy 10:5 it is the receptacle for the tablets of the law, hence, no doubt
the title 'Ark of the Covenant'.

When King David captured Jerusalem, the roaming Ark of the Covenant finally
came to rest in that city, and the first permanent Temple building was subsequently
constructed by David's son, King Solomon. For many centuries, however, other
sanctuaries retained their religious functions until King Josiah (c. 640–609 BCE)
established the Temple of Jerusalem as the only place of sacrifice within the
Kingdom.

When King Solomon built the Temple, he modelled it on the Sanctuary. As a result
of this, the most important feature within all synagogues after the Torah scrolls, is
the Holy Ark.

In synagogues in western countries, the Aron Kodesh is always placed in the east wall of the synagogue, as this is the direction of Jerusalem. It acts as a representation of the golden box in which the Ten Commandments were stored in the original Temple in that city, and today contains the Sefer Torah scrolls. There is usually a richly decorated parochet that is hung in front of it; again a symbol of the curtain that separated the Holy of Holies from the outer chamber in the original Temple.

The actions and treatment surrounding the Aron Kodesh also act as reminders to Jews of the holiness of the Temple in Jerusalem. For example, rabbinic tradition states that it is forbidden to make any secular use of it, and when it is no longer usable it cannot be destroyed, but must be stored away. Neither must one sell the Aron Kodesh, even in order to use the money to build a new synagogue. It is also customary to stand while it is being opened.

It is related that Rabbi Jacob Halevi (known as the Maharil) used to bow three times to the Aron Kodesh when he passed it on leaving the synagogue, just as a disciple would do on taking leave of their master.

The Aron Kodesh

Key quote

One must show great honour to the Torah scrolls and it is a mitzvah to set aside a special place for them, to honour that place, and to beautify it. (Talmud)

The social role of the synagogue as meeting place for the Jewish community – bet k'nesset (house of meeting); the synagogue as a place of study and Torah reading – bet midrash (house of study) or 'school' (shul)

Specification content

Its social role: as meeting place for the Jewish community – bet k'nesset (house of meeting); the synagogue as a place of study and Torah reading – bet midrash (house of study) or 'school' (shul).

AO1 Activity

As you read through this section, make a list of the various activities that take place at a typical synagogue. Use your list to create a virtual notice board for a synagogue, noting, for example, events, dates, and times for activities which are likely to take place in a typical month.

Key terms

Bet k'nesset: house of meeting

Bet midrash: house of study

Shul: school

Yiddish: a language based on German that is written in Hebrew characters, and originally spoken by Jews of central and Eastern Europe

The word 'synagogue' refers to a Jewish place of worship; however, the Hebrew language has a number of different words for synagogue. Many Jews refer to it as the **bet k'nesset** (house of meeting), **bet midrash** (house of study) or **shul** (a **Yiddish** word) meaning 'school'. These terms highlight the fact that, apart from worship, the synagogue has an important role to play in the wider Jewish community. The name 'bet k'nesset' reflects the fact that as well as a place of prayer and worship, the synagogue plays a valuable role as that of a social centre, where various activities take place just as at the original Temple in Jerusalem.

quickfire

4.6 What are the Hebrew names for 'house of meeting' and 'house of study'?

Key quote

Throughout the centuries, when the vast majority of Europe was illiterate, Jews maintained an educational infrastructure as their highest priority. It is no exaggeration to say that this lay at the heart of the Jewish ability to survive catastrophe, negotiate change and flourish in difficult circumstances. (Rabbi Jonathan Sacks)

Key quote

These are the Lord's appointed festivals, the sacred assemblies you are to proclaim at their appointed times. (Leviticus 23:4)

Modern synagogues are usually built with meeting rooms or classrooms incorporated into the building. There will sometimes be a hall for community use, which acts as a venue for a variety of events such as bar mitzvah and wedding celebrations. The synagogue therefore acts as a hub for all ages, holding youth club meetings, hosting lectures, and providing a meeting place for senior citizens.

Alan Unterman draws a distinction between the bet k'nesset and the bet midrash: 'In effect there are two kinds of synagogue, the bet k'nesset ... which is the synagogue proper used for prayers and other liturgical rites, and the bet midrash ... which is used for study as well as regular services.'

He also notes that the halakhic status of these two types of building differs: '... thus while the former should be the tallest building in the locality and one should neither sleep nor eat in it, these rules do not apply to the latter'.

The bet k'nesset is furnished for worship and prayer, and contains the Aron Kodesh; the raised platform or bimah in the centre; and pews for seating. It provides the environment within which the Sefer Torah scrolls can be stored, and where they can be read three times a week: small sections on Mondays and Thursdays, and the main reading on the morning of Shabbat.

The name 'bet midrash' underlines the fact that education is very important in Jewish life. The Torah says, 'And these words which I command you today shall be in your heart. You shall teach them diligently to your children ....' (Deuteronomy 6:6–7). The terms 'bet midrash' and 'shul' refer to the role of the synagogue as a place of study, and many synagogues have classrooms and a library where this can take place.

For many Jewish children who attend secular schools, there is no opportunity to study Hebrew as part of the mainstream curriculum. For this reason, Jewish children are able to attend Hebrew classes that are held at the synagogue. At these classes they are taught how to read from the Torah, and can prepare by practising the portion that they will read at their Bar/Bat mitzvah.

However, education does not stop with children. It is a process that is ongoing throughout life, and classes are also run for adults. Often a text from the Torah or Talmud is studied and sometimes there are lectures or discussion groups. Indeed, it has been suggested that the emphasis upon both the communal and educational aspect of the synagogue has been vital in contributing to the survival of the Jewish faith throughout the difficult times in its history.

Study tip

You will now be close to revision. Try arranging a 'study group' with friends to help revise. Use tips and techniques for peer learning that you have developed here.

The religious role of the synagogue: its central role in Jewish festivals

The Jewish year is full of festivals and special days, which provide opportunities for Jews to celebrate important events from their history, or to mark the different seasons of the year. As family and community are both very important in Jewish life, both the home and the synagogue have a role to play in such celebrations.

The reading of the Torah is an important part of Sabbath, festivals and fasts, and as this can only take place at the synagogue, the synagogue retains a central role in Jewish festivals. Melanie J. Wright claims that: 'Collectively, these festivals are fundamental to the experience of being Jewish', and underlines their importance by noting that even largely secularised Jews take part in, and attend the synagogue at certain festival times.

During the New Year festival of Rosh Hashanah, for example, the morning service at the synagogue can last from four to six hours. Rosh Hashanah is followed by the Day of Atonement (Yom Kippur) where prayers continue through the day, and the synagogue is usually very well attended. Philo of Alexandria, a first century Jewish philosopher, noted that Yom Kippur was observed 'not only by the **pious** and holy but by those who never act religiously in the rest of their lives'. Norman Solomon recognises that this still seems to be the case: 'For many people, however, putting in a brief appearance at the synagogue on Yom Kippur is a statement of Jewish identity rather than a religious commitment.'

Notwithstanding, attendance at the synagogue during festival times allows the wider Jewish community to meet together, and thus strengthen their bonds. The atmosphere is a solemn one when the congregation joins together for the evening service on Yom Kippur when they stand before God in awe. The final service of the festival ends with the chanting of the prayer known as **Avinu Malkenu** ('our father, our king), whereby the unity of God is declared by the congregation in unison.

One particular festival that is celebrated in Orthodox synagogues is **Simchat Torah**. This is the day on which the annual reading of the Torah is completed with the final reading from Deuteronomy; and immediately begun again starting from the first chapter of Genesis. This acts as a reminder that the study of the Torah is a cycle that never ends.

The Torah scrolls are carried in a joyous procession around the synagogue, usually accompanied by singing and dancing, and as many people as possible are given the honour of reciting a blessing over them as well as carrying them.

Such is the joyous nature of this festival that 'it spills over into the home and even the street, with singing and dancing, and a certain amount of alcoholic indulgence'. (De Lange)

The customs and rituals of this particular festival serve to emphasise the importance of the Torah, and its place of safe-keeping: the synagogue. It is the Torah that contains the words of God, and it is these words that have shaped the Jewish religion as a living faith that is centred upon both the home and the synagogue.

The synagogue as a place of prayer

Jews believe that a person can pray to God whenever or wherever they wish, although regular opportunities are provided through daily communal prayer services at the synagogue. The synagogue can therefore also be designated as a **bet tefillah** (house of prayer).

On each day a Jew is able to attend one of three services that offer an opportunity for communal prayer. There is arvit (evening prayer), shacharit (morning prayer) and minchah (afternoon prayer). According to the Talmud, the three daily services are intended to correspond with the times when sacrifices were offered at the Temple in Jerusalem. At Orthodox synagogues, a minyan is required before the act of communal prayer can take place.

Prayers are taken from the siddur, which is the main prayer book, and set prayers are offered at various stages of the synagogue service including the Shema, Amidah and Kaddish. In the United Kingdom, prayers for the Royal family are also offered as well as for the State of Israel.

Jews acknowledge that praying at regular times can be helpful as it provides a timetable in which a person can set aside time for devotion. Such regular prayers at the synagogue keep a person conscious of the bigger context in which they live, and many make the effort to join the wider synagogue congregation in prayer as often as is possible. Rabbinic tradition teaches that there is more merit in praying with a group than there is in praying alone.

Simchat Torah celebrations in the synagogue

Key terms

Avinu Malkenu: 'our father, our king'; a prayer

Bet tefillah: house of prayer

Pious: religiously devout

Simchat Torah: meaning 'rejoicing in the Torah'

quickfire

4.7 Which Jewish festival celebrates the day on which the annual reading of the Torah is completed?

Specification content

The religious role of the synagogue as a place of prayer.

Key quote

Better prayer without synagogue than synagogue without prayer. (Heschel)

quickfire

4.8 Name the three prayer services that are held every day at the synagogue.

Specification content

The religious role of the synagogue as a place for ritual – some contain a mikveh (pool) for religious and physical cleanliness.

> **Key terms**
>
> **Menstruation:** a woman's monthly period
>
> **Mikveh:** 'a place where water has gathered'; a special pool attached to a synagogue where Jews can immerse to purify themselves

Key quote

I will sprinkle clean water on you, and you will be clean; I will cleanse you from all your impurities and from all your idols. (Ezekiel 36:25)

Key quote

The principles of purity and impurity ... are not reckoned among those things that the human mind has determined; they are among the chukim. (Maimonides)

quickfire

4.9 What is the purpose of a mikveh?

Key quote

If a man immerses himself, but without special intention, it is as though he has not immersed himself at all. (Maimonides quoting from the Sages)

The synagogue as a place of ritual

There remains within Judaism today a tradition regarding ritual and spiritual purity. This has its foundation in the ritual of the ancient Temple in Jerusalem where a priest had to be ritually pure to participate in the Temple service. Touching a corpse or a dead animal (other than that killed for food or sacrifice) made a person impure; and so did **menstruation**. People could only regain their purity by immersion in water, and this would have been provided in the form of a designated pool in which rainwater had collected.

Many synagogues continue to provide a facility for this ritual to continue, and this is done by means of a **mikveh**. Mikveh means 'a place where water has gathered', and refers to a special pool where Jews can immerse to purify themselves. The mikveh is usually a private area attached to the synagogue, and there are separate areas for men and women.

Nowadays, the main use of the mikveh is for women. Orthodox Jewish women use the mikveh following their monthly period, and after the birth of a child. As she comes out of the water, a woman is considered to be 'pure' once more, and can resume sexual relations with her husband.

The purpose of immersion in a mikveh is not physical, but spiritual cleanliness and even Maimonides acknowledged that: 'It is plain and manifest that the laws about uncleanness and cleanness are decrees laid down by Scripture and not matters about which human understanding is capable of forming a judgement.' He also distinguished between physical and spiritual cleanliness: 'Now "uncleanness" is not mud or filth which water can remove, but a matter of scriptural decree and dependent on the intention of the heart.' In other words, immersion without proper intent is not considered to be worth anything.

Attendance at the mikveh is open to all members of the Jewish community. For example, it is prescribed that all Jews should bathe in the mikveh on the day before Yom Kippur as a sign of repentance. Many observant Jews also visit the mikveh every week before Shabbat, and it is traditionally used before getting married, or before conversion to Judaism.

A mikveh

A mikveh is also used for the immersion of kitchen utensils (unless they have been manufactured by a Jewish company, under the supervision of a rabbi). This practice has come about in response to the kosher food laws, and its intention is to prevent the use of any item that may have come into contact with non-kosher food products. Usually there is a separate mikveh for such immersion as it would be unsafe to immerse glasses or cups, which might be dropped and broken, and thus become a hazard to those using the mikveh afterwards.

The synagogue's legal status and role: its use as a rabbinical court or bet din (house of judgement)

Specification content

The synagogue's legal status and role: its use as a rabbinical court or bet din (house of judgement).

In areas where there is a large Jewish population there is usually a bet din attached to the synagogue. The bet din serves two primary functions for members of the Jewish community:

- Making judgements on civil disputes using Jewish law
- Ruling on religious matters.

In the United Kingdom, there is no central bet din, but each of the main branches of Judaism that are represented in this country has their own rabbinic authority. However, it is sometimes assumed, wrongly, that Jewish communities in the United Kingdom have a recognised system of courts that act outside the national law of the land: 'The great misnomer is that the Jews have been given the right to have their courts. Nobody gave us that right.' (David Frei)

Nevertheless, as Crown Court Judge Dawn Freedman says: '... just determining Jewish law for a host of areas to do with Sabbath observance, medical ethics and the like. We have a remit which is far beyond acting as a court of law.'

The establishment of the bet din has a biblical origin. Exodus 18:13–16 tells us: 'The next day Moses took his seat to serve as judge for the people ...' Also, when questioned by his father-in-law about why he was doing this, Moses replied, 'Because the people come to me to seek God's will. Whenever they have a dispute, it is brought to me, and I decide between the parties and inform them of God's decrees and instructions.'

A bet din is made up of a panel of three judges (known as dayanim) who listen to people presenting their cases and question witnesses themselves. The judges then reach a verdict and give their decision. The judges are usually very experienced rabbis with a good deal of communal experience between them. In Orthodox Judaism, the bet din will consist of three men; whilst in Progressive communities, women serve as well.

Sometimes Jews will bring their business disputes before the bet din and will request that they reach a judgement on the matters. They are also responsible for issuing Jewish divorce certificates; ensuring that food products can be declared kosher; and issuing labels and licences for butchers. The bet din also tests people who wish to convert to the Jewish faith.

Key quote

Follow justice and justice alone, so that you may live and possess the land the Lord your God is giving you. (Deuteronomy 16:20)

quickfire

4.10 Identify the two primary functions of the bet din within a Jewish community.

Key quote

But select capable men from all the people — men who fear God, trustworthy men who hate dishonest gain — and appoint them as officials over thousands, hundreds, fifties and tens. (Exodus 18:21)

Study tip

When carrying out extra research, you will be aware that many specialist Jewish terms can be spelled in more than one way (e.g. bet din/beth din). To avoid confusion, it is advisable to use the spellings that have been used in the specification content.

AO1 Activity

Use the websites of the Manchester Beth Din and the London Beth Din in order to carry out further research about the activities of a rabbinical court. After you have done your research, create the content for a webpage that provides information about the services that the bet din has to offer.

Key terms

Bet din: meaning 'house of judgement'; a rabbinical court

Dayanim: religious judges attached to a rabbinic court

Key skills

Knowledge involves:

Selection of a range of (thorough) accurate and relevant information that is directly related to the specific demands of the question.

This means you choose the correct information relevant to the question set NOT the topic area. You will have to think and focus on selecting key information and NOT writing everything you know about the topic area.

Understanding involves:

Explanation that is extensive, demonstrating depth and/or breadth with excellent use of evidence and examples including (where appropriate) thorough and accurate supporting use of sacred texts, sources of wisdom and specialist language.

This means that you demonstrate that you understand something by being able to illustrate and expand your points through examples/supporting evidence in a personal way and NOT repeat chunks from a textbook (known as rote learning).

Further application of skills:

Go through the topic areas in this section and create some bullet lists of key points from key areas. For each one, provide further elaboration and explanation through the use of evidence and examples.

AO1 Developing skills

It is now time to reflect upon the information that has been covered so far. It is also important to consider how what you have learned can be focused and used for examination-style answers by practising the skills associated with AO1.

Assessment objective 1 (AO1) involves demonstrating knowledge and understanding. The terms 'knowledge' and 'understanding' are obvious but it is crucial to be familiar with how certain skills demonstrate these terms, and also, how the performance of these skills is measured (see generic band descriptors Band 5 for AS AO1).

▶ **Your new task is this:** below is a list of indicative content that could be used in response to a question requiring an examination of the different roles of a synagogue in Judaism. The problem is that it is not a very full list and needs completing! It will be useful, as a group, to consider what is missing from the list. You will need to add at least five points that you would use to improve the list and/or give more detail to each point that is already in the list. Then, as a group, agree on your final list and write out your new list of indicative content, remembering the principles of explaining with evidence and/or examples.

If you then put this list in order of how you would present the information in an essay, you will have your own plan for an ideal answer.

List of indicative content:

- Synagogue as the centre of Jewish life
- Social function
- Educational function
- Religious role
- Place for ritual purification
- Legal function
- *Your added content*
- . *Your added content*
- Etc.

Issues for analysis and evaluation

Whether the synagogue has a main 'use' or 'purpose' within Judaism

Specification content

Whether the synagogue has a main 'use' or 'purpose' within Judaism.

The synagogue has served as an important place for Jews to meet since the period of the Babylonian exile. The Temple in Jerusalem had been destroyed, and the synagogues developed as the focal point for Jews as a place where they could meet and ensure that their cultural and religious identity was preserved. Their main use or purpose has therefore been to allow Jews to continue practising their faith during the many periods in their history when they have been forced to live in exile, estranged from their historic homeland.

Throughout Jewish history, synagogues have been established wherever Jews are to be found in the world thus indicating their continued use and importance within the religion. It could be argued that the synagogue, especially as a place of education, has been a major factor in the survival of the Jewish faith. Rabbi Jonathan Sacks is in agreement with this view: 'Throughout the centuries, when the vast majority of Europe was illiterate, Jews maintained an educational infrastructure as their highest priority. It is no exaggeration to say that this lay at the heart of the Jewish ability to survive catastrophe, negotiate change and flourish in difficult circumstances.'

Synagogues have a variety of purposes as seen in the different names that can be ascribed to them: the title bet k'nesset denotes a place for prayer and worship. It also reflects the use of the synagogue as a hub for all ages, a social centre where various activities can take place, just as at the original Temple in Jerusalem. A typical synagogue is also the location for the community's bet midrash or shul.

Some major synagogues also provide the services of a bet din where decisions and rulings regarding Jewish law and judgements regarding disputes can be made by three judges. The synagogue is also important as a place of ritual by providing the facilities of a mikveh.

It could be argued that the Jewish home is just as important as the synagogue, as it is the place where children receive the majority of their education and upbringing in the Jewish lifestyle.

The study of the Torah has always been the foundation of the Jewish faith, and this can take place anywhere.

Jews also believe that a person can pray to God whenever or wherever they wish, and indeed all that is required is a minyan which can meet anywhere.

Nicholas De Lange says that a group of people who happen to be together for whatever purpose, 'for example for a meeting, or because they work nearby, may decide to constitute a minyan to say their prayers together. This minyan may sometimes develop into a fixed gathering that becomes in a sense an alternative to the regular synagogue worship.'

In conclusion, the synagogue provides the location for a variety of religious and non-religious activities. However, it was only meant to be temporary until the Temple is rebuilt in Jerusalem once more.

AO2 Activity *Possible lines of argument*

Listed below are some conclusions that could be drawn from the AO2 reasoning in the accompanying text:

1. Its main use or purpose is to provide a place where Jews can meet as an alternative to the Temple, which was destroyed during the period of the Babylonian exile.

2. Its continued use throughout Jewish history underlines its importance as the means by which Jewish cultural and religious identity has been preserved.

3. It has a variety of uses: prayer and worship; social centre; place of education; bet din; and provides the facilities for ritual purity.

4. What goes on in the Jewish home is more important than the synagogue.

5. Study of the Torah and prayer can take place anywhere, and so the synagogue is not really required for these important things.

Consider each of the conclusions drawn above and collect evidence and examples to support each argument from the AO1 and AO2 material studied in this section. Select one conclusion that you think is most convincing and explain why it is so. Now contrast this with the weakest conclusion in the list, justifying your argument with clear reasoning and evidence.

Specification content

The extent to which the synagogue is the heart of a Jewish community.

The extent to which the synagogue is the heart of a Jewish community

The synagogue as an institution provides the location for all aspects of Jewish life: the title bet k'nesset denotes it as a place for prayer and worship. It also reflects the use of the synagogue as a hub for all ages, a social centre where various activities can take place, just as at the original Temple in Jerusalem. A typical synagogue is also the location for the community's bet midrash or shul which is a school for the study of the scriptures and the learning of Hebrew. The Jewish community would be weakened without the availability of these things.

One particular and important aspect of the synagogue is that it provides the community with the facilities for ritual purification. In many synagogues this is done by means of the provision of a mikveh. Attendance is open to all members of the Jewish community, and its purpose is that of spiritual cleanliness.

For Orthodox Jews, in particular, the synagogue acts as a temporary replacement for the Temple in Jerusalem which was destroyed in 586 BCE. When King Solomon built the Temple he modelled it on the Sanctuary. As a result of this, the most important feature within all synagogues after the Torah scrolls themselves, is the Holy Ark, and the actions and treatment surrounding the Ark act as important reminders to Jews of the holiness of the Temple in Jerusalem.

However, the Jewish home is just as important as the synagogue. It is the place where children receive their earliest education and upbringing in the Jewish faith. Parents teach their children the ways of the Jewish faith by living according to the mitzvot. Keeping kashrut, observing Shabbat, for example, as well as the festival rituals which take place in the home, might be said to have more of an impact than attendance at the synagogue. Also parents have the responsibility to teach their children the Shema, thus emphasising the important role that parents have in passing on the faith to the next generation.

It is possible to be a Jew without attending the synagogue as one is born into the religion by virtue of having a Jewish mother. Indeed, apart from one or two occasions every year, such as at Pesach and Yom Kippur, many Jews do not attend at all.

Nevertheless, it is the place where Jews meet for the major events of life: Bar/Bat mitzvah ceremonies celebrate coming of age, for example, and the reading from the Torah scrolls is symbolic of the young man/woman reaching the age when they can take personal responsibility for keeping the mitzvot. This is acknowledged within the wider Jewish community that can provide future support should it be required.

In conclusion, it could be argued that it cannot really be denied that the synagogue is the heart of a Jewish community as it brings together the Jewish community in all aspects of religious and social life. However, it must also be stated that, according to this line of reasoning, the conclusion is acknowledging how it functions for a Jewish community and not Judaism itself as it is clear from the above arguments presented that there is much more to Jewish living than just congregating at a synagogue.

AO2 Activity *Possible lines of argument*

Listed below are some conclusions that could be drawn from the AO2 reasoning in the accompanying text:

1. Without having a synagogue at the heart of the community, it would be harder to maintain a Jewish lifestyle, and assimilation into the wider community might ensue.

2. The synagogue provides a venue for all aspects of Jewish religious and social life.

3. It acts as a temporary replacement until the Temple, the most sacred place within Judaism, is rebuilt in Jerusalem once more.

4. The Jewish home could be said to have a more central role within a Jewish community; it is possible to be Jewish without attending the synagogue on a regular basis.

5. Major events of Jewish life are celebrated at the synagogue; thus including all members of the faith community.

Consider each of the conclusions drawn above and collect evidence and examples to support each argument from the AO1 and AO2 material studied in this section. Select one conclusion that you think is most convincing and explain why it is so. Now contrast this with the weakest conclusion in the list, justifying your argument with clear reasoning and evidence.

AO2 Developing skills

It is now time to reflect upon the information that has been covered so far. It is also important to consider how what you have learned can be focused and used for examination-style answers by practising the skills associated with AO2.

Assessment objective 2 (AO2) involves 'analysis' and 'evaluation'. The terms may be obvious but it is crucial to be familiar with how certain skills demonstrate these terms, and also, how the performance of these skills is measured (see generic band descriptors Band 5 for AS AO2). Obviously an answer is placed within an appropriate band descriptor depending upon how well the answer performs, ranging from excellent, good, satisfactory, basic/limited to very limited.

▶ **Your new task is this:** below is a list of indicative content that could be used in response to a question requiring an evaluation of whether the synagogue still has a useful purpose within Judaism. The problem is that it is not a very full list and needs completing! It will be useful, as a group, to consider what is missing from the list. You will need to add at least six points (three in support and three against) that you would use to improve the list and/or give more detail to each point that is already in the list. Remember, it is how you use the points that is the most important factor. Apply the principles of evaluation by making sure that you: identify issues clearly; present accurate views of others, making sure that you comment on the views presented; reach an overall personal judgement. You may add more of your own suggestions, but try to negotiate as a group and prioritise the most important things to add. Then, as a group, agree on your final list and write out your new list of indicative content, remembering the principles of explaining with evidence and/or examples. If you then put this list in order of how you would present the information in an essay, you will have your own plan for an ideal answer.

List of indicative content:

In support

- Remains the central meeting place for the Jewish community
- It has a variety of uses
- *Your added content*
- *Your added content*
- Etc.

Against

- The Jewish home is important
- Many aspects of Jewish worship can take place anywhere.
- *Your added content*
- *Your added content*
- Etc.

Key skills

Analysis involves identifying issues raised by the materials in the AO1, together with those identified in the AO2 section, and presents sustained and clear views, either of scholars or from a personal perspective ready for evaluation.

This means that it picks out key things to debate and the lines of argument presented by others or a personal point of view.

Evaluation involves considering the various implications of the issues raised based upon the evidence gleaned from analysis and provides an extensive detailed argument with a clear conclusion.

This means that the answer weighs up the various and different lines of argument analysed through individual commentary and response and arrives at a conclusion through a clear process of reasoning.

Specification content

The significance of the 'Passover' event for Jewish identity with reference to: the popularity of observing Pesach amongst Jews today reflecting redemption of the Jewish people from Egypt; the redemption of the world under God's command.

quickfire

4.11 Which event from their history are Jews remembering at Pesach?

quickfire

4.12 Give another name for the festival of Pesach.

Key terms

Haggadah: means 'telling', the text recited at the Seder meal

Pesach: means to 'pass over'

Redemption: the act of being saved

Seder: means 'order', and refers to the ritual service and ceremonial dinner which takes place in the Jewish home at Pesach

Unleavened: (of bread) made without yeast or any other raising agent

Z'man heyruteinu: the season of our freedom

B: The role of festivals in shaping religious identity – Pesach

Introduction

The Jewish festival of Pesach (meaning literally to 'pass over') is known as a pilgrim festival. It remembers the Jews escaping from slavery in Egypt, and it is held in the spring. The Torah states that Jews are to observe Pesach for seven days beginning on the 15th day of the Jewish month of Nissan, which usually falls in April. As well as its common name of Pesach, it can also be known as the festival of unleavened bread.

The focal point of the festival is a special meal called the seder. The seder meal is full of symbolism and follows a set order during which Jews recall the slavery and Exodus from Egypt. The order is set down in a book called the Haggadah.

The significance of the 'Passover' event for Jewish identity: the popularity of observing Pesach amongst Jews today reflecting redemption of the Jewish people from Egypt; redemption of the world under God's command

Pesach is one of the most popular of all of the Jewish festivals, and one that is celebrated even by non-observant Jews. The theme of redemption is at the heart of the festival's celebrations. Pesach is rooted in the story of the Exodus from Egypt when the Israelites were freed from slavery. Exodus 12:14–17 contains the command from God that the event is to be recounted every year at Pesach: 'This is a day you are to commemorate; for the generations to come you shall celebrate it as a festival to the Lord … Celebrate the Festival of Unleavened Bread, because it was on this very day that I brought your divisions out of Egypt. Celebrate this day as a lasting ordinance for the generations to come.'

It is through the rituals of this festival that Jews today can continue to experience the sensations and emotions of making the journey from slavery to freedom. It is a festival in which the Jewish people as individuals and as a community celebrate 'z'man heyruteinu' that means, 'the season of our freedom'.

As well as physical redemption, Pesach also represents spiritual redemption: the Jews were no longer slaves to another nation, and neither were they bound to pagan gods. It was in this state of freedom that Moses was able to deliver God's message to the Jewish people, and to offer them the hope of freedom, and the promise of redemption.

This idea of spiritual redemption at Pesach is demonstrated by the idea that each subsequent generation of Jews is obliged to immerse themselves in the Exodus experience. Melanie J. Wright expresses this notion in the following way: 'Each generation of participants is encouraged to regard itself as standing on the edge of redemption, emphasising the important links between the sense of history and contemporary identity with the Jewish people.'

However, not only does Pesach commemorate the historical redemption of the Israelites from Egypt, it also looks forward to the redemption of the world under the rule of God. The seder itself includes many allusions to the coming of the Messiah. One of the most significant parts of the ritual comes at the end of the meal when a cup of wine is filled, and a blessing said over it. The cup of wine is set aside for the prophet Elijah, whom, it is believed, is the forerunner of the Messiah, and is supposed to come at Pesach in order to do this. At this point, the front door of the house is also opened for a short while. Both the offering of wine and the opening of the door are marks of hospitality for Elijah, in the hope that this will be the night when the world will be redeemed by God.

The importance of Exodus 12–15

The historical background to the festival of Pesach is to be found in Exodus chapters 12–15. This is a significant story in the history and identity of the Jewish people as the retelling of the story celebrates Jewish teachings about redemption and hope.

The book of Exodus tells us that Moses petitioned the Pharaoh for the freedom of the Israelites from slavery; however, the Pharaoh refused, and as a result of this God sent ten plagues upon Egypt. The last plague was the worst: God told Moses that the firstborn in every Egyptian family would be killed. We read in Exodus 12 of the instructions to the Israelites to smear the blood from a lamb on the doorposts of their houses. By doing this, God would know that they were not Egyptians, and the angel of death would pass over, thus sparing their children from loss of life. This is how the festival acquired its name.

That night there was terrible tragedy. Pharaoh's son died and he begged Moses to leave with the Israelites. They set off on their journey across the desert; however, Pharaoh changed his mind and he set off in pursuit with a large army. Exodus 14 tells us that by this time the Israelites had got to the Red Sea (or Reed Sea), and we have a miraculous account of God parting the waters so that the Israelites could pass through. The Egyptians rushed to follow, but the waters came crashing down upon them and they were drowned.

Exodus 15 contains an ancient song of praise, which is sung by Moses and the people in praise of the God who has redeemed them:

'Then Moses and the Israelites sang this song to the Lord:

"I will sing to the Lord,

for he is highly exalted.

Both horse and driver

He has hurled into the sea.

The Lord is my strength and my defence;

He has become my salvation."'

(Exodus 15:1–2)

B.W. Anderson underlines the significance of this passage from Exodus when he says, 'In this poetic portrayal the event is more than a deed of liberation. It is the event of the creation of a people.'

quickfire

4.13 Identify the two forms of redemption that are at the heart of Pesach.

Specification content

The importance of Exodus 12–15.

Key quote

Properly understood, the seder ceremony is no mere act of pious recollection, but a unique device for blending the past, present, and future into a single comprehensive and transcendental experience … The seder narrative relates the whole story of how the Israelites move progressively from darkness to light. **(Rabbi Ronald Isaacs)**

quickfire

4.14 Where, in the Torah, can the historical background to the festival of Pesach be found?

The smearing of the blood of the lamb

Reading from the Haggadah

quicKpire

4.15 What is the name of the book that
acts as a guide to the seder meal?

Key term

Recline: to lean back in a resting
position

Key quote

The customs give our children
a strong Jewish identity and the
sense that they are part of a nation
chosen by God to be beacons of
goodness and holiness in this world.
(Likkutei Sichot)

The symbolism of the seder plate and use of the Haggadah; the role of the Jewish community of believers in remembering and maintaining Jewish identity; hope for the future ('next year in Jerusalem'); the coming of Elijah to announce the arrival of the Messiah

Study tip

There are many things used at the seder meal which have a symbolic meaning.
When revising, make cards that have the name of the item/practice on one side,
with the significance of its use on the other.

The high point of the festival is the seder meal that is held on the eve of Pesach.
It is a meal that is full of symbolism and follows a set order during which Jews
recall the slavery and Exodus from Egypt, with each item of food on the table
representing something that happened at that event. It is clear from one of the
volumes of the Talmud, called Pesachim, that a large part of the ritual for the Seder
meal was already established prior to the destruction of the Temple in 70CE.

The order is set down in a book called the Haggadah, which contains instructions,
prayers, blessing and stories as a guide to the seder meal. By following the text,
Jews are reminded of the fourteen steps of the story of the Jews in Egypt, the
Exodus and the revelation of God.

At set times during the story everyone at the table eats the symbolic foods that are
set out on a seder plate, and drinks four glasses of wine. The symbolic nature of the
meal emphasises Jewish teachings about redemption and hope for the future.

The telling of the story of the Exodus begins with the youngest child of the family
asking four questions:

Why on this night do we eat unleavened bread?

Why on this night do we eat bitter herbs?

Why on this night do we dip our herbs?

Why on this night do we recline?

The four questions are an essential part of the seder, and must therefore be asked
even if no child is present. Talmud Pesachim instructs that even at a seder attended
by only two Torah scholars, both of whom are experts in the laws of Pesach, one
scholar must ask the four questions of the other. And if one should be alone, one
must ask the questions to oneself.

It is the job of the head of the family to give the answers to these questions whilst
pointing out the various symbols that are displayed on the Seder plate. The reply to
the four questions begins:

'We were Pharaoh's slaves in Egypt. The Lord our God brought us out from there by
power and force. And if the Holy One, blessed be He, had not brought our ancestors
out of Egypt, then we, our children, and our grandchildren would continue to be
enslaved to Pharaoh in Egypt. That is why, however wise or clever or old we are,
however knowledgeable in Torah, we must obey the command to talk about the
Exodus from Egypt. The more one talks about it, the more praiseworthy it is.'

This is followed by comments on the biblical account of the Exodus, although
different families have their own traditions, and some add their own explanations,
and their own observations on the theme of liberation. De Lange explains that this
is because 'the theme of Passover is not only the historical Exodus but everything it
symbolises, including the contemporary political implications of freedom as well as
its moral and spiritual dimensions, and also the future redemption.'

Each item of food on the table represents something which happened at the original Pesach and is presented on the seder plate:

Matzah: this is one of the most important symbols on the seder table. Matzah is a piece of unleavened bread. There are three matzot on the table at the seder meal and they act as a reminder that there was no time to wait for the bread to rise before the Israelites escaped from Egypt. When Jews eat this at Pesach, it helps them to feel a connection with their ancestors. It also links them with all other Jews who are celebrating across the world.

A roasted lamb shank bone commemorates the lamb sacrifice made the night before the Israelites fled from Egypt, when they marked their doorposts with the blood of a lamb so that the angel of death would pass over their homes, and their firstborn would not be killed:

'On that same night I will pass through Egypt and strike down every firstborn of both people and animals ... The blood will be a sign for you on the houses where you are, and when I see the blood, I will pass over you. No destructive plague will touch you when I strike Egypt.' (Exodus 12:12–13)

Maror is a bitter herb, usually horseradish. Bitter herbs bring tears to the eyes when eaten, and recall the bitterness of slavery. It is a symbol of the bitter times when the Jews were enslaved in Egypt.

Charoset is a sweet paste made of apple, cinnamon and raisins. It symbolises both the mortar which was used by the slaves, as well as the sweetness of their redemption.

Karpas is a green vegetable, usually parsley, which is a symbol of spring. It is dipped into salt water that symbolises the tears and sweat of slavery. Some families use boiled potatoes for karpas, especially those descended from Eastern Europe where it was difficult to obtain fresh green vegetables.

A roasted egg is also present, but not eaten, and its presence recalls the sacrifice that would have been made in the ancient Temple in Jerusalem.

There is also a ritual of drinking four cups of red wine during the meal, which recalls the fourfold promise of redemption in Exodus 6:6–7:

'I am the Lord, and I will bring you out from under the yoke of the Egyptians. I will free you from being slaves to them, and I will redeem you with an outstretched arm and with mighty acts of judgement. I will take you as my own people, and I will be your God.'

The central theme of the festival is thus encapsulated: God will 'bring out', 'free', 'redeem' and 'take' his people.

After the symbolic food has been represented, a festive meal is eaten, and finally the grace is recited in conclusion. A blessing is said over a cup of wine, which is drunk. Another cup is poured and set aside for the prophet Elijah who is believed to herald the Messiah, and who, it is believed, will come at Pesach to do this. The door to the house is opened for a while at this point for Elijah to enter. The meal ends with the words 'Next year may we be in Jerusalem; next year may we be free'.

AO1 Activity

Make a list of all the things that happen during Pesach which highlight/emphasise the theme of redemption.

Study tip

You will be close to revision now so try using the techniques of exam preparation found in the developing skills sections as a way of directing and focusing your revision.

Key terms

Charoset: a sweet paste made of apple, cinnamon and raisins

Karpas: a green vegetable

Maror: a bitter herb

Matzah: a piece of unleavened bread

Matzot: plural of 'matzah'

Mortar: a mixture of sand, water and cement used in bricklaying

Seder plate

Cup of Elijah

Key quote

He who does not stress these rituals on Passover does not fulfil his obligations: the paschal lamb, matzah, and maror. (Rabban Gamaliel)

quickfire

4.16 Name the item on the seder table which represents the sweetness of redemption.

Key quote

Passover's ability to accommodate historical and theological change within the structured framework of its rituals means that in many ways it epitomises Judaism. The existence of unity alongside diversity, tradition without stagnation, is vital to Jewish expression. (M. J. Wright)

quickfire

4.17 Why is a cup of wine poured and set aside for Elijah?

Key skills

Knowledge involves:

Selection of a range of (thorough) accurate and relevant information that is directly related to the specific demands of the question.

This means you choose the correct information relevant to the question set NOT the topic area. You will have to think and focus on selecting key information and NOT writing everything you know about the topic area.

Understanding involves:

Explanation that is extensive, demonstrating depth and/or breadth with excellent use of evidence and examples including (where appropriate) thorough and accurate supporting use of sacred texts, sources of wisdom and specialist language.

This means that you demonstrate that you understand something by being able to illustrate and expand your points through examples/supporting evidence in a personal way and NOT repeat chunks from a textbook (known as rote learning).

Further application of skills:

Go through the topic areas in this section and create some bullet lists of key points from key areas. For each one, provide further elaboration and explanation through the use of evidence and examples.

AO1 Developing skills

It is now time to reflect upon the information that has been covered so far. It is also important to consider how what you have learned can be focused and used for examination-style answers by practising the skills associated with AO1.

Assessment objective 1 (AO1) involves demonstrating knowledge and understanding. The terms 'knowledge' and 'understanding' are obvious but it is crucial to be familiar with how certain skills demonstrate these terms, and also, how the performance of these skills is measured (see generic band descriptors Band 5 for AS AO1).

You are now nearing the end of this section of the course. From now on the task will have only instructions with no examples; however, using the skills you have developed in completing the earlier tasks, you should be able to apply what you have learned to do and complete this successfully.

▶ **Your new task is this:** you will have to write a response under timed conditions to a question requiring an examination of how Pesach reflects Jewish beliefs about redemption. You will need to focus for this and apply the skills that you have developed so far:

1. **Begin with a list of indicative content. Perhaps discuss this as a group. It does not need to be in any order.**

2. **Develop the list using examples.**

3. **Now consider in which order you would like to explain the information.**

4. **Then write out your plan, under timed conditions, remembering the principles of explaining with evidence and/or examples.**

Use this technique as revision for each of the topic areas that you have studied. The basic technique of planning answers helps even when time is short and you cannot complete every essay.

Issues for analysis and evaluation

The extent to which Pesach is the central festival within Judaism

Pesach is certainly one of the most popular festivals, and the fact that it is celebrated by so many, including non-observant Jews, underlines its centrality as a festival which unites the Jewish community across the world. Its celebration in the home, by eating a special symbolic meal, ensures that the traditions and values of the faith can be nurtured and passed down to the younger generations.

It has great significance since it commemorates the time when the Jewish people escaped from slavery in Egypt and entered into the covenant relationship with God at Mount Sinai. It was this act that established them as a nation. Jews remember God as their protector and redeemer, which is central to their relationship with God.

Not only does Pesach commemorate the historical redemption of the Israelites from Egypt, but it also looks forward to the spiritual redemption of the world under the rule of God, at the arrival of the Messiah. This idea of spiritual redemption at Pesach is demonstrated by the idea that each subsequent generation of Jews is obliged to immerse themselves in the Exodus experience. Melanie J. Wright expresses this notion in the following way: 'Each generation of participants is encouraged to regard itself as standing on the edge of redemption, emphasising the important links between the sense of history and contemporary identity with the Jewish people.'

The seder itself includes many allusions to the coming of the Messiah. One of the most significant parts of the ritual comes at the end of the meal when a cup of wine is filled, and a blessing said over it. The cup of wine is set aside for the prophet Elijah, who, it is believed, is the forerunner of the Messiah, and is supposed to come at Pesach in order to do this. At this point the front door of the house is also opened for a short while. Both the offering of wine and the opening of the door are marks of hospitality for Elijah, in the hope that this will be the night when the world will be redeemed by God.

There are other festivals which have equal claims. Rosh Hashanah is a serious, solemn time for reviewing the deeds of the past year and repenting. It is important to put right one's relationships with other people when they have faltered, as well as preparing for God's judgement. This festival is at the height of Jewish spirituality, as well as encouraging a deeper understanding of the nature of humanity.

Yom Kippur could be considered to be the central festival because of its emphasis upon reconciliation. It is the holiest day of the Jewish year, and many Jews who do not normally attend the synagogue will be there on the day. It brings the joy of forgiveness through repentance, and is important as a time for the confession of sins and making a fresh start.

Those who would conclude that Pesach is the central festival in Judaism would do so on the basis of its link to the Mosaic covenant and its indication of, and exploration of, the relationship between God and human beings within this covenant. However, perhaps the best conclusion is that it is just one of the central festivals within Judaism as for other equally convincing reasons, the festivals of Rosh Hashanah and Yom Kippur could make the very same claim.

This section covers AO2 content and skills

Specification content

The extent to which Pesach is the central festival within Judaism.

AO2 Activity *Possible lines of argument*

Listed below are some conclusions that could be drawn from the AO2 reasoning in the accompanying text:

1. The way in which Pesach is celebrated ensures that the traditions and rituals of the festival are passed down to the younger generations.

2. It commemorates a significant event from the history of the Jews when they entered into the covenant relationship with God.

3. It is a festival that continues to have relevance for the present as well as for the future.

4. The theme of Rosh Hashanah, on the other hand, is also a serious and important one.

5. Other festivals, such as Yom Kippur, for example, are equally as popular and well attended.

Consider each of the conclusions drawn above and collect evidence and examples to support each argument from the AO1 and AO2 material studied in this section. Select one conclusion that you think is most convincing and explain why it is so. Now contrast this with the weakest conclusion in the list, justifying your argument with clear reasoning and evidence.

Specification content

Whether the notion of redemption
has any relevance for Judaism today.

Whether the notion of redemption has any relevance for Judaism today

The theme of redemption is one which finds expression in all manner of Jewish ritual and worship. The daily prayer, the Amidah, includes requests that spiritual and physical needs be met including the final redemption by the Messiah. Likewise, the Shema contains an expression of hope of the coming age when the world will be redeemed under God's command.

Redemption is at the heart of the festival of Pesach. As well as physical redemption, the festival also represents spiritual redemption: the Jews were no longer slaves to another nation, and neither were they bound to pagan gods. It was in this state of freedom that Moses was able to deliver God's message to the Jewish people, and to offer them the hope of freedom, and the promise of redemption.

Not only does Pesach commemorate the historical redemption of the Israelites from Egypt, but it also looks forward to the redemption of the world under the rule of God, with the ritual of the Cup of Elijah. This is a significant ritual that occurs at the end of the seder meal when a cup is filled with wine, and a blessing said over it. The cup of wine is set aside for the prophet Elijah, who, it is believed, is the forerunner of the Messiah, and is supposed to come at Pesach in order to do this. At this point the front door of the house is also opened for a short while. Both the offering of wine and the opening of the door are marks of hospitality for Elijah, in the hope that this will be the night when the world will be redeemed by God.

The seder meal is a symbolic re-enactment of the events of the Exodus, and the different elements place great emphasis upon redemption and hope for the future.

Different groups within Judaism offer varying perspectives about future redemption. Orthodox Jews believe in a personal Messiah, who will come at the time of God's choosing, and who will lead all humanity back to God.

Reform Jews view redemption in a different way; they reject the notion of a personal Messiah, and place their belief in the notion that they have been chosen to spread the monotheistic truth and morality over all the earth. Reform Jews believe that it is their role to live in such a way as to demonstrate God's will for humankind, and as such humanity would accomplish its own redemption.

Redemption also has its place as an important goal within the mystical branch of Judaism. Only after death can a person hope that their soul will reach a complete and permanent state of devekut with God, and the final state of bliss will not be achieved until the redemption, after the coming of the Messiah, when all just Jews will live together eternally in the state of devekut.

In the light of all the above, it would be wrong to say that redemption has no value for followers of Judaism today as it is clearly a central theme that runs throughout the history of Judaism and is remembered within the festivals. Perhaps the best conclusion would be to argue that the idea of redemption is relevant today in that it is part of the future of Judaism when one considers the significance of the phrase 'next year in Jerusalem' and the beliefs that surround the Messianic Age. In this sense, the teaching of redemption in Judaism remains relevant in an indirect way as indicated by the festival observances and therefore functions as a crucial reminder for all involved of the final piece of the long saga of the Jewish people and making it a very relevant concept for Judaism today.

AO2 Activity *Possible lines of argument*

Listed below are some conclusions that could be drawn from the AO2 reasoning in the accompanying text:

1. Redemption is an important theme within Jewish ritual and worship.

2. Redemption is the theme at the heart of the celebration of Pesach.

3. Orthodox Jews believe in future redemption with the arrival of a personal Messiah.

4. Redemption has a different emphasis within Reform Judaism.

5. The mystical branch of Judaism emphasises the importance of redemption as an important goal that can only be achieved by attaining devekut.

Consider each of the conclusions drawn above and collect evidence and examples to support each argument from the AO1 and AO2 material studied in this section. Select one conclusion that you think is most convincing and explain why it is so. Now contrast this with the weakest conclusion in the list, justifying your argument with clear reasoning and evidence.

AO2 Developing skills

It is now time to reflect upon the information that has been covered so far. It is also important to consider how what you have learned can be focused and used for examination-style answers by practising the skills associated with AO2.

Assessment objective 2 (AO2) involves 'analysis' and 'evaluation'. The terms may be obvious but it is crucial to be familiar with how certain skills demonstrate these terms, and also, how the performance of these skills are measured (see generic band descriptors Band 5 for AS AO2).

Obviously, an answer is placed within an appropriate band descriptor depending upon how well the answer performs, ranging from excellent, good, satisfactory, basic/limited to very limited.

You are now nearing the end of this section of the course. From now on the task will have only instructions with no examples; however, using the skills you have developed in completing the earlier tasks, you should be able to apply what you have learned to do and complete this successfully.

▶ **Your new task is this:** you will have to write a response under timed conditions to a question requiring an evaluation of the claim that Pesach is the central festival within Judaism. You will need to focus for this and apply the skills that you have developed so far:

> 1. **Begin with a list of indicative content. Perhaps discuss this as a group. It does not need to be in any order. Remember, this is evaluation, so you need different lines of argument. The easiest way is to use the 'support' and 'against' headings.**

> 2. **Develop the list using examples.**

> 3. **Now consider in which order you would like to explain the information.**

> 4. **Then write out your plan, under timed conditions, remembering to apply the principles of evaluation by making sure that you: identify issues clearly; present accurate views of others making sure that you comment on the views presented; reach an overall personal judgement.**

Use this technique as revision for each of the topic areas that you have studied. The basic technique of planning answers helps even when time is short and you cannot complete every essay.

Specification content

The origins of the rituals of these festivals and their significance; the extent to which these festivals are observed; the impact and purpose of their observance.

quickfire

4.18 What is the name of the Jewish New Year Festival?

quickfire

4.19 Which Jewish festival is also known as the Day of Atonement?

Key terms

Atonement: the act of making up for a wrongdoing or sin

Rosh Hashanah: meaning 'the Head of the Year'; the Jewish New Year Festival

Yom Kippur: the Day of Atonement

quickfire

4.20 What name is given to the period of time between Rosh Hashanah and Yom Kippur?

Specification content

Rosh Hashanah. The importance of the machzor and the amendments to the Amidah as confirming unity and identity of the Jewish people.

Key term

Machzor: a special prayer book for Rosh Hashanah and Yom Kippur

C: Rosh Hashanah and Yom Kippur

Introduction

The festivals of **Rosh Hashanah** (meaning 'the Head of the Year') and **Yom Kippur** (Day of Atonement) are called High Holy Days as they are among the most important and holiest days of the Jewish year. Although they are two separate festivals, rabbinic tradition has created a strong link between them.

Rosh Hashanah is the Jewish New Year Festival that occurs on the first and second days of the Jewish month of Tishri. It is the anniversary of the day when God created Adam and Eve. Jews believe that on this day, God judges all people for the deeds that they have carried out in the past year, and writes the names in one of three books. Rabbi Yohanan, writing in the 3rd century BCE describes them thus:

'Three books are opened in Heaven on Rosh Hashanah, one for the completely wicked, one for the completely righteous and one for those in between. The completely righteous are immediately inscribed in the book of life. The completely wicked are immediately inscribed in the book of death. The fate of those in between is suspended until Yom Kippur. If they do well, they are inscribed in the book of life; if not, in the book of death.' (Mishnah Rosh Hashanah 16b)

There are ten days between Rosh Hashanah and the festival of Yom Kippur, which are known as the Ten Days of Returning. It is during this period that Jews are provided with the opportunity to consider their behaviour in the past year and to repent. Indeed, Rabbi Soloveitchik, a 20th-century Jewish philosopher, proposed that true repentance begins with a confession: '... and a tormented soul finds peace in confessing'. During this time, Jews will make the effort to contact anyone they might have wronged in the past year in order to ask for their forgiveness. At the same time, prayers are inserted into the order of worship that emphasise teshuvah (repentance and returning to God).

In summary:

- At Rosh Hashanah, Jews believe that God judges all people for their deeds during the previous year.
- Ten days later at Yom Kippur, God's decisions are finalised.
- The two festivals are linked by the themes of judgement, repentance and **atonement**.
- They are considered to be important festivals because their main focus is on people and their relationship with God.

Rosh Hashanah

C.M. Pilkington claims that: 'It could well be argued that to understand the High Holy Days is to understand Judaism. Repentance and atonement stand at the height of Jewish spiritual life. Many would say ... that they lie at the heart of human life in general. Certainly, the need to face up to mistakes, to let go of resentments, to feel that others have let go of resentments towards you, and to feel the genuine chance of a fresh start are vital parts of much experience. From the Jewish point of view, the designer of the whole enterprise is the one to whom to turn for such renewal.'

Pilkington continues by noting that the liturgy of Rosh Hashanah has less of a focus on human beings as sinners and more on God as king. Sin is scarcely mentioned in fact. The Reform **Machzor** says, 'On New Year we acknowledge Him as king; may He reign over us and within us.'

One might expect the liturgy to start with the cleansing of sins before a person is presented in a state of purity to God. However, this is not the case; first is the need to restore 'a sense of God in the world, the sense of the spiritual that is a prerequisite for atonement' (Pilkington).

For many Jews, the month preceding Rosh Hashanah is a time of preparation for the spiritual demands of the High Holy Days that are to follow. Preparation takes the form of reciting selichot (prayers for forgiveness). The aim of selichot is to encourage self-examination, and to raise one's spiritual awareness. On the eve of Rosh Hashanah, the last day of the old year, special selichot are said at the synagogue at a service that is held at midnight. All members of the Jewish community are represented, and the rabbi preaches a sermon.

The actual selichot are a collection of Torah verses and poems, which focus on asking God for forgiveness on both a personal and communal level. However, the central point of the service is the recitation of the 'Thirteen Attributes of Mercy', which it is believed God revealed to Moses on Mount Sinai as a means by which the people could beg for compassion when required. They are based upon Exodus 34:6–7:

'The Lord, the Lord, a God merciful and gracious, slow to anger, and abounding in steadfast love and faithfulness, keeping steadfast love for thousands, forgiving iniquity and transgressions and sin ...'

According to rabbinic tradition, the Thirteen Attributes are as follows:

1. The Lord (Adonai) – God is merciful before a person sins
2. The Lord (Adonai) – God is merciful to sinners
3. God (El) – this name for God denotes might, strength and power
4. Compassionate
5. Gracious
6. Slow to anger
7. Abundant in goodness
8. Abundant in truth
9. Merciful
10. Forgiver of iniquity
11. Forgiver of those who sin
12. Forgiver of errors (sins committed through thoughtlessness)
13. One who cleanses (wiping away the sins of those who repent).

It is traditional to wear white at Rosh Hashanah, and this comes from the belief that as it is the Day of Judgement, Jews wish to present themselves before God as being clean of all sin. Alan Unterman refers to the following passage from the Talmud by way of explanation:

'The usual practice is for a man who is to be tried in court to dress in black and let his beard grow, since he does not know how his case will go. But Israel is not so. Instead they wear white, trim their beards, eat, drink and rejoice. For they know the Holy One will perform miracles for them.'

At the synagogue, the covers on the bimah, ark and lectern are also draped in white.

The festival of Rosh Hashanah starts with prayers at the evening synagogue service. During the High Holy Days, a special prayer book called the machzor takes the place of the siddur. The machzor is important as it offers additional prayers that focus on the themes of malkhiyot ('Kingship'), zikhronot ('Remembrances'), and shofarot ('shofar blasts'). The prayers emphasise the sovereignty of God: a God who sits in judgement over the world; who is asked to accept, once again, the kingship of the world. This includes asking God to remember humankind, as well as acting as a reminder to all Jews that they must not forget the things which God has done for them. The prayers also focus on the Torah and the Promised Land.

quickfire

4.21 What are 'selichot'?

Key quote

For not listening to Your voice within us

For denying the needs of our soul

For making this world a god

Forgive us, pardon us and grant atonement ...

(Extract from a selichot prayer)

Key terms

El: name for God denoting might, strength and power

Iniquity: sinfulness

Lectern: a stand with a sloping surface for holding a book; used for someone to read or preach from

Malkhiyot: kingship

Selichot: prayers for forgiveness

Sermon: a talk on a religious or moral subject

Shofarot: the blasts on the shofar

Zikhronot : remembrances

Key quote

Though your sins are like scarlet, they shall be as white as snow. (Isaiah 1:18)

quickfire

4.22 Note down the three significant themes of the machzor.

At Rosh Hashanah, the usual format of the daily prayer known as the Amidah is also recited with some amendments including references to God's kingship, remembrance and shofarot. The order of the three additional themes and the relationship between them is explained by Rabbi Reuven Hammer:

'We accept God as our ruler, we ask to be "remembered" by God, and we declare our desire for redemption – for individual and national freedom – by the sounding of the shofarot.'

On leaving the synagogue, Jews bless each other with the words 'May you be written down for a good year'; these words making reference to God's judgement. Jews believe that God balances a person's good deeds over the last year against their bad deeds, and decides what the next year will be like for them. It is believed that God sets these things out in the Book of Life, which is finalised on Yom Kippur.

The high point of Rosh Hashanah is the blowing of the **shofar** at the morning service. Unlike during the month preceding the festival, when only a few notes are sounded, on Rosh Hashanah itself 100 notes are blown.

The festival is also observed at home. It is customary to have round **challot** rather than the usual plaited ones during the festive meal. It has been said that it is round to represent a crown, thus reflecting the coronation of God as king of the world. Its shape also symbolises the cycle of life and the cycle of the year.

De Lange says that it is within the home that 'the sweetness of the festival comes out'. For example, challot are baked with raisins in the dough, and the top is brushed with honey to symbolise the 'sweet new year'. Likewise, apples dipped in honey are also eaten at this time.

Another custom is the eating of a new fruit (one that has not been eaten during the past season). It is usually a pomegranate because it is said that this fruit contains 613 seeds, just as there are 613 mitzvot. Another suggestion as to the reason for this tradition is that Jews wish that their good deeds in the new year will be as many as the seeds of the pomegranate.

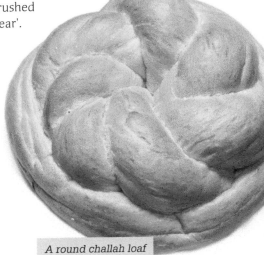

A round challah loaf

Key terms

Challot: special loaves of bread used on Shabbat and festivals

Shofar: a ram's horn trumpet

quickfire

4.23 Give two reasons for the eating of a pomegranate at Rosh Hashanah.

Key quote

Blessed are you, Lord our God, King of the universe, who creates the fruit of the tree. May it be Your will to renew for us a good and sweet new year. (**Words spoken before eating a piece of apple dipped in honey.**)

It is customary to eat apple slices dipped in honey at Rosh Hashanah

Another tradition at Rosh Hashanah is the eating of pomegranates

The significance of the shofar in the Hebrew scriptures

A shofar is a trumpet made from a ram's horn, and is one of the earliest musical instruments. It was developed by the early Hebrews.

The high point of Rosh Hashanah is the blowing of the shofar at the morning service. This ritual originates in Leviticus 23:24, which commands, 'Say to the Israelites: "On the first day of the seventh month you are to have a day of Sabbath rest, a sacred assembly commemorated with trumpet blasts"'. The fact that the shofar is created from a ram's horn is significant as it calls to mind the time when Abraham showed absolute faith in God and was prepared to sacrifice his son Isaac on God's command. At the very last minute, however, God intervened and spared Isaac's life by providing a ram for sacrifice.

The shofar has played a significant part in Jewish history. For example, it was sounded when the Jews entered into the covenant with God at Mount Sinai and accepted the Torah: 'As the sound of the trumpet grew louder and louder, Moses spoke and the voice of God answered him' (Exodus 19:19). The sound of the shofar in the synagogue therefore reminds Jews of their responsibility to keep God's commandments. It was also used during worship at the Temple in Jerusalem, and is a reminder for Jews to pray for the rebuilding of God's holy place.

The notes that are sounded at Rosh Hashanah have three distinct qualities. The first, *tekiah*, is a single long note that calls for attention; the second, *shevarim* consists of three shorter notes; and the third, *teruah*, nine or more very short notes blown in staccato. There is also a final blast that lasts for ten seconds. It has been suggested that the sounds all represent different types of crying, expressing the yearning of the soul calling out to be reunited with God.

Repentance is the theme, and the blasts mark the start of the period known as the Ten Days of Returning. Just as the prophets called out to the Jewish people to improve their ways, so the shofar calls out to the Jews of today. They are reminded that God does not wish to punish, but to provide an opportunity for them to put right the things that have been wrong during the year gone by.

Maimonides interpreted the use of the shofar as a device to wake the people from their slumber; to remind them that they need to make a new start with God at the centre of their lives: 'Awake sleepers from your sleep ... Scrutinise your deeds and return to repentance and remember your creator ... Look to your souls, better your ways and deeds.' (Hilchot Teshuvah)

Specification content

The significance of the shofar horn in the Hebrew scriptures.

Key quote

The great shofar is sounded; a gentle whisper is heard; the angels quaking with fear, declare: 'The day of judgement is here ... so dost thou make all living souls pass before thee; thou does count and number thy creatures, fixing their lifetime and inscribing their destiny.'
(Rosh Hashanah prayer)

quickfire

4.24 What is a 'shofar'?

Key terms

Shevarim: three short notes sounded on the shofar

Tekiah: a single long note sounded on the shofar

Teruah: nine or more very short notes blown in staccato on the shofar

A shofar

Specification content

The meaning and significance
of tashlikh.

Key terms

Pagan: religious beliefs other than
those of major religions

Tashlikh: meaning 'to cast'; the ritual
of symbolically casting away the sins
of the previous year

quickpire

4.25 Describe the ritual of tashlikh.

Tashlikh

At Rosh Hashanah, many
traditional Jewish communities
observe a ritual called **tashlikh**
(literally meaning 'to cast') which
involves the symbolic casting
away of the sins of the previous
year by tossing pieces of bread
into a body of flowing water. The
origin of tashlikh is unknown,
but it appears to have developed
from a biblical passage in Micah
7:19 that says, 'And you will cast
all their sins into the depths of the
sea'. De Lange notes that there
is no mention of this practice

The ritual of tashlikh

before the fifteenth century, and as such, it may represent a Jewish adaptation of
a **pagan** ritual.

In addition to throwing bread into the water, many Jews will shake their clothes,
and empty their pockets of crumbs as a symbol of casting off every trace of sin.
This event usually takes place following the afternoon service on the first day of
Rosh Hashanah. However, if the first day of the festival falls on Shabbat, it will be
moved to the Sunday.

> **AO1 Activity**
>
> It is important to be able to identify the Rosh Hashanah rituals as well as the
> meanings behind each one. A good way to do this is to create a table with
> two columns entitled ritual and significance. Use the table to note down the
> practices that are traditionally observed at this festival, whilst also noting the
> meaning (significance) for each one in the adjacent column.

Specification content

Yom Kippur. Kol Nidrei. The challenge
of a 25-hour fast and its value.

Key quote

Create in me a clean heart, O God
and put a new and right spirit
within me. (Psalm 51:10)

Key term

Shabbat Shuvah: Sabbath of
Returning

Yom Kippur

The period of time from Rosh Hashanah to Yom Kippur is known as the Ten Days
of Returning, and is focused upon the theme of repentance. The Hebrew word for
repentance is 'teshuvah' that literally means 'returning'.

The Shabbat that falls during this week is called **Shabbat Shuvah**, and the
scriptural reading on this day comes from Hosea 14, and urges the Jews to turn to
God:

'Return, Israel, to the Lord your God.

Your sins have been your downfall.

Take words with you

And return to the Lord.

Say to him:

"Forgive all our sins and receive us graciously."'

(Hosea 14:1–2)

This period of ten days provides the opportunity for each Jew to take stock of their
life. Jews believe that God does not forgive a wrong done to another person unless
one has first asked that person for forgiveness. During this time therefore, Jews try
to contact anyone they might have wronged, to ask them for forgiveness.

The day before Yom Kippur is a time of preparation. Some families give donations to charity as this is a time of the year when concern for the poor is emphasised. This goes back to the time of the Temple when there was a ceremony in which a goat was driven out of Jerusalem after the sins of the people had been symbolically transferred to it. It was a symbol of the sins of the past year being cleaned away, leaving a clean slate for the New Year. This was known as the scapegoat.

After the Temple in Jerusalem was destroyed, the custom developed of slaughtering a chicken instead and giving it to the poor for the festive meal held before Yom Kippur. Some very Orthodox Jews still do this, but most give money to charity instead. This act shows that people wish to make amends for the wrong that they have done. Sometimes men visit the mikveh as a symbol of spiritual cleansing. It is the only time of the year when men are obliged to go.

On the eve of Yom Kippur, there is a special meal. It is a very festive event that is followed, in contrast, by a 25-hour fast. As well as abstaining from food and drink during this time, Jews will refrain from bathing in a luxurious way, using perfume, having sex and wearing leather shoes.

The 25-hour fast can be a challenge for many Jews; however, the spiritual benefits are considered to outweigh the difficulties. The fast has been interpreted in a number of ways. For example, the discomfort that one feels during the fast atones for every sin committed that hasn't been atoned for in another way. Also, the point of the fast is not to punish, but to take a person's mind off physical needs so that they are able to concentrate on spiritual matters. Fasting can also show that one is sincere in asking for forgiveness. It also encourages self-discipline, which is much needed at the New Year when thinking about the resolutions that need to be kept.

After the meal, and before the evening prayers begin, many Jews change their clothing. They do not wear leather shoes as this is a symbol of luxury, and the men might put on a white garment called a kittel. This symbolises purity and repentance as a verse in the book of the prophet Isaiah says: 'Even if your sins will be as red as scarlet they will become as white as snow.' (Isaiah 1:18) The women will wear white dresses, or clothes that are predominantly white for the same reason. Gold jewellery is also removed.

Just before sunset, the candles are lit and the holy day begins.

The five services of Yom Kippur

Yom Kippur is considered to be the most important and holiest festival in the Jewish calendar. As a result, many Jews who do not go to the synagogue at all during the rest of the year will take part and attend the synagogue on this day. De Lange notes that there is a popular expression 'a Yom Kippur Jew', meaning one who attends the synagogue only once a year.

It is an important festival because it is the day when each individual has the opportunity to make themselves right with God by repenting for all the bad things done, and making amends. As Leviticus 16:29–30 states:

'In the seventh month, on the tenth day of the month, you shall afflict your souls, and you shall not do any work … For on that day he shall provide atonement for you to cleanse you from all your sins before the Lord.'

Five services are held at the synagogue on this day, and in older times, Jews would stay there for the whole 25 hours of the fast. Nowadays there is a break for the night, as well as a short interlude in the afternoon.

The white kittel will be worn, a symbol explained by Franz Rosenzweig: 'Man is utterly alone on the day of his death, when he is clothed in his shroud, and in the prayers of these days he is also alone. They too set him, lonely and naked, straight before the throne of God.'

Key terms

Kittel: a white ceremonial robe

Scapegoat: the goat upon which the sins of the people were transferred by the Jewish high priest

A kittel

Key quote

This is the fast I desire:
To unlock fetters of wickedness,
And untie the cords of the yoke
To let the oppressed go free;
To break off every yoke.
(Isaiah 58:6)

The opening service of Yom Kippur is called **Kol Nidrei**, named after a part of the liturgy that is chanted during the service. The Kol Nidrei declaration takes the form of a statement that all vows that will be uttered in the coming year are to be declared null and void:

'All vows and oaths, all promises and obligations, all renunciations and responses, that we shall make from this Yom Kippur to the next ... all of them we retract. May we be absolved of them all, may we be released from them all, may they be null and void, may they be of no effect. May these vows not be vows, may these oaths not be oaths, may these responses not be responses.'

The declaration only applies to religious vows, and it has its background at times in history when many Jews had been forced to live outwardly as Christians by swearing vows to be faithful to the church. Nowadays the prayer is an acknowledgement that one can't always keep the promises that are made to God. However, they are also remembering the times in history when Jews took great risks by living as Jews. The prayers act as a review of Jewish history and hope for the messianic future.

The morning service is followed by **Musaf**, an additional service that includes a step-by-step account of the Temple procedure, including details of the ritual involving the goat carrying the sins of the people away (Leviticus 16). The aim of the service is to release people from feeling guilty for the past so that they can feel free to start again.

The afternoon service includes the reading of the Book of Jonah with its powerful theme of repentance.

The day's worship concludes with **Neilah**, 'the closing of the gates'. It is unique to Yom Kippur, and is the final service before the decrees made by God on Rosh Hashanah are sealed. Throughout this service, the doors of the Ark, symbolising the gates of heaven, remain open. At the end of the Neilah, each person makes three declarations of faith:

'Hear O Israel, the Lord is our God, the Lord is One.' This is the daily declaration of God's oneness and it is said once.

'Blessed is the name of His glorious kingdom forever and ever.' This is said three times.

'The Lord is God.' This is said seven times.

When nightfall comes, there is a single blast on the shofar that announces that the fast is now over. At home, the **havdalah** ceremony is performed and the fast broken.

quickfire

4.26 What is the name of the opening service of Yom Kippur?

Key term

Havdalah: a ceremony performed at the end of Shabbat and festivals

Kol Nidrei: meaning 'annulment of vows'

Musaf: a fourth prayer that is added on Shabbat and festivals

Neilah: literally meaning 'the closing of the gates'; the final prayer on Yom Kippur

quickfire

4.27 What is the name of the final service held on Yom Kippur?

Key quote

Yom Kippur is a day of awe. Yet the Talmud calls it one of the most joyous days of the year ... God has given us free will and thus the strength to turn from bad to good. He has granted us a Day of Atonement, and thus the chance ... to find forgiveness. (Rabbi Jonathan Sacks)

AO1 Activity

Create a running order of the events that take place during the festival of Yom Kippur. Add brief explanations, where appropriate, for the rituals and practices that occur.

Study tip

Even though there is a strong link between Rosh Hashanah and Yom Kippur, it is vital that you remember that they are separate festivals. When answering questions on one, the other, or both, make sure that you do not confuse the two.

AO1 Activity

Create flash cards based upon the rituals of Rosh Hashanah and Yom Kippur. They can be used for two purposes: (1) To test yourself on the meanings behind the rituals, and (2) to identify in which of the two festivals they can be found.

AO1 Developing skills

It is now time to reflect upon the information that has been covered so far. It is also important to consider how what you have learned can be focused and used for examination-style answers by practising the skills associated with AO1.

Assessment objective 1 (AO1) involves demonstrating knowledge and understanding. The terms 'knowledge' and 'understanding' are obvious but it is crucial to be familiar with how certain skills demonstrate these terms, and also, how the performance of these skills is measured (see generic band descriptors Band 5 for AS AO1).

You are now nearing the end of this section of the course. From now on the task will have only instructions with no examples; however, using the skills you have developed in completing the earlier tasks, you should be able to apply what you have learned to do and complete this successfully.

▶ **Your new task is this:** you will have to write another response under timed conditions to a question requiring an examination of the rituals of Rosh Hashanah and their significance. You will need to do the same as your last AO1 Developing skills task but with some further development. This time there is a fifth point to help you improve the quality of your answers.

> 1. **Begin with a list of indicative content. Perhaps discuss this as a group. It does not need to be in any order.**

> 2. **Develop the list using examples.**

> 3. **Now consider in which order you would like to explain the information.**

> 4. **Then write out your plan, under timed conditions, remembering the principles of explaining with evidence and/or examples.**

> 5. **Use the band descriptors to mark your own answer, considering carefully the descriptors. Then ask someone else to read your answer and see if they can help you improve it in any way.**

Use this technique as revision for each of the topic areas that you have studied. Swap and compare answers to improve your own.

Key skills

Knowledge involves:

Selection of a range of (thorough) accurate and relevant information that is directly related to the specific demands of the question.

This means you choose the correct information relevant to the question set NOT the topic area. You will have to think and focus on selecting key information and NOT writing everything you know about the topic area.

Understanding involves:

Explanation that is extensive, demonstrating depth and/or breadth with excellent use of evidence and examples including (where appropriate) thorough and accurate supporting use of sacred texts, sources of wisdom and specialist language.

This means that you demonstrate that you understand something by being able to illustrate and expand your points through examples/supporting evidence in a personal way and NOT repeat chunks from a textbook (known as rote learning).

Further application of skills:

Go through the topic areas in this section and create some bullet lists of key points from key areas. For each one, provide further elaboration and explanation through the use of evidence and examples.

**This section covers AO2
content and skills**

Specification content

Whether Jewish festivals are effective in reinforcing Jewish identity.

AO2 Activity *Possible lines of argument*

Listed below are some conclusions that could be drawn from the AO2 reasoning in the accompanying text:

1. Jewish identity is more usually linked to lifestyle practices.

2. The weekly celebration of Shabbat is synonymous with Jewish identity.

3. Certain festivals within the Jewish year are considered to be so significant that they even bring those Jews who are usually non-observant back to the synagogue.

4. Festivals bring the Jewish community together and act, through the liturgy, as reminders of the important themes that underpin Jewish identity.

5. There is no single accepted definition as to what makes a person Jewish.

Consider each of the conclusions drawn above and collect evidence and examples to support each argument from the AO1 and AO2 material studied in this section. Select one conclusion that you think is most convincing and explain why it is so. Now contrast this with the weakest conclusion in the list, justifying your argument with clear reasoning and evidence.

Issues for analysis and evaluation

Whether Jewish festivals are effective in reinforcing Jewish identity

Judaism has been described as a 'lifestyle', which suggests that Jewish identity is more closely linked to the rituals and practices that occur on a daily or weekly basis rather than the things that occur during festival celebrations. Everyday routines such as the Orthodox Jewish practice of keeping the kosher food laws might be seen as a more effective way to reinforce one's Jewish identity.

The weekly festival of Shabbat, however, is regarded by many as the centrepiece of Jewish life, and is synonymous with Jewish identity. It is a day of rest and celebration, whereby Jews follow the commandment of God to desist from work.

Nevertheless, it could be argued that festivals *are* significant in reinforcing Jewish identity by virtue of the fact that those Jews who are usually non-observant, and who do not usually attend the synagogue on a regular basis, make a special effort for Yom Kippur. This could provide the justification for saying that they are definitely effective if they bring otherwise non-observant Jews back to the synagogue.

Festivals, by their very nature, allow Jews to meet with fellow believers, and thus to be reminded of the common themes which underpin Jewish identity. The use of the machzor in place of the siddur during Rosh Hashanah and Yom Kippur, as well as the amendments to the Amidah at this time both emphasise the sovereignty of God; a God who sits in judgement over the world; who is asked to accept, once again, the kingship of the world. This includes asking God to remember humankind, as well as acting as a reminder to all Jews that they must not forget the things which God has done for them. The prayers also focus on the Torah and the Promised Land.

Likewise, one of the purposes of the Kol Nidrei is to act as reminder of the times in history when Jews took great risks by living as Jews. The prayer act as a review of Jewish history, and includes hope for the messianic future, an important theme which reinforces Jewish identity.

In conclusion, we also need to note that there is no clear-cut way by which to define Jewishness. For some it is to be born to a Jewish mother; for others it is a national identity. Without a clear definition, it can be difficult to judge the effectiveness of the Jewish festivals in reinforcing Jewish identity.

Overall, the issue is not whether or not the festivals are the only way of stating Jewish identity but rather that they are effective means of reinforcing Jewish identity. Seen in this light, despite there being very many other ways of acknowledging Jewish identity, it could be argued that the best possible solution to this debate is to recognise the role of festivals in contributing towards Jewish identity in conjunction with other elements of Judaism. In defence of this, it can be clearly seen from studying festivals such as Pesach, Rosh Hashanah and Yom Kippur that they celebrate Jewish identity through reminding Jews of their relationship with God and indirectly, or directly, with the covenants. This means, therefore, that Jewish festivals can be viewed as an effective means of reinforcing Jewish identity.

Whether the regular acknowledgement of sins and penitence is an admission of failure in spiritual development

Repentance and atonement stand at the centre of Jewish spiritual life, indeed it can be said that this reflects a need that can be found in human life in general.

The festivals of Rosh Hashanah and Yom Kippur make time on a regular yearly basis for Jews to reflect specifically upon their deeds of the past year, and to be awarded the opportunity to put things right; to wipe the slate clean; to start again. This is a very human need and is by no means a sign of failure in spiritual development.

Indeed the liturgy, in preparation for the High Holy Days, is designed to provide the means by which a Jew's spiritual awareness can be raised through a period of self-examination: therefore, there is an acknowledgment within Judaism that an opportunity to admit to one's sins and practise repentance is required on a regular basis. The selichot, for example, work on a communal as well as an individual level.

The focus on sins and penitence also serves another purpose: that of striving to restore, as Pilkington says, 'a sense of God in the world': actually acting to bring a person closer to God. The Reform Machzor says, 'On New Year we acknowledge Him as king; may He reign over us and within us'. Thus Jews are required to restore the sense of the spiritual before atonement can be achieved.

Spiritual development can take many forms. For many Jews it means developing a sense of godliness that can be displayed through the acts of everyday living, such as adhering to the mitzvot, for example. Indeed Jews would acknowledge that they are inherently connected to God through the covenant made with Abraham. And yet, whilst they believe that God is finite, they readily acknowledge that humans are limited and would never be capable of achieving perfection in either their spiritual or non-spiritual daily lives.

Hasidic Jews, in particular, whilst striving for devekut, would not accept that the acknowledgement of sins and penitence is an admission of failure in spiritual development, rather than that it is a good habit to cultivate in order to maintain an attachment to God which allows a person to have God always at the forefront of their mind in whatever they are doing. In this case, it would be the non-acknowledgement of one's sins and the lack of an expression of regret that would be considered to be a failure in spiritual development.

In conclusion, there might be a question as to what is meant by the term 'regular'. It could be considered as meaningless if there was never any true intention to pay anything other than lip service to the acknowledgement of sin. And if penitence were not truly sought after then that indeed might be considered to be a failure in spiritual development.

However, this all seems very negative and possibly the best solution would be to argue that the whole purpose of the regular acknowledgement of sins and practices of penitence within Judaism is not meant to focus ultimately on failure. Rather, such practices and acknowledgements in acknowledging failure simultaneously develop the humility within a follower of Judaism that enables the greater picture of the maintenance of the Jewish covenant relationship with God to be recognised and celebrated. This is, surely, the end purpose of acknowledging sins and acts of penitence in that it reminds Jews of this and therefore can only serve to enhance spiritual development.

Specification content

Whether the regular acknowledgement of sins and penitence for them is an admission of failure in spiritual development.

AO2 Activity *Possible lines of argument*

Listed below are some conclusions that could be drawn from the AO2 reasoning in the accompanying text:

1. Rosh Hashanah and Yom Kippur provide Jews with the opportunity to acknowledge their sins and to seek penitence on an annual basis.

2. The liturgy of the High Holy Days is focused upon self-examination, providing an opportunity for Jews to admit to sin and to achieve atonement.

3. Acknowledging sin brings people back to God.

4. Spiritual development is not based purely upon the acknowledgement of sin and penitence.

5. We need to consider what is meant by the term 'regular acknowledgement'.

Consider each of the conclusions drawn above and collect evidence and examples to support each argument from the AO1 and AO2 material studied in this section. Select one conclusion that you think is most convincing and explain why it is so. Now contrast this with the weakest conclusion in the list, justifying your argument with clear reasoning and evidence.

Key skills

Analysis involves identifying issues raised by the materials in the AO1, together with those identified in the AO2 section, and presents sustained and clear views, either of scholars or from a personal perspective ready for evaluation.

This means that it picks out key things to debate and the lines of argument presented by others or a personal point of view.

Evaluation involves considering the various implications of the issues raised based upon the evidence gleaned from analysis and provides an extensive detailed argument with a clear conclusion.

This means that the answer weighs up the various and different lines of argument analysed through individual commentary and response and arrives at a conclusion through a clear process of reasoning.

AO2 Developing skills

It is now time to reflect upon the information that has been covered so far. It is also important to consider how what you have learned can be focused and used for examination-style answers by practising the skills associated with AO2.

Assessment objective 2 (AO2) involves 'analysis' and 'evaluation'. The terms may be obvious but it is crucial to be familiar with how certain skills demonstrate these terms, and also, how the performance of these skills is measured (see generic band descriptors Band 5 for AS AO2). Obviously, an answer is placed within an appropriate band descriptor depending upon how well the answer performs, ranging from excellent, good, satisfactory, basic/limited to very limited.

You are now nearing the end of this section of the course. From now on the task will have only instructions with no examples; however, using the skills you have developed in completing the earlier tasks, you should be able to apply what you have learned to do and complete this successfully.

▶ **Your new task is this:** you will have to write another response under timed conditions to a question requiring an evaluation of whether the Jewish festivals are effective in reinforcing Jewish identity. You will need to do the same as your last AO2 Developing skills task but with some further development. This time there is a fifth point to help you improve the quality of your answers.

> 1. **Begin with a list of indicative content. Perhaps discuss this as a group. It does not need to be in any order. Remember, this is evaluation, so you need different lines of argument. The easiest way is to use the 'support' and 'against' headings.**

> 2. **Develop the list using examples.**

> 3. **Now consider in which order you would like to explain the information.**

> 4. **Then write out your plan, under timed conditions, remembering to apply the principles of evaluation by making sure that you: identify issues clearly; present accurate views of others making sure that you comment on the views presented; reach an overall personal judgement.**

> 5. **Use the band descriptors to mark your own answer, considering carefully the descriptors. Then ask someone else to read your answer and see if they can help you improve it in any way.**

Use this technique as revision for each of the topic areas that you have studied. Swap and compare answers to improve your own.

Questions and answers

Theme 1

AO1 question area: *Examining the role of Abraham in Judaism*

A strong answer

According to tradition, the Jewish religion began with a man called Abraham who entered into a special relationship, or covenant, with God. We are told that he was originally called Abram but that God changed his name to Abraham, meaning 'the father of many'. He was born in about 1800 BCE in the city of Ur, which was in an area of the Middle East which is nowadays known as Iraq. Jews regard Abraham as the first Patriarch of the Jewish people. A Patriarch is the name given to the male head of a tribe, and as Anderson points out, it was common for a cult to be traced back to a special relationship between a deity and the cult founder. **1**

Monotheism was born as a result of Abraham questioning the accepted view of the time that there were many gods. He was the first to teach that there was One God who was responsible for creating Heaven and earth. A reference to this can be found in Genesis 14:22: 'I have sworn an oath to the Lord, God Most high, Creator of Heaven and earth'. The Jewish religion of today is based upon this belief. **2**

Genesis chapter 12 tells us that God chose to make a covenant with Abraham. This became known as the Abrahamic covenant. The terms of the covenant were as follows: first that Abraham would be the father of a great nation; second that he would have lots of descendants, and third that he would be given a land to call his own: 'I will make you into a great nation, and I will bless you.' **3**

The Abrahamic covenant was known as an unconditional covenant, which means that it was made between two parties, but where only one of the parties was required to do something. The outward, physical sign of the covenant was circumcision or brit milah, which is still an important ritual for Jewish families. Abraham was commanded by God to circumcise himself and all males of his family: 'Every male among you shall be circumcised ... it will be a sign of the covenant between me and you' (Genesis 17). It is also seen as a spiritual act showing that that Jews are still subject to God's commands. **4**

Abraham's total faith in God can be seen in Genesis 22 when God asked him to sacrifice his son Isaac. God had promised Abraham that he would have descendants through his son, therefore it is difficult to understand why he should be asked to kill Isaac. However, it can be seen as a test of faith, for at the very last minute God provided a ram for sacrifice instead. **5**

In conclusion, it can be said that Abraham's faith is significant, as it was through him that God established a special relationship with the Jewish people. This relationship offered future blessing to the descendants of Abraham, and thus Abraham lived up to his new name 'the father of many' and founder of the Jewish faith. **6**

Commentary

1 This is a very good introduction that presents Abraham as the founder of Judaism. Key terms such as 'covenant' and 'patriarch' have been used correctly, and reference has been made to a scholarly opinion.

2 This paragraph makes a key link between Abraham's belief in monotheism to the fact that it is still the main tenet of the Jewish religion today.

3 This is a good paragraph which shows a clear understanding of the terms of the Abrahamic covenant.

4 The covenant has been identified correctly as one which is unconditional, and an accurate explanation of brit milah as the outward sign of the covenant has been included.

5 The incident of Abraham being told to sacrifice Isaac is presented as the ultimate test of Abraham's faith.

6 The conclusion is concise and shows the significance of the role of Abraham in Judaism.

Summative comment

Overall the answer has a good structure: introduction, conclusion, paragraphs on monotheism; the covenant and its nature; brit milah as a sign of the covenant: all with a focus upon the significance of the role of Abraham in Judaism. It also includes relevant quotations from the Torah, as well as a reference to a scholarly opinion. If anything is lacking, then a reference to the scholarly debate surrounding the concept of monotheism as an anachronistic understanding of the term would have improved it further.

AO2 question area: *Evaluating the extent of the covenant's universality*

A weak answer

It has been argued that the covenant is universal and applies to everyone. [1]

There have been earlier covenants which were universal but they failed because Adam and Noah sinned and didn't listen to God. [2]

Some Jews say that the covenant is only for them because they are God's favourites in the world and are better than everyone else. This is why they circumcise the boys in each family. [3]

In conclusion, I believe that it is far more important for Jews to eat kosher food and to go to the synagogue every Friday night. This is because all Jews do this. [4]

Commentary

[1] This is a vague introduction that is really self-evident.

[2] There is no evidence of evaluation or critical analysis: furthermore, the point made is not entirely accurate.

[3] An attempt has been made to offer a viewpoint, but it lacks meaningful analysis and is inaccurate regarding the concept of covenant in Judaism.

[4] The conclusion has no connection at all to what has been written above. A conclusion always needs to follow on from what has gone before.

Summative comment

This is a poor answer with confusion, inaccuracies and a very basic level of understanding of the issue. There is not a meaningful line of reasoning or argument that links any of the points made, and its conclusion is irrelevant.

Theme 2

AO1 question area: *Examining the nature of the Shema as an aid to faith and remembering*

A weak answer

The Shema is very important to Jews and they teach it to all members of the family, but it is very important especially for children to learn it so that they can say it at the synagogue. [1]

The Shema is said in three parts and these three parts act as an aid to faith and remembering for all Jews. Without it Jews would not know how to carry out their Jewish faith. [2]

Many Jews wear tefillin when they pray because the Shema tells them to do so. They wind leather straps around their head and one of their arms so that they are thinking of God, and have God in their hearts. [3]

Jews also use a box on the doorposts of their houses, except for the toilets. It contains the Torah and reminds them of the word of God. [4]

Jewish men also wear prayer shawls called tzitzit with fringes on them. [5]

The Shema is therefore a very important thing which acts an aid to faith and remembering for Jews. [6]

Commentary

[1] There is no definition of what the Shema is, let alone an awareness or explanation of its significance in Judaism.

[2] This is very vague indeed, merely repeating the words of the question without any accurate evidence or examples. Neither does it give any indication as to the scriptural basis for the Shema.

[3] This is the best bit of the answer so far, and it does make sense. However, it lacks a link to the relevant portion of the Shema.

[4] Even though it is accurate to say that Jewish houses have a box on the doorpost, the specialist term 'mezuzah' should have been used. Also there was a missed opportunity to quote from Deuteronomy 6:9, which would have given the practice its scriptural basis.

[5] The term 'tzitzit' is also used inaccurately as the name for a prayer shawl. This part of the answer also fails to develop the link between the Shema and the practice of wearing prayer shawls with fringes.

[6] This is not a summary at all, it merely reiterates the theme of the question, with nothing new to add, and has no depth of understanding.

Summative comment

This is a poor answer with confusion, inaccuracies and a very basic level of understanding and with no substantial explanations or examples. The summary is merely just an assertion with no explanation and therefore no evidence of understanding.

AO2 question area: *Evaluating the Shema as providing a detailed guide to Jewish belief and practice*

A strong answer

It has been said that Judaism is a way of life which is based upon a set of practices. These practices are based upon commandments from God called mitzvot, and are a requirement of the covenant relationship between God and humankind. I shall therefore be analysing the extent to which the Shema is capable of providing a detailed guide to what Jews believe and do. **1**

In the first instance, it could be suggested that a prayer which is made up of three paragraphs would not be capable of summing up the full extent of the Jewish religion as well as outlining all of its beliefs and practices. This is not to downgrade its importance, however, as it unquestionably holds a central place within Judaism. Its significance can be shown by the very fact that it is one of the first things taught to a Jewish child, and that devout Jews wish it to be the last words spoken before death. **2**

It is important to realise, however, that the principles of Jewish belief and practice have developed over a long period of time. Generations of rabbis have interpreted the mitzvot which are to be found in the Torah, and it is from the rabbinic tradition that Jews have been able to formulate their practices. **3**

However, even though we might argue that the Shema does not provide a detailed guide to Jewish belief and practice, it certainly does contain a number of mitzvot that Jews are required to keep. The words of the prayer are taken literally in the use of the tefillin, mezuzah, tallit and tzitzit, which are all items that act as aids to faith and reminders of God's commandments. However, even in this case, the Shema is not precise about what particular form each of these must take, and current Jewish practice has evolved over many thousands of years of rabbinic interpretation. **4**

In conclusion, it is clear that the Shema is important to Judaism; however, rather than acting as a guide for Jewish practice, it is perhaps better seen as having been developed for the purpose of summing up the very essence of Jewish belief that there is One God who demands total obedience from the Jewish people. **5**

Commentary

1   This is a good introductory paragraph that shows an understanding of the issue, and proposes the focus for the discussion which needs to take place.

2   A good evaluative style introducing a particular line of argument with clear examples and evidence to support it.

3   Another example has been introduced here with an explanation to support it.

4   A very good counter-argument is introduced which tackles 'the extent to which' as proposed in the introductory paragraph.

5   This is a good conclusion, demonstrating that it has considered the evidence and arrived at a judgement.

Summative comment

The answer has a very balanced approach that is well sourced and structured, with clear justification for each point of view. The conclusion is directly linked to the evidence presented and makes an evaluative judgement. Quotations and reference to examples from rabbinic tradition may have further enhanced the answer.

Theme 3

AO1 question area: *Examining the relevance of the mitzvot for Orthodox and Reform Jews*

A strong answer

Mitzvot is the Hebrew word for 'commandments', and Jews use this term when speaking of the rules that God wants them to keep as set out in the terms of the covenant made with Moses. The Torah states that the Jews must 'walk in obedience' and 'keep the Lord's commands' (Deuteronomy 10:12–13). **1**

In all, there are 613 mitzvot, and they cover every area of life; 248 of them are positive (meaning that Jews must carry them out), and 365 are negative (meaning that Jews must not do these things). Over the centuries, Jewish scholars have compiled a complete list of the mitzvot, for example Maimonides, who is probably the most notable. **2**

For the majority of Jews, the mitzvot are still relevant to their faith. However, we need to take account of the diversity that can be found regarding their relevance in modern society. **3**

For Orthodox Jews, the mitzvot are extremely relevant. This is because they believe that the Torah is the direct revelation of God, and as such that they must obey the mitzvot contained within it. The purpose of keeping the mitzvot in everyday life leads to a disciplined life. However, it must be noted that many of the mitzvot can no longer be observed as they are rules relating to the ritual that must take place in the ancient Temple that was destroyed in 70CE. **4**

Many people have questioned how rules made many thousands of years ago can still be relevant today. However, rabbis over the centuries have discussed the original mitzvot and have adapted them to meet new circumstances. A good example of this is the ethical issue of organ donation. This has been placed in the category of pikuach nefesh, a commandment to preserve life at all costs. Brian Close claims that this ability to adapt is the reason why the mitzvot have remained relevant and real in the lives of Orthodox Jews. **5**

In order to discover the mitzvot, Orthodox Jews refer to the halakhah (meaning 'the path that one walks'). Halakhah refers to the complete body of rules that Jews are obliged to follow. It has its source in the Torah, rabbinic thought and long-standing tradition. A Jew might say 'what does the halakhah say about ...?' when wondering how to interpret the mitzvot for a particular situation. **6**

Let us now turn our attention to Reform Judaism. Although Reform Jews believe the Torah contains many divine truths, and that it remains the foundation of their religion, they are different from Orthodox Jews as they consider it to be a product of human minds. In other words, they believe that God revealed the Law to Moses, but that this revelation was not dictated word for word to him. Rather that the revelation from God inspired others to write. This belief is reflected in the Pittsburgh Platform, which states that Reform Jews accept only 'moral laws'. **7**

If the Torah is the word of God interpreted by human minds, then it is possible for mistakes to be made. Reform Jews believe it is important to look at the mitzvot carefully when faced with a new challenge in modern society. Reform Jews therefore feel that it is fine to adjust the mitzvot or even to stop following some of them if it feels right. For example, Reform Jews have a different attitude to divorce from Orthodox Jews, and accept civil divorce rather than divorce through the Jewish courts. **8**

This does not mean that Reform Jews disregard the mitzvot entirely, as they still believe that it is their duty to live ethical and moral lives. Likewise, it is very important for Orthodox Jews that they continue to live according to the mitzvot as they believe that they will be judged eventually on the way in which they have kept the terms of covenant made with God, through Moses. **9**

Commentary

1. A very good general introduction that shows an accurate understanding of the term 'mitzvot'. Very good use has also been made of a relevant quotation from the Torah.

2. The answer then provides a more developed overview of the mitzvot, with the addition of reference to Maimonides, a notable Jewish rabbi and scholar.

3. A good connecting paragraph follows which focuses on the theme of the question.

4. This explains why the mitzvot are relevant to Orthodox Jews.

5. This is a correct explanation of the way in which the mitzvot have remained relevant throughout the centuries. Pikuach nefesh has been succinctly explained with a good example, and the premise of the paragraph has been summed up concisely by referring to a scholar of Judaism.

6. The role of halakhah is very relevant within Orthodox Judaism, and its explanation is well-placed here.

7. The Reform Judaism element of the answer has been introduced well by means of a comparison with the beliefs of Orthodox Jews. The reference to the Pittsburgh Platform is also very important.

8. A good explanation with an appropriate example.

9. The conclusion demonstrates the continuing relevance of the mitzvot for both Reform and Orthodox Jews.

Summative comment

This is a very confident answer with correct use of technical terms, relevant use of quotations, and the inclusion of scholarly insight. It is extremely well structured and gives a direct answer to a question about the relevance of the mitzvot for Orthodox and Reform Jews. It is an example of an excellent answer that also manages to draw comparisons between the two Jewish groups throughout.

AO2 question area: *An evaluation of the contribution of the mitzvot to spirituality in Judaism*

A weak answer

All Jews live according to the mitzvot as they believe that they were given by God to Moses on Mount Sinai. They form the basis of the covenant relationship, and enable them to live a disciplined, moral lifestyle in accordance with God's wishes. **1**

In Judaism, however, there are different attitudes to the mitzvot. On the one hand, Orthodox Jews believe that the mitzvot, as found in the Torah, contain the actual words of God, dictated to Moses. As the mitzvot are directly from God then it follows that they must be followed in order to live in obedience to God. There are 613 mitzvot, but Orthodox Jews no longer keep some of them because they relate to ritual and sacrifice in the Temple, which was destroyed in 70 CE. **2**

Reform Jews, on the other hand, hold a different interpretation of the mitzvot. Even though they agree with Orthodox Jews that the mitzvot come from God, they don't believe that God's revelation was dictated directly to Moses. Instead, they say that the revelation inspired others to write. This means that Reform Jews feel free to interpret the mitzvot in a much wider way. They even disregard some of the things like keeping kosher, as they do not see how things like this are relevant in everyday life. However, they still aim to live a good moral and ethical life. **3**

Hasidic Jews are very spiritual, and this has led to the development of a mystical tradition known as the Kabbalah. The main text of the Kabbalah is the Zohar, the content of which helps a Jew to achieve devotion to God. Hasidic Jews believe that God is everywhere in the universe, and they are therefore mindful of the need to live ethical and moral lives. **4**

In conclusion, I would therefore say that Hasidic Jews are more spiritual than either Orthodox or Reform Jews. **5**

Commentary

1 This is a good introduction in terms of content, but it does not introduce the issue of spirituality.

2 This is a very good account of Orthodox attitudes to the mitzvot BUT it is NOT EVALUATIVE.

3 The answer explains the attitude of Reform Jews to the mitzvot, but does not link it to spirituality and therefore it is NOT EVALUATIVE.

4 This gives an indication that spirituality is an important part of Hasidic tradition, and yet it doesn't address the theme of the question in an evaluative way.

5 The conclusion is NOT EVALUATIVE and no relevant judgement is made.

Summative comment

Overall, this is clearly an able candidate who has not recognised the difference between knowledge and understanding (AO1) and evaluation (AO2), and therefore in presenting the incorrect assessment skills writes a very weak answer. The lack of focus on the evaluation issues means that it is NOT EVALUATIVE, missing the whole point of the issues raised, and it is sad to say that it would not even be judged as A level standard.

Theme 4

AO1 question area: *Examining the rituals of Rosh Hashanah and their significance*

A weak answer

Rosh Hashanah is the name of a Jewish festival. The Jewish year is full of festivals with some being much more important than others. **1**

Yom Kippur is another Jewish festival and it is linked to Rosh Hashanah because they are ten days apart. **2**

The rituals at each Jewish festival are different, and so Rosh Hashanah is not like Passover, for example. **3**

The rituals of Rosh Hashanah are very significant. **4**

The new year is a good time to make resolutions and to show that you are sorry for all the bad things done in the past year. It is all about turning over a new leaf. **5**

In conclusion, therefore I think that this is the reason why Rosh Hashanah is the most important of all of the Jewish festivals. **6**

Commentary

1 This sentence is very weak as an introduction. It is very vague, and says nothing more about Rosh Hashanah other than it is one of many festivals.

2 This is a classic digression from the answer. The question is about Rosh Hashanah, and here we have the introduction of another festival. There *is* a link between Rosh Hashanah and Yom Kippur, but the question requires attention to be paid to Rosh Hashanah alone. The statement that they are linked 'because they are ten days apart' is also meaningless.

3 The answer then gives another irrelevant statement.

4 The theme of the question has merely been repeated in this sentence without any evidence, examples or explanation.

5 This is the only aspect of the answer that comes close to the theme of the question, but it is very vague.

6 One might assume from the conclusion that the question was about the relative importance of the Jewish festivals.

Summative comment

Overall this is clearly a very weak answer. The lack of focus, detail and accurate information means that it would not even be A level standard.

AO2 question area: *An evaluation of whether Jewish festivals are effective in reinforcing Jewish identity*

A strong answer

One line of argument that might be taken is that festivals, by their very nature, provide important opportunities for believers to meet together and as a result, to be reminded of the common themes that underpin Jewish identity. Jews are a minority religious group in the UK, and to be able to meet for times of celebration and joy must surely give rise to the reinforcement and strengthening of their common religious identity. **1**

Furthermore, certain festivals in the Jewish calendar have the power to draw in Jews who, for the rest of the year, are usually non-observant. For example, many Jews make a special effort to attend the synagogue at Yom Kippur. This could provide the justification for saying that festivals are definitely effective if they bring otherwise non-observant Jews back to the worshipping community where they express themselves once more as Jews. **2**

The festival of Shabbat is synonymous with Jewish identity, and is regarded by many as the weekly focal point of Jewish life. It is a day of rest and celebration, and its purpose is to recognise that God rested from creative practice on the seventh day of creation, and commanded the Jewish people to do likewise. **3**

However, Judaism has been described as a 'lifestyle', which suggests that Jewish identity is more closely linked to the things that occur on a daily basis rather than the things which happen during specific festival celebrations. **4**

Surely one of the most important things therefore in reinforcing Jewish identity, is living a life in accordance with the mitzvot as set out by God on Mount Sinai. Living a life that is true to the Torah allows God to be part of each and every aspect of a Jewish person's life. **5**

Everyday routines such as the Orthodox Jewish practice of keeping the kosher food laws might be seen as a more effective way to reinforce one's Jewish identity. Also the clothes that many Jewish people wear, such as the tallit or the kippah, might be said to have greater significance as they act as visible reminders. **6**

In conclusion, it is important to note that it is actually quite difficult to define what makes a person Jewish, even within Judaism itself. For some, it means being born into the faith by virtue of having a Jewish mother; for others it is a term that denotes national identity which is not necessarily linked to religious practice. Therefore, without a clear definition, it can be difficult to judge the effectiveness of the Jewish festivals in reinforcing Jewish identity. **7**

Commentary

1 This is a good evaluative style introducing a particular line of argument with a clear example and evidence to prove it.

2 Another reason is offered with an explanation to prove it.

3 The answer provides a final reason to support this line of argument.

4, **5** and **6** The answer provides a clear counter-argument through an opposing line of reasoning, giving clear evidence, explanation and examples to support there being other means of reinforcing Jewish identity.

7 This is a good conclusion demonstrating that the crux of the matter depends upon how one defines 'Jewishness'.

Summative comment

The answer has a very balanced approach that is well-sourced and structured, with three clear justifications for each point of view. An excellent conclusion introduces an interesting viewpoint which suggests that the debate is much more complex.

Quickfire answers

Theme 1

1.1 The father of many.

1.2 It was because he was considered to be 'blameless' amongst those in his generation.

1.3 One in which only one of the parties is required to do something.

1.4 Circumcision was to be an outward, physical sign in the flesh of the eternal covenant between God and the Jewish people.

1.5 When Abraham was a 100 years old, and Sarah, his wife was 90, she gave birth to a son.

1.6 God asked him to sacrifice his son Isaac.

1.7 Moses.

1.8 Pharaoh attempted to weaken the Hebrew nation by killing all their male newborn babies.

1.9 Moses heard the voice of God speaking to him from a bush which flamed but did not burn.

1.10 One in which two or more parties agree to look after each other's interests so that they will all benefit.

1.11 Jews were now told what they were required to do as their side of the agreement.

1.12 By living according to the mitzvot, thus cultivating a lifestyle which reflects the holy nature of the covenant relationship.

1.13 'Instruction' or 'teaching'.

1.14 Genesis, Exodus, Leviticus, Numbers, and Deuteronomy.

1.15 The Jewish Bible.

1.16 They reject laws which have a ritual rather than a moral basis, such as the Jewish dietary laws, for example.

1.17 Rabbi Eliezer ben Yose, Rabbi Shimon ben Lakish, Rabbi Akiva (choose two from three).

1.18 Chumash.

1.19 'And you shall teach it to your children.' (Deuteronomy 6:7)

1.20 To explain in greater detail how to adhere to the commandments of the written Torah when a fuller explanation was needed.

Theme 2

2.1 The first of the Ten Commandments: 'You shall have no other gods before me.' (Exodus 20:3), and the Shema.

2.2 The first verse in the Jewish scriptures reads: 'In the beginning God created the heavens and the earth.' (Genesis 1:1).

2.3 Having no physical body or physical substance and therefore no material existence.

2.4 Protector.

2.5 God's power has no limits at all. God is totally in control of the universe, and this includes all activities of nature and humans.

2.6 Adonai which means 'Lord'.

2.7 Kavod and shekinah.

2.8 The Hebrew word for 'image' which refers to the nature or essence of a being.

2.9 Judaism teaches that body and soul are separate, yet co-exist in human life.

2.10 The Talmud allows for the breaking of the laws of the Sabbath in order to save the life of another person.

2.11 Teshuvah means 'return', and is the word used to describe the concept of repentance in Judaism.

2.12 A mezuzah or mezuzot.

2.13 By wearing tefillin.

2.14 The tallit gadol is a large prayer shawl draped round the shoulders; whereas the tallit katan is a four-cornered garment with a hole for the head; it fits over the shoulders and drapes over the back and front of the body.

2.15 Isaiah and Jeremiah.

2.16 He predicted that the Messiah will restore the kingdom of David to its former glory, restore the Temple and gather the Jews together as a nation once more. The Messiah will also be a ruler who will reign according to the commandments contained in the Torah.

2.17 It refers to the branch of theology dealing with death, divine judgement, and life after death.

2.18 Paragraph 7 of the Pittsburgh Platform states that: 'Reform Judaism rejects the idea of bodily resurrection but accepts the view that the soul is immortal and that the spirit is divine.'

Theme 3

3.1 613.

3.2 Ritual and ethical acts.

3.3 Reform Jews believe that God revealed the Laws to Moses, but that the revelation was not dictated word for word to him. Rather that the revelation from God inspired others to write.

3.4 Hasidic males usually have a long beard and ear locks. This is in obedience to the mitzvah, which states: 'Do not cut the hair at the sides of your head or clip off the edges of your beard.' (Leviticus 19:27)

3.5 The Zohar explains the Torah by use of mystical insights.

3.6 Devotion to God.

3.7 Tefillah (prayer) provides an opportunity for a Jewish believer to reflect upon the nature of God, thereby coming to a greater understanding of the path God wants them to take in life.

3.8 A basic understanding the significance of the words which are being said; an awareness of being in the presence of God.

3.9 Arvit (evening prayer), shacharit (morning prayer) and minchah (afternoon prayer).

3.10 A minyan is a group of ten men over the age of 13, that is needed before an act of communal prayer at the synagogue can take place.

3.11 'There will always be poor people in the land. Therefore, I command you to be open-handed toward your fellow Israelites who are poor and needy.'

3.12 Friends and neighbours helping out when there is illness in a family; helping to look after children if a parent is ill; providing a meal; attending a funeral service in order to show your respect.

3.13 Family members will use them by depositing their small change after shopping, with the money collected going to charity.

3.14 Help the poor to rehabilitate themselves by lending them money, employing them, or giving them work.

3.15 Aseret ha-D'ibrot.

3.16 Number 3: 'You shall not take the name of the Lord in vain.'

3.17 They recite the Kaddish for 11 months after the death of a parent.

3.18 Sins relating to speech, such as slander; evil reports about another person; rumours; and the relating of unpleasant facts.

Theme 4

4.1 To gather together.

4.2 The Temple was destroyed by the Babylonians in 586 BCE.

4.3 Jeremiah.

4.4 To house the two tablets of stone given to Moses at Sinai.

4.5 King Solomon.

4.6 Bet k'nesset (house of meeting); bet midrash (house of study)

4.7 Simchat Torah.

4.8 Arvit (evening prayer), shacharit (morning prayer) and minchah (afternoon prayer).

4.9 It is used to regain ritual and spiritual purity by immersion in water.

4.10 Making judgements on civil disputes using Jewish law, and ruling on religious matters.

4.11 The Exodus, or the escape from slavery in Egypt.

4.12 Passover, or the festival of unleavened bread.

4.13 Physical (historical) redemption, and spiritual redemption (redemption of the world).

4.14 Exodus chapters 12–15.

4.15 Haggadah.

4.16 Charoset.

4.17 It is believed that Elijah will come at Pesach to herald the arrival of the Messiah.

4.18 Rosh Hashanah.

4.19 Yom Kippur.

4.20 The Ten Days of Returning.

4.21 Prayers for forgiveness.

4.22 Malkhiyot ('Kingship'), zikhronot ('Remembrances'), and shofarot ('shofar blasts').

4.23 (1) It is said that this fruit contains 613 seeds, just as there are 613 mitzvot. (2) Jews wish that their good deeds in the new year will be as many as the seeds of the pomegranate.

4.24 A shofar is a trumpet made from a ram's horn, and is one of the earliest musical instruments.

4.25 It involves the symbolic casting away of the sins of the previous year by tossing pieces of bread into a body of flowing water. In addition to throwing bread into the water, many Jews will shake their clothes, and empty their pockets of crumbs as a symbol of casting off every trace of sin.

4.26 Kol Nidrei.

4.27 Neilah.

Glossary

Abraham: meaning 'the father of many'

Absolute monotheism: the belief that there is only one God; the ultimate cause of existence

Acronym: a word made from the first letters of other words

Acrostic: a form of writing in which the first letter of each line spells out a word.

Adonai: meaning 'Lord'

Akedah: referring to 'binding' of Isaac

Alms: donations of food, money, etc., to the poor

Amidah: literally means 'standing'; one of the principal prayers of the Jewish liturgy

Amidah: the name of a daily prayer

Anachronistic: to attribute something to a historical period in which it did not exist

Aniconism: opposition to the use of idols, images and the worship of objects which are symbolic of a deity

Ani Ma'amin: a poetic form of Maimonides' Thirteen Articles of Faith which is recited every day after morning prayers at the synagogue

Anointing: to put oil on someone's head, usually as part of a religious ceremony

Anthropomorphism: the attribution of human characteristics, feelings or behaviour to a god, animal or inanimate object

Apostate: someone who rejects a belief

Aron Kodesh (1): the 'Holy Ark' or cabinet in which are kept the Sefer Torah scrolls at the synagogue

Aron Kodesh (2): originally the name given to the wooden box, covered in gold, in which were stored the two tablets of stone given to Moses at Sinai

Arvit: evening prayer

Aseret ha-D'ibrot: the Ten Sayings

Aseret ha-D'varim: the Ten Principles

Atone: to make amends for a wrong-doing

Atonement: the act of making up for a wrongdoing or sin

Avinu Malkenu: 'our father, our king'; a prayer

Avodah shebalev: meaning 'service of the heart'

Baal Shem Tov: literally means 'Master of the Good Name' (i.e. the name of God)

Bakashah: section 2 of the Amidah

Bar mitzvah: 'son of the commandment'; the coming of age ceremony for a Jewish boy at 13 years of age

Baruch atah Adonai, melech ha'olam: Blessed are you, Lord, our God, sovereign of the universe

Bat mitzvah: meaning 'daughter of the commandment'; the name given to the coming of age ceremony for a Jewish girl at 12 years of age

BCE: Before the Common Era

Benevolence: act of kindness or generosity

Berakah: blessing (singular)

Berakot: blessings (plural)

Bet din: meaning 'house of judgement'; a rabbinical court

Bet k'nesset: house of meeting

Bet midrash: house of study

Bet tefillah: house of prayer

Bimah: a raised reading desk in the synagogue where the Torah is read

Blasphemy: an act that insults God

Brit milah: circumcision

CE: referring to the Common Era; the period beginning with the traditional birth year of Jesus

Celestial: relating to heaven

Challot: special loaves of bread used on Shabbat and festivals

Charoset: a sweet paste made of apple, cinnamon and raisins

Chukim: commandments for which no particular reason has been given for having to keep them

Chumash: a printed text containing the Five Books of Moses

Civil divorce: divorce according to the laws of the country

Cohen: a man descended from the old priestly families of ancient Israel

Conditional covenant: a covenant in which two or more parties agree to look after each other's interests so that they will all benefit

Consecrating: making someone/something sacred; setting them apart for holy use

Consecration: the act of dedicating to God's service

Corporeal: having a bodily form

Covenant: an agreement or contract

Covet: the desire to possess something (especially something which belongs to someone else)

Cultic: a system of religious beliefs

Dayanim: religious judges attached to a rabbinic court

Debauched: immoral, corrupt behaviour

Decalogue: the Ten Commandments

Deities: gods or goddesses

Devekut: devotion to God; having God permanently in the mind

Didactic: intended to teach or instruct

Divine: belonging to; relating to; or coming from God

Ego: the consciousness within us

El: name for God denoting might, strength and power

El male rachamim: a funeral prayer

El Olam: a name for God within Judaism, meaning the everlasting or eternal One

Eschatology: the branch of theology dealing with death, divine judgement, and life after death

Ethical: to live according to a set of moral principles

Etz chaim: meaning 'tree of life'; the name given to the wooden pole on a Sefer torah scroll

Exile: enforced absence from one's country of origin

Exiles: people who have been forced to leave a country

Ex nihilo: a Latin phrase meaning 'out of nothing'

Exodus: a departure, a going out, usually of a large group of people

Extrapolate: to draw conclusions from known facts

Gehinnom: a place of spiritual punishment and/or purification

Gemara: a rabbinical commentary on the Mishnah, forming the second part of the Talmud

Gemilut hasadim: 'the giving of loving kindness'; doing good deeds

Gentiles: the general term for people who are not Jewish

Haggadah: means 'telling', the text recited at the Seder meal

Halakhah: literal meaning: 'the path that one walks'; Jewish law

Hasidim: literally means 'the pious ones'; an ultra-orthodox wing of Judaism

Havdalah: a ceremony performed at the end of Shabbat and festivals

Heretic: someone whose religious views are in conflict with the majority

Hittite: the name given to a nation of people from Asia Minor

Hoda'ah: section 3 of the Amidah

Idol: an image or symbol, especially of a god, which is used as an object of worship

Idolatrous: worship of idols

Immutable: unable to be changed

Incomparable: unable to be compared with anything else

Incorporeal: without bodily substance

Indivisible: unable to be divided or separated

Iniquity: sinfulness

Intercede: to make an appeal on someone's behalf

Investiture: a formal ceremony giving a special role to someone

Judicial: referring to the decisions of a judge

Kabbalah: Jewish mystical tradition

Kaddish: a prayer said by a mourner

Karpas: a green vegetable

Kashrut: religious dietary laws

Kavod: literally means 'heavy' or 'weighty', but often denotes honour or glory. It attempts to describe the experience of standing in the presence of God

Kavvanah: literal meaning is 'intention'; used to denote a state of mental concentration and devotion at prayer

Kittel: a white ceremonial robe

Kol Nidrei: meaning 'annulment of vows'

Kosher (1): meaning 'fit' or 'proper'

Kosher (2): food which a Jew is permitted to eat; food prepared in accordance with Jewish dietary laws

Lashon hara: literally means 'evil tongue'; derogatory speech about another person

Lectern: a stand with a sloping surface for holding a book; used for someone to read or preach from

Machzor: a special prayer book for Rosh Hashanah and Yom Kippur

Malkhiyot: kingship

Mantle: a decorated cover for the Sefer Torah

Maror: a bitter herb

Matriarch: the female head of a community or tribe

Matzah: a piece of unleavened bread

Matzot: plural of 'matzah'

Mediator: someone who acts between two parties in order to bring about an end to a disagreement

Melachot: the 39 types of work forbidden on Shabbat

Menstruation: a woman's monthly period

Mercy: the characteristic of God to be forgiving

Messiah: the 'anointed one'; one who will usher in a new era for humanity, which will be established under the rule of God

Mezuzah: a small parchment scroll fixed to the right-hand doorpost of every room in a Jewish house (except bathroom and toilet)

Mezuzot: plural of mezuzah which is a small parchment scroll fixed to the right-hand doorpost of every room in a Jewish house (except bathroom and toilet)

Midrash: 'to search' or 'to root out' and is a reference to the method of interpretation of the Hebrew Scriptures

Mikveh: 'a place where water has gathered'; a special pool attached to a synagogue where Jews can immerse to purify themselves

Minchah: afternoon prayer

Minim: relating to those who belong to a sect, whose views differ from the mainstream

Minyan: congregation or assembly; a group of ten males over the age of 13 required before an act of communal prayer can take place at the synagogue

Mishnah: meaning 'a teaching that is repeated'; a collection of oral laws

Mitzvah: commandment (singular)

Mitzvot: commandments (plural)

Mohel: a qualified person who carries out the rite of circumcision

Monotheism: belief that there is only one God

Mortar: a mixture of sand, water and cement used in bricklaying

Mosaic: relating to Moses

Moses: which means 'to draw out' or to 'extract'

Musaf: a fourth prayer that is added on Shabbat and festivals

Nazoraeans: early Jewish Christians

Nefesh: a term meaning 'soul'

Neilah: literally meaning 'the closing of the gates'; the final prayer on Yom Kippur

Noachide Laws: the minimal moral duties required by all people (not just Jews)

Nomadic: not living a settled life in one place

Olam ha-ba: literally 'the world to come'; the afterlife

Omnibenevolent: having absolute goodness

Omnipotent: all-powerful

Omniscient: all-knowing

Pagan: religious beliefs other than those of major religions

Parity: the condition of being equal

Parochet: curtain

Parshiot: sections of the Torah read in the synagogue

Patriarch: the term given to denote the male head of a family or tribe

Pesach: means to 'pass over'

Pesikta Rabbati: a medieval Midrash

Petition: to request; to make an appeal, usually to a higher authority

Pharaoh: the title of the kings of ancient Egypt

Pikuach nefesh: the sanctity of life

Pious: religiously devout

Plurality: a large number or variety

Polytheism: belief in more than one god

Predicate: the part of a sentence which tells us what the subject of the same sentence is or does

Progressive Revelation: the concept that old laws of the Bible are no longer applicable in modern society in which new ethical, moral and spiritual values have been 'revealed'

Promised Land: the land of Canaan which had been promised by God to Abraham and his descendants

Prophet: a person chosen to express the will of God

Prophetic: having the characteristics of a prophet

Pushkes: collection boxes for charity

Qodesh: holiness of God

Rabbinic tradition: teachings which come from the rabbis

Ratify: to give formal consent to a treaty or agreement

Rebbe: the title given to the spiritual leader of Hasidic Jewish communities

Recline: to lean back in a resting position

Redemption: the act of being saved

Repentance: to regret the bad or evil things one has done in the past, and change one's behaviour as a result

Resurrected: to bring back to life

Retroject: to project into the past

Revelation: the act of revealing a divine truth

Ritual: an often repeated procedure or set of actions

Rosh Hashanah: meaning 'the Head of the Year'; the Jewish New Year Festival

Sabbath: the seventh day of the week; the day of rest according to the Ten Commandments

Sanctuary: a holy or sacred place

Scapegoat: the goat upon which the sins of the people were transferred by the Jewish high priest

Secular: relating to things which are not religious

Seder: means 'order', and refers to the ritual service and ceremonial dinner which takes place in the Jewish home at Pesach

Sefer Torah: 'Scroll of the Torah'

Selichot: prayers for forgiveness

Seminary: a theological college

Sermon: a talk on a religious or moral subject

Shabbat: the seventh day of the week; the day of rest according to the Ten Commandments

Shabbat Shuvah: Sabbath of Returning

Shacharit: morning prayer

Shekinah: means 'dwelling' or 'settling' and denotes the divine presence of God in the world

Shema: means 'hear'; Jewish prayer declaring the oneness of God

Shemonah Esray: meaning 'the eighteen', and referring to the 18 original benedictions of the Amidah

Shevach: section 1 of the Amidah

Shevarim: three short notes sounded on the shofar

Shofar: a ram's horn trumpet

Shofarot: the blasts on the shofar

Shul: school

Shulchan Arukh the Code of Jewish Law

Siddur: prayer book

Simchat Torah: meaning 'rejoicing in the Torah'

Sofer: scribe

Subjugation: to be in a state of domination by another nation

Subordinate: lower in importance or rank

Suzerain: a ruler that exercises control over another state, whilst allowing it to retain some autonomy

Synagogue: comes from a Greek word meaning 'to gather together'; the name given to the Jewish place of worship

Tabernacled: relating to the sanctuary for the Ark of the Covenant

Tallit: a woollen or silk shawl worn by Jewish males during morning prayer

Tallit gadol: large prayer shawl

Tallit katan: a four-cornered garment with a hole for the head; it fits over the shoulders and drapes over the back and front of the body

Talmud: 'teaching' or 'study': the work of the collected scholars as a running commentary to the Mishnah

Tanakh: Hebrew name for the Bible

Tarry: to be slow or late in coming; to linger

Tashlikh: meaning 'to cast'; the ritual of symbolically casting away the sins of the previous year

Tefillah: prayer

Tefillin: two small leather boxes with compartments that contain passages from the Torah

Tekiah: a single long note sounded on the shofar

Teruah: nine or more very short notes blown in staccato on the shofar

Teshuvah: means 'return', and is the word used to describe the concept of repentance in Judaism

Theophany: the manifestation of God to humans

Tithe: the giving of a tenth of one's income, after taxes have been taken, to charity

Torah: means 'instruction' or 'teaching' and refers to the first five books of the Jewish scriptures; it can also refer to the whole of Jewish teaching

Tzaddik: meaning 'righteous man'

Tzedakah: 'charity'; literal meaning is 'justice' or 'righteousness'

Tzelem: the nature or essence of a being

Tzitzit: fringes attached to each corner of the tallit

Unconditional covenant: an agreement between two parties, but when only *one* of the parties is required to do something

Unleavened: (of bread) made without yeast or any other raising agent

Vayyitzer: meaning 'formed'

Vicissitudes: unpredictable changes of circumstance

Wilderness: a wild and uncultivated region: in this case, a desert

Yad: a pointer in the shape of a hand with outstretched finger which is used when reading from the Torah

Yahweh: a form of the Hebrew name for God

Yeshiva: a Jewish academy for Talmudic studies

Yetzer hara: evil inclination

Yetzer hatov: good inclination

Yiddish: a language based on German that is written in Hebrew characters, and originally spoken by Jews of central and Eastern Europe

Yom Kippur: the Day of Atonement

Zikhronot : remembrances

Zohar: the classical text of Kabbalah; a mystical interpretation of the Torah

Z'man heyruteinu: the season of our freedom

Index